Christmas

love from Laurie & Sally

TV reviews

and of course

Victor

First published in Great Britain in 2012
by Badastral Books
123 Pall Mall
London
SW1Y 5EA
UK
www.badastralbooks.com

© Victor Lewis-Smith, Paul Sparks

All rights reserved. No part of this publication may be reproduced stored in or introduced into a retrieval system, or transmitted in any form or by any means (electronic, mechanical, photocopying, recording or otherwise) without the prior written permission of both the copyright owner and the publisher of this book.

ISBN-13: 978-1481156066
ISBN-10: 1481156063

Design: Jay Huggins

Victor Lewis-Smith's

satirical, hilarious, and scathing television reviews - including celebrity assassinations - from the Evening Standard, Volume I

TV reviews

Dedication

This book is dedicated to Mr Justice Eady, a man who has done more than any other during the past decade to promote freedom of speech in the United Kingdom. Cynics may point out that he was repeatedly rebuked by the Court of Appeal for his conduct during the 2009 Desmond *v.* Bower libel case; that the Court of Appeal ruled he had "erred in his approach" over the Simon Singh libel case in 2010, and had invited the court "to become an Orwellian ministry of truth;" and that in April 2011 he granted a restraining order "*contra mundum*" (against the world), even though his legal powers did not extend beyond Britain. But frankly, I regard all such criticisms as bogus (a word, incidentally, of which the Court of Appeal decided he did not know the correct meaning).

Acknowledgements

Thanks to the following – the good guys – all of whom have influenced this book in some form of another: Ray Galton and Alan Simpson. All at Associated Newspapers, including Bernice Davison, Doug Wills, Jeannette Arnold, Max Hastings, and all the hard-working TV desk researchers (too numerous to mention, but much appreciated). From the TV world, Kevin Lygo, James Hunt, Sophie Turner Laing, Andrew O'Connell, and Dawn Airey, none of whom have ever confused my TV reviewing work with my TV production work (unlike some others, who did). Thanks, as well, to Danny Baker, Alan Bennett, Trevor Beattie, Dave and Barb, Barry Cryer, Michael Mansfield QC, Mark Borkowski, John Pitman, Jeremy Fox, all at Viz, Brian and Lynne Basham, all at Private Eye, Keith and Tamzin, Bob Windsor, Tim Gardam, Lin Cook, Michael Ember, Ian Gardhouse, Graham Pass, Mark Twigg, Cath Royle, The Spanish Airforce, Burt Coleman, Laurie and Sally, John McVicar, Piers Morgan, Richard Corrigan, Fergus Henderson, Phil Dirtbox, Jerry Sadowitz, and my co-writer Paul Sparks (who doesn't receive all the bouquets, but also doesn't get assaulted in the street). Also, the sadly departed Liam Carson, Peter Langan, Bob Robinson, Noel Botham and Tim Hodlin. And thanks to all the disgusting, fat, bloated, money-grabbing and corrupt Establishment scumbag lawyers who have tried, and – more often than not – failed to neuter my writing, or otherwise incommode me over the years (you know who you are and fuck you all).

And most of all, my rock, Virginia.

Contents

Acknowledgements	5
Introduction	8

Chapter 1 GASTROTELLY — 11

Blumenthal In Search Of Perfection	12	Floyd Around The Med	38
Return Of The Chef [Fanny Cradock]	14	Rick Stein	43
The Real Fanny Cradock	16	Cutting Edge	46
Ainsley's Barbecue Bible	19	Two Fat Ladies	49
Ainsley's Gourmet Express	21	The Hairy Bikers	51
Jamie's School Dinner	23	If You Can't Stand The Heat	55
Kitchen Chemistry [Blumenthal]	26	Delia's How to Cook	56
Grow Your Own Veg	29	Carluccio's Feast	60
Christmas Live	32	Celebrity Cook	62
Floyd Uncorked	36	Airport	64

Chapter 2 SANK WITHOUT TRACE — 66

The Baby Channel	67	Real Estate TV	87
Win TV	70	Ceefax	89
Quizmania	72	C4 The Ten Commandments	92
The Musicians Channel	75	Sin Cities	95
Forecourt TV	77	Artsworld	97
Japanorama	80	Your Destiny TV	99
The Advert Channel	83	Are You Being Cheated	101
London TV	85		

Chapter 3 SACRED COWS — 103

The Life of Mammals	104	Great Romances	121
Esther Rantzen	108	Royal London	124
Band Aid	112	Trooping The Colour	126
Geldorf In Africa	114	William's Women	128
Wogan: Now and Then	116	Top Gear	132
One on One – Terry Wogan	119	Parkinson	134

Chapter 4 LIVE AND DIRECT   137

Children In Need	138	The O'Reilly Factor	164
Two Minutes Silence	140	God TV	167
Big Brother	143	Working Lunch	170
Big Brother	145	This Morning	172
Great Food Live	149	Last Night Of The Proms	175
Market Kitchen	151	Nigella	177
Trooping the Colour	153	The Lord Mayor's Show	180
Test Board	156	The X Factor	183
Inauguration Of Pope Benedict XVI	158	Pick Of The Day	185
Late Junction	161		

Ch 5 SCIENCE   188

Intimate Relations	191	Embarrassing Illnesses	212
Trust Me I'm A Doctor	194	Under The Influence	215
Sweeney Investigates	196	Science Shack	217
The Future Of the Car	198	The Sky At Night	219
Christmas Lectures	201	The Truth About Gay Animals	222
The Science Of Lying	203	Look Around You	224
Horizon	205	Rough Science	227
Constant Craving	207	The Gadget Show	229
Meeting with Remarkable Trees	209		

Chapter 6 RAGBAG   232

Cottage Cheese	232	Mumbai Calling	252
The Office	234	Dragons' Den	255
The Gulf War	237	Comedy Awards	258
The Downing Street Patient	239	The Last Days Of The Routemaster	260
Underground Ernie	243	Bless This House	262
The New Mr & Mrs Show	244	Urban Myth	265
Would like To Meet Esther	246	Doctor Who	267
Viagra: The Hard Sell	248	Kenneth Williams In His Own Words	270
The Truth About Richard and Judy	250		

INTRODUCTION

What is the point of television critics? That's a question that I often pondered during my years in the *profession* as television critic for the London Evening Standard. Theatre and opera critics have a genuinely useful function to perform, because directors and actors at the start of a long run can learn from their reviews, and adjust future performances, while their observations may usefully inform the general public about what's hot and what's rot. But television reviewers can only give their opinions after the programme is over, so surely they're about as much use (and as pathetic) as a frustrated passenger standing alone on a railway station, impotently heckling a train that's already left the platform?

Equally pathetic is the narcissistic urge that motivates most performers to try to appear on television in the first place, which is why the smart money is on never appearing inside the magic rectangle at all. Television is a mask that eats away at the face, and for decades it has been devouring the souls of those who spend too long appearing on it. And the situation has lately become worse, because television has now begun to eat away at itself.

So, to return to my opening question, what is the point of TV critics? Beyond the necessary business of pricking the pomposity of overinflated egos, and (hopefully) amusing the reader, their most useful function is surely to keep an eye on the state of the industry. And as I've been re-reading the thousands of reviews that I wrote during the 1990s and 2000s, I have realised that this book is really a chronicle of the decline of British television. Alright, it's not *A History of the English-Speaking Peoples* (thank God), but over the past couple of decades, television has undoubtedly fragmented and degenerated, from a medium where a mighty handful of well-resourced channels offered us a communal viewing experience, into a world of a thousand satellite channels (many of which are barely watched or funded at all). Older viewers increasingly search in vain for anything worthwhile to watch, while the younger generation is increasingly abandoning television's dubious pleasures altogether, in favour of the Internet.

I witnessed the decline of television in sorrow and in anger, and can fairly claim to have seen it coming. Indeed, while writing for another newspaper back in the late 1980s, I prophesied what would happen when Mrs Thatcher first encouraged multi-channel satellite television in the UK. In every branch of entertainment, I wrote, there is an immutable law of inverse proportions between quality and quantity. If you open thirty theatres on a single street in a small town that can barely sustain one local rep company, then expect execrable productions from all of them. Why does anyone expect multi-channel television to fare any better?

However, this isn't simply an "I told you so" book about settling scores, or about the rehashing of minor skirmishes from the past (fun though that is). Its true purpose is to take the temperature of television – then and now – and to discover whether the patient has survived, or has become a lifeless cadaver in urgent need of burial. That's why, at times of desperation, some of these reviews may seem to be metaphorically taking the temperature with an anal thermometer, and wiping it all over the screen.

Given the visceral contempt that runs through many of my reviews, the casual reader might think that I hate television, but the reverse is true. I have always *loved* television at its best, but during my many years as a critic, I was professionally required to watch a great deal of television at its very worst. Hence the working title of this book (which was to have been called *Before Turning the Gun on Himself...*), reflecting the genuine desperation I that I increasingly felt, as television producers and presenters scraped right down to the very bottom of the barrel, then carried on scraping through until they reached another barrel beneath, the existence of which had hitherto never even been suspected.

I am compelled to thank my loyal readers who, during my nearly two decades with the *Evening Standard*, refrained from writing to tell me that I had, yet again, repeated a joke (which I did with alacrity and without a shred of guilt). You will see more repeated and recycled jokes in this very tome (as proof of my ecological leanings).

When I was first asked to compile a selection of my television journalism, I wondered whether reviews of five-or-ten-year-old pro-grammes would still be relevant to readers. But a quick perusal of the TV schedules soon put my mind to rest on that score, because little, if anything, seems to have changed in the intervening years. Many of the reviews in this book are preceded or followed by a www link to a relevant piece of footage or a news item, and those of you reading this book as a PC download will be able simply to click on those links. However, those of you reading it on Kindle (or on paper) won't want to keep typing in long strings of web addresses. So instead, you can simply use your PC or iPad to access the Badastral Books website, where you will find all the relevant items helpfully placed together.

And, finally, three cheers to Janice Hadlow, long-time friend and colleague, now Controller of BBC2, who once phoned me at home and said "if you don't like the programme I made that's on tonight, please don't review it." I didn't like the programme, I did review it, and she hasn't spoken to me since.

Victor Lewis-Smith, St Omer, France, November 2012

The back cover shows an image of the very first television star – "Stookie Bill." This disembodied head of a ventriloquist's dummy was used by John Logie Baird during his early experiments in the early part of the last century. In many ways, Stookie was the perfect "presenter" for the new medium of television. He had an IQ of zero and he sported a permanent ear-to-ear grin. However, he had one tragic flaw: he was made of wax and, if left in front of the hot studio lights for more than a few minutes, he would start to melt...

CHAPTER 1

GASTROTELLY: HALF-BAKED AND OVERDONE

As well as being a TV critic, I was also a restaurant critic of many years' standing (why the waiters won't ever let me have a chair is something I've never understood). Let's face it, reviewing TV and restaurants wasn't exactly the most arduous way to earn a living. In fact, had bed-tester been on the list at the local job exchange, you wouldn't have had to suffer my outpourings in print at all.

Having eaten far and wide in this country, I can tell you that the oft-repeated statement that "British food has never been so good" is garbage, because over the years, I've had almost as many dreadful gastronomic experiences as I've had hot dinners. Throughout this land, I've eaten sausages that have been nothing more than condoms filled with sawdust, the piece of cod that passeth all understanding, and roadkill in a bun served on a tablecloth so filthy that it looked as though it had recently passed through a Yogi's digestive tract, during his quest for inner cleanliness.

Great cooking is a time-consuming blend of art and science, creating esculent masterpieces that can only truly be savoured and appreciated in a restaurant, not a TV studio. Why? Because a single complex dish often requires many different cooking processes to come to a climax simultaneously, and that's a feat that can only be achieved by an experienced and skilful team, working together in perfect synchronisation. Chefs who love their art know this, which is why many of the greatest names in gastronomy are virtually unheard of outside of their own profession; they refuse to fritter away their time and their talent for the benefit of TV cameras, and know that, if you can stand the heat, then you shouldn't get out of the kitchen.

Alright. Perhaps that sounds a trifle harsh, but before sitting down to write, I'd just spent an hour attempting to make Provençal grand aioli, and it ended up looking like a bowlful of snot, so I wasn't in the greatest mood. But one thing is beyond doubt. Far too many intelligent and basically decent chefs have allowed themselves to be seduced by the lure of the lens, and have ended up by abandoning the serious pursuit of their profession altogether, in favour of joining the ranks of the "celebrity chef." But as they do so, they should remember one thing. Celebrity is the mask that eats away the face, and that's ultimately a very grim feast indeed.

TV reviews

HESTON BLUMENTHAL:
IN SEARCH OF PERFECTION
BBC2 2006

With Christmas gifts already being marketed in the shops, it's time for the launch of my new Alphabetti Touretti board game. Combining obscene lexicography with complete gastric mayhem, this great new game requires each contestant to eat twenty cans of alphabetti spaghetti without chewing, roll a dice, then select a mystery card from the "Chunder Pile," and perform the required forfeit. This will involve them watching a powerful visual emetic (such as "Saint Jamie Oliver Educating Our Kids" or "Gordon Ramsay Swearing"), then vomiting their unmasticated pasta up against a wall, the winner being the first player to throw up a suitably filthy (yet correctly spelt) description of the celebrity chef in question. So hurry. Boxed sets of Alphabetti Touretti will soon be available in all branches of Toys R Us, except in the West Country, where they'll be stocked by Toys Be We. Or, if Michael Jackson is visiting you over the Yuletide period, why not purchase the junior edition from Boys R Us?

"Visual emetic" accurately sums up the physiognomical state of the average tellychef nowadays, because few of the current batch could honestly be described as "dish of the day." Antony Worrall Thompson looks increasingly like an obese Robin Cook (though not as full of life), Gordon Ramsay resembles... (well, let's just say "it must be a face, it's got ears"), and now we have *Heston Blumenthal: In Search of Perfection* to help boost sales of my Alphabetti Touretti game. He's undoubtedly a talented chef, but there's something about his bald head, slightly sinister name, white "mad scientist" coat, and fondness for dry ice that makes him seem uncomfortably like a James Bond villain. That similarity is further increased by a title sequence which offers glimpses of the chef through 007-style white circles on a black background, and is completed by his inquisitorial approach to cuisine, because this man doesn't just cook food – he tortures it until it confesses its secrets.

"People have called my approach to food 'molecular gastronomy'," he told us last night, though he prefers to call it "cookery with a bit of science thrown in," but however it's described, there's certainly nothing original about what he's doing. Back in the 1950s, Edouard de Pomiane (an eccentric Franco-Polish genius whose *French Cooking in Ten Minutes* is one of the great works of gastronomic philosophy) pioneered the science of "gastrotechnie," and showed how chefs could turn their kitchens into laboratories; but he wisely viewed this approach as a mere novelty, whereas

Ch 1 GASTROTELLY

Blumenthal has turned it into a culinary fetish. Vowing to "reinvent the way we cook in the twenty-first century," he promised "to revolutionise the nation's favourite dishes," and I suddenly recalled the words of another great French gastronaut, Clement Vautel, who'd loathed the fashion for "snobbish gastronomy" that prevailed in the 1920s. "The curious thing is that snobbish gastronomes always look for a traditional classic to adapt," he'd observed, and as Blumenthal set about deconstructing the archetypal British dish of sausage and mash, it seemed that Vautel had got him banger to rights.

What followed was a mixture of standard techniques and perverse gimmickry that simply made a familiar dish ten times harder to prepare. Making mash by baking potatoes in the oven before scooping out the insides isn't remotely new (I've made mash that way for years, though asbestos hands would be an advantage), but poaching his bangers made them look as anaemic as those disgusting *weisse* sausages that middle-aged Bavarian women consume in restaurants, swallowing them whole as though they were porn stars in a remake of *Deep Throat*. There wasn't anything particularly scientific about the chef's cunning ploy "to reinforce the onion flavour" (by adding onions), or "to reinforce the bready flavour" (by adding bread), and as for holding some fat over smoking logs to capture "the smell of the fat dripping into the fire at a barbecue," that seemed to veer dangerously close to anthropophagy. Well, in my experience, the dominant smell at most barbecues is sizzling human flesh, after a drunken guest decides to pour a can of petrol over the coals "to get it going," and ends up wondering why they now look like Simon Weston.

Blumenthal is a world-class chef who hasn't yet developed the monstrous ego of an Oliver or a Ramsay, but the premise of his entire series seems woefully half-baked. I doubt if one viewer in a million is ever going to source their own "middlewhite pig meat" or purchase their own "natural hog casing," because people watch TV food programmes as a *substitute* for doing any serious cookery themselves, just as they watch football to save themselves the bother of running around a field, and watch porn to avoid having serious sex. Where Blumenthal could do us all a favour would be by marketing his own brand of top-quality sausages that we could all buy ready-made off the shelf, and I'd certainly be willing to give those a try. Perhaps Gordon Ramsay should market some, too, with a picture of him stabbing into one and the words "prick with a fork," to be interpreted as an instruction or a description, according to taste.

TV reviews

I understand that in February 2009, there was an unfortunate case of food poisoning at The Fat Duck causing the restaurant to be closed down for a short time. Prior to that, over 500 cases of illness were reported over a period of a couple of months.

A detailed report by The Health Protection Agency about the poisoning can be seen by clicking on link #1 on the **TV Reviews** page on *www.badastralbooks.com*.

The restaurant has since re-opened without problems. Although I still suffer from nausea whenever I see Mr Blumenthal's face on my screen.

The only poisonous thing about Fanny Cradock was her tongue. Shortly before she died, I saw her gloriously eviscerate a young chat show host called Jonathan Ross. She took him to pieces without so much as leaving his giblets behind. A feast fit for a King. I praised her in passing in the following.

RETURN OF THE CHEF

C4 2005

Let us pause to pay tribute to Fanny Cradock, one of television's first celebrity chefs, whose seminal *Kitchen Magic* series began on the BBC exactly fifty years ago. Sporting lipstick that was applied so wildly that she looked as though she'd been sipping from a rough-edged glass (*aka* "the Joker-from-Batman" look), this cross between Margaret Thatcher and Baby Jane conducted herself in the studio like a one-woman paramilitary division of the Women's Institute, shouting and swearing at technical staff, and informing viewers that "I can't bear it when I'm told to hurry up on television." Although she lied compulsively about her private life, her approach to gastronomy was always honest, but it must be said that she was a stranger to environmental health regulations, idly fondling her breasts (of poultry) before touching other ingredients, then blithely insisting that "it's alright, I have sterilised the knives" (an excuse marginally less convincing than "there can be no whitewash at the White House"). Overall, her performance was a mixture of hysteria and listeria, but she was a genuine TV original, and now rests in peace beside her husband Johnny, a man who was half-Jewish and half-Mormon. How odd. Perhaps his parents came from Salt Beef City.

Ch 1 GASTROTELLY

Although viewers learned a good deal about Fanny and Johnny's relationship during her programmes, there was never any doubt that the food always came first. But regrettably, half a century later, most tellychefs are more concerned with showing us the tedious minutiae of their private lives than with actually doing any cooking, and that's certainly the case with the presenter of C4's *The Return of the Chef*. Back in 2003, John Burton-Race expected us to watch him playing the role of Alpha Mayle with his family in a farmhouse near Provence, and now he's inviting us to follow him to Devon, as he sets up a new restaurant and home in Dartmouth. "It's the biggest gamble of their lives," said the narrator at the start of last night's episode, and I suppose it might have been, if only the entire enterprise hadn't been underpinned by a lucrative deal with C4, hours of free advertising for his restaurant, and a new cookbook (*Coming Home*, available from all good bookshops, price £20).

As I watched the Burton-Races embark on their move, I suddenly understood the true significance of Heisenberg's Uncertainty Principle. That theory states that the presence of an observer will affect the result of an experiment, and it certainly applied last night, because almost every scene looked fake, as though it was being artificially staged and re-enacted for the benefit of the TV crew ("take twos" as they're known in the biz). Phone conversations sounded stilted and false, arguments seemed wooden and contrived, and the level of artifice was shocking.

"They have to open up in six weeks," gasped the narrator in a desperate attempt to create excitement by turning the restaurant's refurbishment into a Burton-Race against the clock. But of course, they didn't *have* to open in six weeks at all, nor did they *have* "to buy a house in three weeks," and as for the will-they-won't-they struggle to get a mortgage, would you believe it, they *could* get one after all. If the family's motivation for the move really was (as we were told) "trying to find the recipe for a slower, saner, more balanced way of life," then perhaps they should have adopted a *modus operandi* that didn't involve being followed everywhere by a film crew, and when I saw shots of the family pets, I began to realise why they'd chosen to relocate to the South-West coast. To be closer to the ultimate purveyors of glutinous, emotional, please-love-me, cookery-as-lifestyle television, Rick Stein and his scarf-wearing cutesie prop-dog Chalkie, the tellychef's answer to the devious street beggar's mutt on a string.

What, I wonder, would the brave and fearless cutting-edge C4 of a generation ago think of the soft, cuddly, bourgeois programming that it now broadcasts each evening? Its late-night schedules can still pack a punch, but watching it between 8 and 9 is like reading a Sunday colour

TV reviews

supplement where every page is the same, because whether the theme is ostensibly cooking, travel, health, real estate, or clothing, they've all become lifestyle programmes. Cutting-edge C4 would certainly be horrified by the disingenuous output of Llewellyn and her ilk, whose shows are as fake and as dimwitted as cosy Bisto ads from the 1960s. O tempora, o mores. How I wish there was a knob on my TV set to turn up the intelligence. There is a knob labelled "brightness" that I've twiddled with, but it doesn't seem to work.

Television didn't always treat gastronomy like a sport or a game show. Which brings us again to one of the pioneers of British televisual cookery, Fanny Cradock, and this tribute to her, made way back in 1997. Despite looking like an explosion in a paint factory, and being plastered with make up that would make even Bozo the clown seem understated (not to mention dyeing her food blue), she was an impressive presence in the TV kitchen, because her down-to-earth style was all about culinary technique, with no juggling about or game-playing with the food. In an era when the likes of Ainsley Harriott can't even peel an onion without spookin' for de white folk while simultaneously conducting a phantom orchestra, the simplicity and honesty of the Cradocks was refreshing. And just to prove you can't get enough Fanny...

THE REAL... FANNY CRADOCK

C4 1998

It's time to play Vic's Family Fortunes! We asked a hundred celebrity telly chefs "what's a wok?" and seventeen percent answered "a wok's something you throw at a wabbit." Then we enquired why the coffee they serve in their restaurants tastes like mud, and thirty-four percent told us "because it was ground this morning." Finally, we asked the same hundred TV chefs what they mostly ate, and a whopping ninety-eight percent admitted that they were full of shitake. Who can argue with that?

Excuse the *double entendres*, but Saturday night's *The Real... Fanny Cradock* (C4) was full of them too, from the moment we heard that the most famous telly chef of the 50s and 60s was a master baker, to the revelation that, as a young man, her partner Johbnnie "was mesmerised by Fanny" (I could almost see them breathless with laughter in the dubbing suite). Smut aside, it soon transpired that when she wasn't creating new dishes in the

Ch 1 GASTROTELLY

kitchen, Fanny had been busy cooking up a glamorous fantasy past, which bore little or no relation to her humble and prosaic origins. Seeing her march onto the stage of the Royal Albert Hall to prepare dinner (wearing couture so haut that she made the Queen Mother look like a slut), it was hard to equate her elaborate reminiscences of an aristocratic childhood ("the tallest footman lit the top of the Christmas tree") with the stark reality of a shabby upbringing, during which she'd fiddled her bus fare and angrily dreamed of glory. "One day I'll be a household name" she vowed, and she was, but she did it the hard way. If being a household name was all she wanted, she could have saved herself a lot of trouble by simply calling herself Miss Windolene J Cloth.

There was plenty of familiar archive of Fanny in her heyday, invariably partnered by Johnnie, his clip-on monocle as phoney as the clip-on aristocratic demeanour they both adopted. In series such as *Chez Bon Viveur* and *Kitchen Magic*, they concocted a mixture of cooking and theatre, their eccentric behaviour and colourful dishes captivating wannabe middle class viewers who were desperate to escape the drabness of grey post-war Britain. Not that everyone approved of the sometimes garish results: "we couldn't stand her food" said neighbours, "because her potatoes were bright green and the eggs were blue." Like prototype Thatchers, the hectoring wife always took charge in public, while the henpecked and gaffe-prone husband took refuge in the odd drink or eight (although he was clearly a great deal smarter and less inebriated than he ever let on), but there was sadly no film of Johnnie's greatest gaffe, when he memorably told viewers that "I hope all your doughnuts turn out like Fanny's." Well, as another contributor remarked, "hygiene was never one of their strongest points."

But beneath this familiar exterior, the programme revealed fascinating discrepancies between the life Fanny claimed to have led, and reality. She hadn't grown up in a grand French chateau at all, but in Leytonstone. She'd married at seventeen, then again at nineteen, and it wasn't long before her two baby sons were receiving their unjust desserts, being abandoned by a mother who desired only the love of an adoring public. Stranger still, she committed bigamy twice (always a bride, never a bridesmaid), and managed to entice four husbands, even though in later life her thickly painted face and gaudy frocks made her look like what the French might call "*mouton habillé comme agneau.*" But by the mid-seventies, her increasing cantankerousness was alienating friends, family, and public alike, and the Cradocks sought refuge in the spirit world – Johnnie in the bottled variety, Fanny in faith healers and Ouija boards. Just as I'd always suspected. Fanny liked nothing better than having the willies put up her.

TV reviews

Do not speak ill of the dead, we are told, yet television nowadays likes nothing better than cutting its own deceased icons down to size. Admittedly they feel no pain, nor can they sue, but Fanny's autobiographical inexactitudes were hardly of Kurt Waldheimian proportions and, as for lying about her age, why that's positively *de rigueur* in the media (I myself am only twenty-three, and intend to remain so for at least another decade). Despite the mild kicking her reputation received from this workmanlike documentary, I confess to feeling a certain admiration for the woman (especially when, in her eighties, she effortlessly wiped the floor with Jonathan Ross), and she undoubtedly deserves credit for having dragged post-war British cuisine a few reluctant steps forward. The colour archive trails for her early TV shows were timeless works of popular art, and it's sad to think that only twelve people turned up for her funeral in 1994. Well, by then she was no longer "hot," as they say in Hollywood. Although paradoxically, down at the crematorium shortly afterwards, she was the hottest she'd been in years.

By the early 1990s, celebrity chefs were taking us into new realms of pointless infantilism as they reduced gastronomy to a branch of light entertainment, despite frequently possessing only a wafer-thin knowledge of the subject they claimed to excel in. No better example of that than Ainsley Harriott, who started his media career by appearing as an extra in Hale and Pace (or Hale and Pacemaker as I like to call them, after one of the double act with two straight men had an infarction of his ventricle), and performing as one half of The Calypso Twins, a pop duo who released a record in the early 1990s called "World Party."

Hear this by clicking on link #2 on the **TV Reviews** page on **www.badastralbooks.com**.

That's not to say Mr Harriot had no experience in gastronomy, prior to becoming a tellychef. He did work in the kitchens of several London hotels in the 1980s and early 1990s, and a friend of mine distinctly remembers seeing him cutting sandwiches in the Long Room at Lord's Cricket Ground.

Ch 1 GASTROTELLY

AINSLEY'S BARBECUE BIBLE

BBC2 1997

I've heard some unlikely titles for food programmes in my time. A US cable station once scheduled *Vegetarian Cooking with Jeffrey Dahmer* (though he never turned up for the transmission) but, for sheer portentousness, *Ainsley's Barbecue Bible* (BBC2) surely takes the briquette. Yet, as I watched Mr Harriott present the first programme of his new series last night, the religious nomenclature began to make sense, because the man spent thirty minutes lovingly preparing a succession of burnt offerings. "Bless me father, for I have singed."

And Lo, out of the wilderness of daytime television there came forth a multitude of the talentless, performing unmiraculous feats with loaves and fishes and searching for the promised land of Prime Time. And yeah verily, leading them towards the land of semi-skimmed milk and honey was (to my knowledge) the world's last "spooking for de white folk" black man: Ainsley Harriott – part David Bellamy, part Rustie Lee – rolling his eyes, waving his hands, holding a banana between his lips to exaggerate his smile, and so generally undignified in his eagerness to pander to every cultural presupposition of his predominantly white audience that he made Charlie Williams look like Nelson Mandela. "Bible" suggests a work of some seriousness, but when Ainsley prepared the meat for his *al fresco* recipes he forgot to trim off the excess fatuousness, which is why the main culinary activity on view last night was the sight of airtime being frittered away by a man who can't even fry an onion without cavorting around as though auditioning to be a backing singer for The Temptations.

"I'll be travelling around the world during this series" he began, "this week, the Uplands Allotments, Birmingham." Not *quite* the global trek we'd been promised but, to be fair, he was surrounded by Brummies from thirty countries who, sitting in front of their rickety sheds on the outskirts of the metropolis, bore an uncanny resemblance to the inhabitants of a Third World shantytown (the sort of residents whose new "front room" furniture had, the previous day, been on a curb on the other side of the city). A fitting backdrop for Ainsley to walk that TV walk and talk that TV talk, though sadly he couldn't cook and think at the same time, and quickly degenerated into a weak adjectival string machine: "beautiful, magnificent, beautiful, lovely, fantastic, wonderful." There was alliteration too ("stir, season, and simmer... and you'll soon be a Barbecue Black Belt"), and even poetry: "white wine vinegar for a tang, English mustard adds a bang." And all that

TV reviews

for the sake of a carrot, a vegetable whose sole function in life is to alert us not to step in pavement sick.

As anyone who works in the emergency services will tell you, barbecues are not for the normal. They're primarily a form of Darwinian culling for the sort of stupid people who pour cans of petrol onto bonfires and then wonder why they end up looking like Ken Dodd. Though avoiding personal injury, Mr Harriott quickly magicked up some Nagasaki sausages on his grill, but by now my interest had become purely clinical as the man – who talked to himself in the third person ("ooh Ainsley... yes indeed Ainsley") – was gripped by literal-itis ("literally leave it for two hours... vegetables literally just come off the allotment"), and promised to show us how to save money by lighting fires in old biscuit tins and discarded lawn mower cuttings boxes, when (as everybody knows) the expensive elements of a barbecue are the charcoal, the lighter fuel, and the food. Predictably, his finished dishes invariably appeared to be charred beyond recall, and that's the problem with making a TV show about this type of cooking. The only redeeming feature of a barbecue is the aroma but, until the boffins finally invent Smellyvision, all the viewer can experience is the unedifying sight of good food being turned into carbon.

"There you go" said Ainsley, and there indeed I went. If food is the new rock'n'roll, then Mr Harriott is Al Jolson, desperately mugging for the cameras and claiming that "you ain't heard nothin' yet" when in fact we've seen and heard it all a thousand times before. We may be turning into a nation of frozen dinner-for-one reheaters, but the less we cook the more we seem prepared to watch others doing it, a sad but compelling explanation of the veritable bulimic orgy of food shows currently in the schedules. As for open-air barbecues in Britain, with weather like ours, forget it. I was given a bowl of soup once, and failed to realise it was raining. It took me seven months to finish. Is this a record?

I thought of Ainsley recently, when I was playing with my prik while staring right up Prince Edward's tradesman's entrance. Don't get me wrong. I was merely eating chillies at the Chiang Mai Thai restaurant in Frith Street, while gazing across the road toward the rear of the Prince Edward theatre. And I suddenly remembered that Ainsley had also made a programme about Thai Cuisine.

Ch 1 **GASTROTELLY**

AINSLEY'S GOURMET EXPRESS

BBC2 2000

Some years ago, I studied Thai cooking in Bangkok, under the great Sansern Gajaseni. The course lasted one week, so there was only time to learn the basics, but I was taught such essential culinary skills as how to differentiate between high and low quality noodles (I now know my Guay Tiaw from my Sen Mee), how to prepare curry pastes, and the difference between Gaeng Phed and Geng Pa. I also learned the wizardry essential to the proper handling of coconut milk, discovered that those expensive packets of Thai fragrant rice on sale in the UK are a waste of money, and realised that Rendang Kok Bung Ghoon is the only dish in the world which sounds like a cross between somebody farting in a bath and a biscuit tin being kicked down stairs. Oh, and they also taught me a little about the ancient craft of carving vegetables, but I never quite mastered it, and only succeeded in making a complete pig's ear out of a carrot.

    Most of all, that week-long course taught me just how much I *didn't* know about the art of Thai cooking, which is why I've been too nervous ever since to make so much as a green curry for my Thai friends (even though I'm sure it would be pretty authentic). But everything's okay now because last night, in a mere twenty-eight minutes, *Ainsley's Gourmet Express* (BBC2) taught me how to make several different Thai noodle dishes, along with Japanese sushi and tempura, and absolutely no previous experience was necessary! Introducing a programme that was reminiscent of Monty Python's famous Blue Peter sketch ("this week, we'll show you how to split the atom, how to unite the Arabs with the Jews, and how to irrigate the Sahara desert"), Mr Harriott declared "I've got more taste than time these days." I suspect he may have recorded that speech prior to the no-nonsense axing of his US network show. These days, he surely has all the time in the world, although (judging from the garish lime green sweater he was wearing) the jury's still out on the question of taste.

    Entering the Itsu Japanese restaurant, he wasted no time in imparting his culinary wisdom to viewers. "Just for people who don't know, sushi means 'raw fish'" he explained. It doesn't. That's *sashimi*, whereas sushi is simply a cake of cold boiled rice which can have many different garnishes. Still, a little thing like accuracy wasn't going to stop the man from telling us how to make it, and he was soon back in his kitchen, sadly parading his recently-acquired and all-too-briefly-required Americanisms ("toona... bay-zel... eggplant"), and singing pointless improvised songs

TV reviews

("one, two, three, four, shake that vinegar galore"), presumably in a bid to become Andrew Lloyd Webber's new lyricist next time his Lordship changes his aristocratic underpants. And looking at the unappealing results of his uncooked piscine endeavours, I finally understood why a friend of mine recently described the act of cunnilingus as "like eating sushi from the floor of a barbershop."

If there was one thing you had to admit about the pre-US Ainsley, it was that he constantly enthused on screen, a sort of human hokey cokey, continually putting his whole self in and shaking it all about. But the NBC experience seems to have left him jaded, and the sudden bursts of song and dance were juxtaposed with periods of calm where he just concentrated on the food, and I gradually came to the conclusion that he's really not a very good chef. To be fair, he'd chosen thoroughly competent professionals with whom to discuss the preparation of the dishes (Clive Fretwell for the Japanese cuisine, Mai Ngoc Henry for the Thai) but, to be fairer, the show suffered from the same problem as the final turgid series of *Wogan* in the early nineties. The interviews would have been so much better without the interviewer.

I'm off for my annual holiday at the weekend (a three-week package tour for TV critics – debeaking chickens on Gruinard Island), and perhaps the recent plethora of cookery shows is starting to make me stir-fry crazy. But even allowing for that, this was a particularly pitiable example of the genre, not least because the photography (with its whip pans, crash zooms, and jump cuts) was yet another unappetising réchauffé of *The Naked Chef*, and although the presenter doesn't swig lager as he talks, he is very much like a bottle of beer. Why? Because he's empty from the neck up, quickly loses his head, is only mildly intoxicating, is brewed from malt, sugar, and hops, and is best served cold with Indian or Chinese food. Oh alright. On second thoughts, perhaps Ainsley Harriott *isn't* very much like a bottle of beer after all. Sorry about that. I've been under a lot of strain lately.

The aforementioned NBC show ran for just one series, after which Ainsley returned to the UK, where his popularity and his spookin' both remained undiminished.

One of the funniest assassinations of Ainsley and his gastrochef peers was performed by Rory Bremner, and it said more in a minute than I could manage in the previous 800 words. It is a masterpiece of timing and of special effects and can be seen by clicking on link #3 on the **TV Reviews** *page on* **www.badastralbooks.com.**

Ch 1 GASTROTELLY

Jamie Oliver started his career as a likeable and unpretentious cook. Clearly a precocious talent, he trained at the River Café, and brought a breath of fresh air to the screen in The Naked Chef in 1999. Back then, many critics insisted on calling him (inaccurately) a "Mockney", with journalists jumping onto the "fake accent" bandwagon, describing him as "a nice middle-class boy... who used to be quite well-spoken before someone stuck a camera in front of him." That was quite untrue, and if they'd bothered to check before filing their copy, they'd have discovered that the young Jamie was, in this respect, the real McCoy.

Indeed, Jamie was initially a refreshingly unpretentious and unaffected chef, and not simply another of the "here's a personality I whipped up earlier" brigade, who usually infest the gastronomic airwaves. I wrote about him glowingly during the airing of that first series, and received a delighted phone call from him in response. I immediately scribbled a note back to him, saying "do me a favour and don't become seduced by your own celebrity," adding that if I ever saw his face on a pot or pan, or on any kitchen implement that was being offered for sale, I'd have to conclude that he'd been corrupted by fame and had sold out, like so many chefs before him.

Sadly, shortly after that exchange, he did indeed start to believe his own publicity, and not only began turning himself into a lucrative multi-national corporation, but also started to believe that he was the long-awaited Messiah of gastronomy, sent to earth to save the poor and dispossessed from culinary deprivation. Which brings me to...

JAMIE'S SCHOOL DINNERS

C4 2005

As I was telling my two children, Niacin and Thiamin (we originally wanted to christen them Pearl and Dean, but the vicar phoned the social workers from the font), "when I were a lad, food were scarce, so father used to raise a litter or two of giblets, which he kept in hutch in t' back yard." I went on to inform them that giblets are small edible creatures with long furry bodies and cute little snouts, which nowadays are reared in battery cages, and used to stuff supermarket chickens. But back before the war, the domestic giblet was a common sight in working-class gardens, where it would be fattened throughout the winter on nose pickings and navel fluff, before being ritually slaughtered in the spring by the entire

TV reviews

family, who would place a pillow over its head and sit on it. A tradition that, in a modified form, lives on to this day, in the annual holiday known as Smothering Sunday.

You probably think that tale is untrue, because nowadays nobody believes anything that journalists write, yet some people will swallow almost any food-related story if it's served up in a TV documentary format. Take Jamie Oliver, whose *faux-naif, homme-du-peuple* routine initially conned me into thinking he was genuine, and continues to fool millions of viewers into believing that he's the inspiring estuary equivalent of Robin Williams in *Dead Poets Society*. The scales fell from my eyes a couple of years ago, when *Jamie's Kitchen* duped vast swathes of the media into ludicrously hailing him as the saviour of the unemployed, and he tried it again last night in *Jamie's School Dinners*, which many hacks seem to believe is an entirely philanthropic venture on his part, to raise the standard of our children's nutrition. "I'm not getting paid for being here... I'm doing it because I want a better cooler cleverer nation," he told us altruistically from a Greenwich school canteen, oddly neglecting to mention that (as owner of Fresh One Productions) he's making a fortune out of the series, and it's that yawning chasm between appearance and reality in his various "charitable" enterprises that leaves a very funny taste in my mouth.

"School dinners are in crisis," we were told, "they've got worse and worse over the past twenty years." Comparing today's burger-and-chips menus with the overcooked and near-inedible slop served up in my day, why should anyone accept that initial premise? The clean plates at Kidbrooke Comprehensive demonstrated that the children enjoyed every mouthful of their 37p-per-portion fast food diet, and I thought back to Loyd "food tsar" Grossman's futile attempts to overhaul NHS catering a few years ago, replacing shepherd's pie with "navarin of lamb with couscous," only to find that it cost twice as much and the patients refused to eat it. "There's shitloads of additives here," Oliver fumed, without ever telling us what's wrong with using chemicals to preserve food and enhance flavour. And his claims that chips have "no vitamin C... too much salt and fat" were simply ill-informed, because as the British Potato Council could have told him – I checked this – a portion of chips contains five times as much vitamin C as grapes, and far less salt and fat than the cheese-and-tomato pizza offered as a "healthy" alternative. Anyway, his gripes were a bit rich, coming from a man who then drove away in a gas-guzzling car, belching fumes that could knock ten points off the IQ of an entire primary school, just by revving up hard outside the main gate.

Worse than his unscientific insistence that additive-free food is inherently superior (something that his former paymasters at Sainsbury's also proclaim when pushing their high-priced organic range), and domestic scenes that smacked of posing for the cameras (he himself admitted that he mostly sees his kids only at photoshoots), was his relentlessly foul language. When he started in TV, he restricted himself to pukka-pukka-pukka, but now every sentence is phukka-phukka-phukka, and swearing so unrestrainedly in front of women old enough to be his mother was disrespectful and distasteful (as was proudly displaying his "cock-shaped bread, hee hee hee"). By the end of the episode, he'd finally produced some alternative meals, but the ingredients exceeded the budget by 200 per cent, required far more costly labour to prepare, and the results were no more popular than the fish fingers the children had been happily wolfing down before. And I was reminded of BBC2's *Food and Drink* programme which, during the height of 80s unemployment, used to promise to show the poor how to make "a nutritious and delicious three-course dinner for only 50p," only to give itself away by telling viewers to "first, take some olive oil, cèpes, and saffron from your store cupboard..."

With Oliver's production company shaping the action and editing, it's not hard to predict that the final episode will end triumphantly, with the children professing a newly kindled love of zucchini and fresh fruit, while shamefaced politicians promise to invest more in school dinners after the next election. But I also predict that, once the cameras have departed, the children and canteen staff will soon return to their comfortable old chips-and-burgers ways, just as most of the formerly unemployed staff of Fifteen quietly quit the restaurant once the buzz of continuous media attention was no longer there to motivate them. As for the boss, his "normal bloke" routine is a Branson-esque disguise, behind which lurks a serious breadhead who's cynically marketing his image, behaving like a ten-year-old who's discovered that swearing attracts attention, or like the Football Association's idea of the perfect soccer fan, who could only exist in an all-seater stadium. C4 won't care, of course, because the ratings will doubtless be huge, but the channel has hit rock bottom with a programme that proves only one thing: that the road to hell is paved with *food* intentions.

In the year following Jamie's pioneering "school dinners" efforts, which were warmly endorsed by Tony Blair and New Labour, the number of school dinners consumed by children fell sharply. As chips and burgers disappeared from school menus, so did the kids, to the point that the provision of school dinners became unviable in some areas. In June 2010, Tory Health Secretary Andrew Lansley bluntly spelt out the truth of this misguided crusade: "The net effect of Jamie Oliver's campaign was that the number of children eating school meals in many of these places went down. Lecturing people is counterproductive."

TV reviews

After I criticised Jamie in print for the first time, I received an out-of-the-blue phone call from him during which he repeatedly told me that I'd got him wrong and that he was "a great guy." I told him he was confusing me with somebody who gave a fuck, and the phone was slammed down on me. Shortly afterwards, I found myself quoted on the back cover of his latest book, talking about him in admiring tones, which was odd (although perhaps his publishers had quoted me without his knowledge). His delusions of grandeur have since continued to grow, to the point that he's gradually turning into a gastronomic Michael Jackson (only thankfully without the kiddie fiddling – and, furthermore, Jamie is technically still alive). Whom should we blame for this? His own vanity, I suppose, but ultimately the finger has to be pointed at his original production company, Optomen, who appear to have taken a genuinely talented and likeable young chef and turned him into a caricature.

Now to Heston Blumenthal who, when he first appeared on our screens, wasn't part of the Optomen stable. And like Jamie, he began his media career with some first-class programmes, like this series from 2005.

KITCHEN CHEMISTRY

DISCOVERY 2005

If poetry is the synthesis of hyacinths and biscuits, then everyday speech is surely a union of kapok and marshmallow. Quotidian language is full of sloppy and meaningless expressions, like the people who approach you at bus stops and ask "has the bus come yet?" as though you would still be standing there in a position to reply to them if it had. Such people also tell you that "life is short" (even though it's the longest thing any of us have), and are wont to walk into a room, clap their hands, and ask "fit?" – to which one must always reply "no thanks, I had a grand mal just before I came out." And as for those who utter the absurd and phatic words "so... what's cooking?" the only sensible response is "cooking is a method of preparing food by using heat to soften the fibres and improve the texture." That usually puts them in their place.

      Or, better still, I could sit them down with a video of *Kitchen Chemistry*, an intelligent and enthralling explanation of the science of cooking that's currently running on the Discovery channel. "The kitchen is a bit like a science lab," observes Heston Blumenthal (the inspired two-star chef at The Fat Duck in Bray) at the start of each edition, and there's something admirably refreshing about his willingness to experiment with

Ch 1 GASTROTELLY

food, and to test the worth of age-old culinary lore through a mixture of theory and practice. As with his restaurant's menu, the series is built around "molecular gastronomy," an approach which seeks to understand exactly what happens when, for example, salt is added to a dish, or why certain food combinations enhance our enjoyment, while others repel. In short, he's set out to answer a simple yet vital question that most chefs will not (or, more probably, *cannot*) explain: "why does food behave as it does when we cook it?"

Last night's programme was devoted to solving the many mysteries surrounding chocolate. No, not why people keep sneaking into your hotel room and leaving a single Mozart chocolate on your pillow every time you pop out for a few minutes, nor why we allow confectioners to sell us high-priced eggs that are 98 per cent cardboard and air every Easter, but "a journey deep into chocolate's molecular heart," to discover how the stuff can be given the properties that chefs require and diners relish. To show how emulsifiers must be sensitively handled in order to stabilise the molecules of cocoa powder, cocoa butter, and sugar, Blumenthal deliberately overheated his ingredients and completely ruined the texture and flavour, something I've noticed that the chefs on *Ready Steady Cook* also do quite regularly. "You may as well throw it away" he said, then repeated the experiment at the correct heat to make a classic and delicious dish, which is something the *Ready Steady Cook* bunch *never* do.

"Give it to a pet," he added, which reminded me of a favourite trick I use to get rid of unwanted visitors: I offer them a bowl of peanuts and then, once they've feasted, say "thanks, the dog ate my false teeth last week, so all I can do with choc-o-nuts nowadays is to suck the chocolate off." Then he introduced us to the miracle of "molecular food profiling" (carried out at the Food and Flavour Expertise Centre in Geneva), a technique whereby predictions can be made as to which combinations of food will taste delicious, and which will be disgusting (basil and coffee is a particularly disastrous coupling, we were warned, so I tried it, and it is). Lastly, he explained that chocolate (like metal) can be "tempered" by heat, so that it forms crystals with a high melting point, and is therefore easier to handle. Apparently, cheap "bad-tempered chocolate" melts on the fingers of customers, thus making them bad-tempered too, though not as bad-tempered as I am when I think of the way that ads during my childhood for Milky Bars used to pronounce Nestles to rhyme with "wrestles," then one day suddenly changed, so that I now have to walk into shops and remember to ask for "Ness-lays."

This was starred first material from Two Four Productions, and from Blumenthal, an unpretentious and ungimmicky TV chef who is worth ten Jamie Olivers, a hundred Worrall Thompsons, and several million

TV reviews

28

Rick Steins. Okay, the animations had an unusual whiff of a 70s school programme about them, while the obsessive, slightly-out-of-focus, macro close-ups of the presenters' teeth and eyes made them look like ambulance men peering at you through your letterbox after you've had the near fatal stroke; but at least the programme was determined to break new ground, both gastronomically and televisually. Best of all, upon being told that the molecular profiles of chocolate and blue cheese combine perfectly, I resolved to commence manufacturing chocolate and Stilton effigies of Christ, under the brand name "Cheeses of Nazareth," because I'm convinced that they'll sell like hot cakes. Not that I've ever seen anyone go into a shop, ask for "a hot cake please," and be offered one for sale. Well, I suppose they'd have already sold out, that being very much the essential nature of the hot cake.

Sadly, Mr Blumenthal joined the Optomen stable (and I choose that word advisedly) a few years later, and his programmes have since become increasingly gimmicky and tasteless. The media mostly seem to fall for his loveable-mad-scientist persona, but then they mostly fall for Jamie Oliver's I'm-the-Messiah-of-food schtick too ("Jamie Oliver is beyond criticism," a BBC channel controller once told me). It all leaves a very nasty taste in the mouth.

If there is a seemingly high level of irritability in several of the following reviews, this brief digression will explain why. Although I was writing for a London paper for 15 years, for almost the entire time, I was filing copy from the middle of the Cumbrian Fells, a full seven-hour drive from the capital (something that shocked my London readers, but delighted me). When I arrived there, I had to arrange for a massive erection (of a TV aerial), and even then I could initially only pick up BBC Cymru in the Welsh language. I phoned my editor, Max Hastings, asking if he'd mind if I reviewed exclusively programmes in Welsh (a language that I do not understand, save for llanfairpwllgwyngyllgogerychwyrndrobwllllantysiliogogogoch) in his London newspaper, and met with a bemused response. A similar response to the one I met with from a subsequent editor, Veronica Wadley, when I called her to say that there was nothing worth reviewing on conventional TV, and asking if I could instead review clips (shot with the rear camera on my Lexus) of me reversing into a tight parking space.

Because I was writing from a farm in Cumbria, and was often looking out of the window as I typed, a lot of my reviews are shot through with countryside references. Although I soon discovered that the countryside was a lot less romantic than erstwhile townies like me had been brought up to believe. On the day we arrived, the love of my life, Virginia, found a "lucky rabbit's foot" in the fields, but we were soon put right by a dour farmer who spotted it hanging over

Ch 1 GASTROTELLY

our door: "It's a sheep penis." This event set the tone for the next 16 years in Cumbria. Often, I'd be staring out of the window, and an event that I witnessed would appear in the column. Such as this extract from a review of Shaun the Sheep:

Spring is in the air, and it's a time of year that I always greet with mixed feelings. On the positive side, the Asperges season will soon be with us (though be careful not to confuse it with Aspergers, or you might end up pouring hollandaise sauce over the victim's head), but on the negative side, another posse of lambs from the neighbouring farm will soon be scrabbling through the hole at the bottom of my garden, and seeking the forbidden source of pleasure that lies secreted within the tyres of my old car. Each generation of sheep somehow teaches its offspring to creep furtively up to the wheels of my vehicle, then bite down on the rubber valves as though they were teats, thus giving their stomachs an exhilarating rush of compressed air that seems as addictive as heroin, judging from the extra bounce I can subsequently detect in their gambol (yes, they gambol too). Still, their short lives will soon be terminated in the slaughterhouse, so I haven't got the heart to deprive them of their cheap temporary thrills, and anyway, I can always exact revenge by walking past their field and whispering the phrase that has made me Britain's number one sheep worrier: "mint sauce."

I am prepared to admit that, the summer before this next review was written, I had battled (and lost the fight with) an army of slugs who had eaten through the carefully nurtured young shoots in my vegetable patch in the space of a single night. It occurred to me afterwards that there should be a TV series which shows viewers "101 delicious ways to cook slugs," because if you attempt to grow vegetables in your own garden, you will always have a plentiful supply of these gastropod molluscs – and frequently little else.

And because truth is stranger than fiction, it turns out that there are nowadays chefs who include slug dishes in their repertoire:

You may see one by clicking on link #4 on the **TV Reviews** page on **www.badastralbooks.com**.

Anyway, instead of tending to my sprouts, I found myself reviewing this:

TV reviews

GROW YOUR OWN VEG!
BBC2 2007

During my New Year vacation, the only television I saw was the gruesome image of Saddam Hussein being hanged (or is it hung? Nobody can decide, and the suspension is killing me). According to Shia and Kurdish leaders, he should have been executed fifty times for his crimes against humanity, and that no-nonsense approach to capital punishment has inspired me to suggest a new system of posthumous hangings for this country, so that murderers who have committed suicide rather than serve out their life sentences can be dug up and made to face the justice they shamefully tried to avoid. I can hear the bulletins already: "The Home Secretary has announced today that Dr Harold Shipman is to be disinterred, whipped, given a cold shower, paraded through the streets, 'dead-legged', then hanged by the neck until he is dead again. Then buried. Then dug up and hanged again. Oh, and gobbed on." As for Fred West (the alcoholic psychopath who once told his prison warder "I could murder a couple of Tennants"), he also deserves a taste of exhumation-execution, because he not only avoided trial by topping himself, but also escaped the misery of slowly rotting away in a room, staring blankly at a TV set for year after year after year. Good God. I hope such a terrible fate never befalls me.

As I write, Saddam's corpse is already turning to mulch in the ground, thereby helping to boost organic vegetable production in the Tikrit area, and it would be a fitting irony if Jerusalem artichokes are now feeding on him. According to Carol Klein on Friday night's *Grow Your Own Veg!*, those tubers grow well in winter and thrive in any type of soil, although they'd surely do even better if a decomposing cadaver was putting some genuine human back into the humus in which they're planted. The presenter (who addressed us in a manner reminiscent of Janet Brown impersonating Margaret Thatcher) would doubtless agree, because she spoke excitedly about "growing my own organic vegetables" and promised us that we too could harvest fresh produce every day of the year, "and all you need is a three-metre-square plot." But as I observed her crumbling the soil in her hands in a quasi-orgasmic manner (a sort of horticultural version of those old Flake ads), it struck me that there's a very fine line between "hobby" and "mental illness," and that I was watching a woman who had simultaneously found and lost the plot.

Within minutes, Carol was digging a trench, chitting potatoes, and insisting that food tastes better when it only travels from garden to table. "I'm planting Red Duke of York because it's a really good eating potato" she told us (as though eating was merely one of many reasons why we might wish to grow spuds), then interviewed two dykey-looking members of the Royal Horticultural Society, who flatly contradicted her by advising us not to bother planting "potatoes, onions, or things you can buy from a supermarket." As they sifted the loam with their hands, I idly wondered if a lesbian with fat fingers could be described as well-hung, and marvelled at the way all of them failed to mention the considerable downside of gardening as a pastime. Slugs, pests, disease, hours of backbreaking digging, and worst of all, trying to convince yourself that the stuff from your garden has more flavour than the stuff you buy in a plastic bag from Tesco – when blind tastings repeatedly demonstrate that it bloody-well does not.

Before long, I'd realised that Carol is one of those women who likes to talk to her vegetables (us, the viewers), and that producer/director Juliet Glaves was mortally afraid of boring her audience. Consequently, many of the on-screen images were absurdly over-directed (with needless macro close-ups and jimmy jibs), the soundtrack was plastered with brief snatches of eclectic but irrelevant music, and there were too many narrative strands, suggesting that the series outline hadn't been plotted nearly as carefully as the neatly-partitioned individual vegetable beds. A visit to the garden of a smiling "grow your own" family straight off a box of wholesome additive-free breakfast cereal confirmed my long-held view (echoed yesterday by Environment Secretary David Miliband) that the organic movement is nothing more than a middle-class lifestyle choice, with no basis whatsoever for the smug air of superiority its aficionados routinely adopt. Not least because Carol arrived there in her gas-guzzling car, rather like those millions of visitors who drive each year to see the energy-saving Eden Project, belching out fumes all the way to Cornwall and back so they can spend an afternoon marvelling at such environmentally friendly greenness.

Frankly, there was more than a whiff of bullshit about this introduction to the wonders of organic vegetable-growing. Any gardening programme that makes you wish for the return of Alan Titchmarsh has surely failed in its purpose, and the sight of Carol and her hubby exulting over the taste of a single boiled Annabelle potato suggested that this wasn't really about gardening or cooking, but about acting out a *Guardian* reader's Good Life eco-fantasy-wank-fest on television. If even the contributors are telling us not to bother growing those vegetables that we can easily find in the supermarket, then really, what's the point? Although I confess that I was pleased to see Carol encouraging rhubarb-growing, because I've kept a patch for years (no maintenance required), and swear by it to keep me regular. You see, I have a bowel movement at 8 o'clock every morning, regular as clockwork. The only problem is, I don't wake up until 9 o'clock.

TV reviews

Like the vegetables I attempted to grow, Carol Klein seemed to rise steadily on British television for a while, then disappear overnight. In 2008, she complained to the press that she'd "hit a grass ceiling," and had been overlooked by BBC bosses, who wanted younger presenters on the screen. Not the first nor the last time that competent TV women presenters of a certain age have made that complaint, and generally with good reason.

I am not ashamed to admit that my eyes misted over when I watched the last edition of Good Food Live. As a regular viewer of this daily two-hour live programme, I often felt as though I'd enrolled on a university course in gastronomy, presided over by the clever and funny Jeni Barnett.

The programme was avidly watched by a coterie of media types. I know that Danny Baker was a huge fan, as was Andi Peters, and Mateus Rosé-lover Saddam Hussein (ok I lied about Saddam – although not about his love of Mateus Rose, which is well-attested, yet seldom listed in his crimes against humanity). Jeni was (and is) a highly intelligent, spontaneous and very very funny presenter, and the show put the BBC's entire output of food programmes to shame. Inevitably, it was therefore axed by some half-man-half-desk of a channel executive, and replaced by the dire Market Kitchen, a cheap imitation with woefully lacklustre presentation. In this chapter, I've included two reviews as tribute to a programme that, throughout the mid noughties, was up there in my top 5 of favourite television programmes. Here's the first of them.

CHRISTMAS LIVE!

UKTV FOOD 2004

Ladies and gentlemen, kindly assume the crash position and brace yourselves for the annual onslaught of Christmas rituals. Over the next ten days, there'll be amateur drunks depositing action paintings on a pavement near you, smashed secretaries leaving office parties on all fours (pursued by optimistic clerks on all fives), waggish revellers singing "Chest hair roasting on an open fire / Jack Straw's blowing out his nose," strange seasonal food which has to be labelled "Eat Me" (otherwise nobody would go near it), and coins cunningly hidden in steamed puddings (a practice surely dreamed up by emergency orthodontists and their BMW dealers). Television will be equally predictable, with wall-to-wall Baby Jesus and his Sky Gods on the screen, interspersed with festive entertainment

Ch 1 GASTROTELLY

which is nothing more than re-heated turkeys: unappetising, tasteless, unsatisfying, half-baked, and frequently inducing the desire to vomit. Be mindful of leaving Christmas as you would wish to find it. Your co-operation is appreciated.

So, with most channels offering us stale fare or intellectual spume over the Christmas period, where can we turn for something that's genuinely stimulating and nourishing? To UKTV Food, and in particular to its daily *Good Food Live* strand, which is unfailingly fresh and innovative, and consistently treats the art of cooking (and I repeat *art*) with the respect it deserves. In a nod toward the Yuletide season, it's temporarily rechristened itself *Christmas Live!*, but retains the same compelling blend of gastronomic seriousness and presentational quixotism that BBC2 is currently trying to emulate in its blatantly derivative *Full On Food*. But despite its far larger budget, the BBC imitation will not succeed, mainly because it lacks one essential ingredient: Jeni Barnett, an accomplished and intelligent presenter who combines the demeanour of a Roedean housemistress with a hint of flirtatiousness, and a soupçon of dominatrix.

The edition I watched yesterday explored the theme of "kitsch Christmas," and I've seldom seen such high-octane campery taking place in a single studio (which at times resembled Frankie Goes to Hollywood's video for "Relax"). Within the first ten seconds, a half-naked Danish man covered in gold paint was seen amusing himself with a feather duster, while co-presenter Oliver Heath discussed cross-dressing with Jeni, who then asked her guests "are you going to show us your cumquats?" More outrageous still was Ercole Moroni, an Italian florist who sounded like Herve Villechaize as Tattoo in *Fantasy Island* ("de plane! de plane!"), kissed Oliver (but not Jeni) fulsomely beneath a piece of mistletoe he'd brought along solely for that purpose, described all his ornate fruit-and-flower arrangements as either "fabulous" or "amazing," and generally gave the impression that his anus is not exclusively an exit. In short, the behaviour was hilariously shameless and brazen, with only the Dane displaying any sort of gilt.

Yet, as always, whenever the talk turned to gastronomy, the recipes were definitely *not* treated as a laughing matter, and nobody played with their food. For anyone who regards canapés as nothing more than little dead things on toast, Andrew Nutter's snowman canapés will have come as a revelation, although I was somewhat alarmed by the cavalier way he stuck his hands into a plugged-in food blender while mixing the cream cheese and smoked salmon, something that the safety manuals warn you never to do (perhaps he was planning a finger buffet). He also created an astonishing chocolate-and-mincemeat bombe that visually resembled a traditional Christmas pudding, while Paul Young created a pink Christmas

TV reviews

cake, made entirely without marzipan. Which reminded me of a birthday party I attended in the 80s, when I dared to suggest to the host (who'd either had his hair combed forward or his face combed back) that the event was so boring that somebody must have mistakenly put Temazepam in the cake, instead of marzipan. I was never asked back.

With its reliable combination of fearlessness, intelligence, and integrity, this daily strand from Prospect Pictures is unselfconscious television at its best; and best of all, there was no mention of what to do with the Turkey leftovers (what would happen if the whole of Britain suddenly decided this year to kick the cold turkey habit, I wonder? Would that mean that we'd all gone cold turkey?). The format works in no small measure thanks to the brilliant Ms Barnett (one of the best TV presenters in the business), and it's surely only a matter of time before one of the terrestrial networks poaches the entire show, because it knocks the spots off anything they have to offer on their own vapid daytime schedules. After the show, by way of celebrating my forthcoming short holiday (and Mr Blunkett's permanent one, to my utter joy), I made myself a snowball, then fell asleep, and had a peculiar dream in which (due to an administrative error during the cabinet reshuffle) Ann Widdecombe was appointed as Minister of Agriculture by Tony B Liar, while I had become a pork butcher in Accrington, and there was Doris Karloff in my shop, telling me that she wanted "some really good boned meat... but give me some tongue first... dripping all over my rashers." What did it all mean? Who cares? Merry Christmas, and may I offer my loyal readers seasonal warmth to your Christmas balls.

When watching great programmes like Good Food Live was not enough to keep me sane, the Evening Standard would allow me to take a break from television and undertake a bout of restaurant reviewing instead. I soon came to realise that, of all the phatic phrases uttered by people in the restaurant business, the most inscrutable is "would you care to see the menu, sir?"

What is anyone supposed to reply to such a meaningless question? "No, don't bother with the menu, we'll just guess what's on offer from the fucking stains on your apron?" Frankly, whenever it happens to me, I superglue a 10p piece to the table as a tip, and leave.

I got Keith Floyd chuckling about this technique when I filmed him for one of my Keith Allen Ch4 documentaries (Keith meets Keith) in 2009. His agent, Stan Green (with whom he acrimoniously parted company, just as we started filming) repeatedly insulted his own client in correspondence with me, referring to him as "very unreliable," "out of control," "a nightmare... totally out of it,"

Ch 1 GASTROTELLY

and telling me that, for Keith Floyd, "nothing gets in the way of a bar." For months, Stan kept finding reasons why it would be impossible for me to make a television programme about Keith, or even to interview him.

When I finally bypassed the agent and contacted Keith directly (after finding his number in the Avignon telephone directory), I discovered that Stan had not even told him about my programme invitation. Keith was utterly delighted to be asked, furious that he'd not been told before, and happily agreed to take part. This show of duplicity by an agent wasn't an unusual experience, by the way. In fact, 99 per cent of agents that I've ever dealt with have been thieving indolent scum (although my lawyer tells me that Mr Green is definitely amongst the 1 per cent who are entirely blameless). "My clients take 85 per cent of my fee," was the statistic once quoted to me by a well-known showbiz agent, and he clearly wasn't joking when he said it. He even expected me to sympathise with him.

Anyway, a week later, Keith Allen, the crew, and I all went to the house in Avignon, to make our documentary. Our first meeting was a shock, because Keith Floyd was the oldest-looking sixty-five-year-old I'd ever seen, and the first glimpse of him in such a depleted state was a sobering moment for the entire crew. He looked a little like Rocky Marciano, coming out for one fight too many. However, for the next day or so, he charmed us all with his stories and his bonhomie, and all went swimmingly until the celebratory farewell lunch we'd planned (attended also by his close friend Celia and his daughter Poppy). During it, he became increasingly drunk and maudlin and sentimental, then collapsed, and for the first time I realised that the agent did at least have some justification for what he'd told me. To catch Keith Floyd on a good day was heaven. To get him on a bad one was hell.

Of course, Floyd built his TV career on drink, as well as on talent, and was regularly seen imbibing so excessively that his series ought to have been subtitled One Foot in the Gravy or Floyd on the Floor. I had always been a fan of his anarchic style, but many of the reviews I wrote about him don't fully reflect this. That's probably because he was already past his prime when I began reviewing, and by the 1990s he had understandably become somewhat jaded and disillusioned with television, after his early glorious successes. To be fair though, he always understood the relationship between presenter and camera as few others have ever done, and he never seemed to be merely going through the motions. Ah well, when you're dealing with food, I suppose that going through the motions is how it all ends up anyway. The first of these two reviews found him concentrating on wine, the second on Greek cuisine. Both series were made for Channel 5.

TV reviews

FLOYD UNCORKED

C5 1998

Because few TV presenters have added appreciably to the richness of the English language, I intend to submit the following words to the OED for inclusion in the next edition. The verb "to Tarrant," meaning to appear on every TV show that asks you to, while simultaneously telling the press that you'll "be doing no TV this year." The gerund "Feltzing," denoting the action of talking half an inch of meaning to every fifty feet of noise. The verb "to Frostrup," meaning to hint in interviews that you have hidden depths, and then appear on TV and reveal hidden shallows. And I'm also suggesting a collective noun for the new breed of telly wine bores, who insist that "I can smell wet nappies in there... and burnt toast... and Sunday newspapers." What better name for a group of pretentious plonk experts than "plonkers"?

Amongst the acronyms I will be submitting is "FU" (derived from C5's *Floyd Uncorked*), to describe a series that raises two metaphorical fingers at wine bores, and gives us plonk without the plonkers. After a couple of lacklustre series on BBC2, Keith Floyd has risen like a phoenix from the clichés, and is currently demystifying wine without demeaning it, while teaching us more in each half hour than I've learned from a decade of listening to Oz ("I'm an actor really, but don't let on") Clarke on *Food and Drink*. Together with "JP" (Jonathan Pedley), he's been touring the vineyards of France, deciphering such acronyms as AOC, exploring the properties of different soils and production techniques, and fearlessly banning all overblown descriptive language from his show. "I find this very easy to drink" was his succinct report on one of last night's wines, and he was right, although I confess it's difficult to imagine any alcoholic beverage that Floyd *wouldn't* find very easy to drink. Unless, of course, the DTs had set in, but even then, I'm sure he'd be fine if you gave him a funnel and a length of rubber tubing.

Last night he traversed the Rhone Valley from Lyon to Avignon, a journey I myself once made on an all-night train, with only a single vaginal Femfresh wipe with which to give myself a bedbath. While Floyd and JP opened their first bottle of Côtes du Rhône Villages, and enthusiastic viewers opened theirs, they discussed the meaning of room temperature (thereby confusing me because, philosophically speaking, isn't *every* room at room temperature?). After settling on 17°C as the ideal temperature (so you *should* put red wine briefly in the fridge on hot days, despite the laughter in *Abigail's Party*), they discussed the wine itself, but whenever

Ch 1 GASTROTELLY

JP displayed the first symptoms of Goolden-itis and started talking about blackcurrants and plums, he was hauled back to reality by Floyd with a "why do we have to have all these funny words about fruit? Why can't we just say this is a Syrah?" And even more refreshing than the beakerful of the warm South in my hand was to hear him declare "a lot of the things you've said about wine – that it tastes of bananas or something – I frankly disagree with. But I've had to go along with it to stay in the programme, otherwise they'd replace me." Not that they'd dare.

But it's his knockabout relationship with viewers that makes Floyd on form such a delight, and we were gently joshed last night with phrases like "my dear gastronauts, my dear little winos," as he whipped up a splendid *pistou* and an agreeable salt cod and snails (a dish I've always associated with the Var, further South), and laced it with freshly-made aioli. Atop the hill of Hermitage, he gazed down upon this famous vineyard and discussed the difference between widely-available Crozes-Hermitage and exclusive Hermitage, balancing out his put-downs of JP with jokes to viewers and almost Shakespearean asides to the crew. I noticed, incidentally, that his cameraman is called Mike. I only hope his sound recordist isn't called Cameron, otherwise there'll be high jinx that even *The Men From The Ministry* couldn't have equalled, before the series is over.

Floyd is a food presenter with depth (dark at that), and one of the few who wouldn't sauté his own liver just to get on TV. Producer Nick Patten is getting the very best out of him (back to the standards with which Floyd delighted us in the late 80s), and together with JP they're giving us one of the clearest, most relaxed, expositions of the art of producing and drinking wine that I've ever seen. Best of all, there are no strings of adjectival nonsense from plonkers in pin stripes, and that makes me feel, reassuringly, at home.

You see, I drink as I dress. Chablis.

Despite the gallons of blood, sweat, and tears shed by generations of professional scriptwriters in the pursuit of comedy, many of the funniest one-liners I've ever seen were penned by untutored but streetwise market traders. When I was filming Floyd he told me two corkers that he claimed he had seen firsthand. One, a Billingsgate fish stall mysteriously warning: "Blind lesbians – beware of confusion." And another he said he'd seen at Spitalfields Market, which read simply, nay poignantly, "Do not feed the animals – they are dead." Humour and gastronomy were at the core of dear old Floyd.

TV reviews

FLOYD AROUND THE MED

C5 2000

It was during a lengthy wait for my suitcase in the French Riviera's principal airport (so nice they named it Nice) that I finally realised the horrific implications of the theory that the rings around Saturn are composed entirely of lost airline luggage. If that's truly the case, then it's entirely possible that my mislaid Calvin Klein mink-lined posing pouch is now circling that distant planet, nestling between John Prescott's unwashed Y-fronts and Charlie Dimmock's carelessly-discarded upper chest support. And that's a distasteful thought because, as I told the then Deputy PM, "your Y-fronts could well be circling Uranus." "I don't know nothing that might not wouldn't be that it the," he retorted in his usual, delightfully cryptic fashion.

Also rummaging for lost luggage on the same carousel at Nice airport was Keith Floyd, who I now realise must have been visiting the côte of many colours to film his new series, *Floyd around the Med* (C5). He seemed to have contracted a touch of the Prescotts last night, at one point introducing a Greek chef as "my friend, with whom I cannot communicate because neither of us speak our mutual languages." But occasional solecisms are all part of the act when this eminently watchable presenter opens his mouth. Standing in front of the Acropolis, he nearly came a cropper listing all the places he'll be visiting during the next nine weeks, "to view their cultural attractions and sample their cuisine." Like a 70s' Monty Python sketch, he "did" the Med in three minutes flat, posing first inside a bullring, then next to the Sphinx, then in a mosque in Istanbul, before announcing that "my journey begins in Athens... let's see what's cooking in grease." Funny. I thought cooking in grease was more Ainsley Harriott's territory.

"Where the olive tree no longer grows, there is no real gastronomic civilisation," he declared, sounding now like Lord Clark fronting *Civilisation* as he reminded us that the Mediterranean laps the shores of Europe, Asia, and Africa, and that the myriad peoples who live on its periphery have many different religions and traditions, but share the same culinary ingredients. Soon he was stuffing a huge fish with lemons, marjoram, and thyme, and basting it with olive oil, and although I've always thought that 50 per cent of the attraction of Mediterranean cuisine is the endless sunshine and timeless atmosphere that accompanies it when eaten *in situ* (the antithesis of life in grey, punctuality-obsessed Blighty), Floyd got as near to recreating that relaxed ambience as any presenter could.

Ch 1 GASTROTELLY

He pointed out that the Greek diet includes many ingredients borrowed from the country's various conquerors (yoghurt from Turkey, pasta from Italy), which set me wondering whether they have tins of alphabetti spaghetti in Athens. If so, then Heinz must have designed a special pasta machine that extrudes letters in the Hellenic alphabet, and monolingual tourists presumably stare glumly at their plates and lament "it's all Greek to me."

A little later, Floyd was atop a sheer cliff, near an ancient monastery, explaining that some Mediterranean people were so poor that they had to cook lamb in ovens made from camel dung. I've even heard that some war-torn regions in the Med are so rough that they have to buy broken leg of lamb from their butchers, but Floyd thankfully cut the crap from his recipe and cooked the meat with apricots and herbs on a butane stove, which must have been hauled laboriously up the hillside by his unlucky assistants. He gave us some useful professional tips, such as adding dried potato powder to thicken sauces (because, unlike wheat flour, it's completely undetectable), and of course stopped from time to time for a generous swig from a bottle. But what was this? Like the *Galloping Gourmet* – who put double cream and butter in everything in the 70s, then recently reappeared preaching the benefits of low-fat fromage frais) – Floyd is now a reformed character, and the bottle contained not wine, but Evian water.

There's something fundamentally likeable about Floyd, and although this series isn't quite as coherent as the splendid *Floyd Uncorked*, he's still one of the best reasons for occasionally tuning into Channel 5. He exudes bonhomie, and (unlike most TV researchers) is adept at making local contacts, even getting himself invited to a Greek wedding after bumping into members of the stag night party the night before. Oddly, he's more formal on C5 than he was in his days as the *enfant terrible* of the BBC, and it seems that his days of debauchery, self-mockery, and unashamed inebriation are finally behind him. After all, he was content simply to observe a Greek monastery from afar last night, whereas a decade ago he'd doubtless have stormed in through the main gates and shown us all how to separate the men from the boys. Probably with a crowbar if I know those Greeks.

In another programme of his that I had reviewed, Keith outraged viewers by cooking ostrich, while surrounded by a flock of the birds. He didn't outrage me, but I wasn't impressed either. I'm no veggie – in fact, I'll happily suck the brains out of a live monkey with a straw if they've got some garlic with them – but there was something profoundly ignoble about cooking chunks of Ostrich au vin with a herd of live birds gathered around him.

TV reviews

*This clip can be seen by clicking on link #5 on the **TV Reviews** page on **www.badastralbooks.com**.*

This scene generated thousands of complaints, and caused Keith huge problems. So, needless to say, when I was making my documentary about him, he begged us to repeat it. Privately, however, he told me that it was the main reason for him parting company with the BBC after a decade of enormously successful programmes. Keith and I kept in touch after the filming was finished. He saw an advance copy of the edited programme a week before it aired, and I was delighted when he told me that he loved it (and the Fray Bentos pie that I had sent him, because they reminded him of home, and he couldn't get them in Avignon). On Sunday 6 September 2009, at 7:13 pm, Keith Floyd wrote:

Dear Victor,
        Seen the DVD, got the steak pie. Many thanks.

It is true to say we [Celia and I] sat hand in hand petrified, waiting for the DVD to start. I am not a critic but I think it's the best programme I've seen on this kind of subject. The clever use of animation, colour and black and white was absolutely dramatic and brilliant. I think Keith A.'s approach to the whole thing was outstanding, and that goes for you and the whole team. I think the only weak point in an otherwise eclectic piece of television was the subject. To wit: – K. Floyd, esq. It is cathartic to see who you really are. I've never before been involved with such an intimate programme and I found it a very emotional experience – both making it and watching it.

I await with fear and trembling to see how many people I will have upset when the papers review it. Many thanks for putting the boot into Stan Green, expect a stream of unpunctuated abuse and threats!

October sounds great by the way.

From the hideout with grateful thanks,
                                    Keith

Ch 1 GASTROTELLY

I replied:

Dear Keith,
Thanks for yours. Sigh of relief. It was one of the most difficult (and emotionally draining) programmes I've ever written/cut/produced.

Dinner on me when next we meet – Celia and Poppy invited. I'll be in touch this week. I really don't think you have anything to worry about.

BW,

Victor

How wrong I was about that. On the night of transmission, an hour before the programme started, he lay down on the sofa to snooze his way through University Challenge. And died.

E-mail from Kevin Lygo (then head of Channel 4)

> Victor,
> Poor old Floyd. The demon drink, eh? Fun for a while and then just pathetic. Bit like being a TV exec.
> See you soon,
> Kevin

Sad though Keith's death was, it was not entirely unexpected, given his state of health. And at least I knew that he liked my programme, and had died happy.

However, his daughter Poppy was not happy with the inclusion of a scene (with Keith arguing and becoming abusive) in the finished programme, and she mentioned it in her eulogy at her dad's funeral in Bristol. That was the only time I have ever turned to anyone at a funeral and said, "I think we had better leg it."

*See that moment by clicking on link #6 on the **TV Reviews** page on www.badastralbooks.com.*

TV reviews

The press obituaries were suitably generous to Keith, including this obituary from The Times:

Keith Floyd left life in the style in which he had lived it – with a glass of wine in one hand and a cigarette in the other. Despite heart problems and a series of operations for bowel cancer, his last meal was a three-course gourmet feast eaten at the restaurant of fellow celebrity chef, Mark Hix, at Lyme Regis, Dorset. Lunch was shared with his close friend of 40 years, Celia Martin, and began with a Hix Fix cocktail – a morello cherry soaked in Somerset apple eau de vie topped up with champagne – on the sun terrace. He followed this up with a glass of white burgundy before moving indoors to the best table in the house, where he enjoyed a plate of oysters and potted Morecambe Bay shrimps... The meal at the Hix Oyster and Fish House finished with apple pie and perry jelly, and several cigarettes. Floyd picked up the £20 bill. He asked to see Mr Hix, the proprietor, but when told he was not there he left him an invitation to the launch of his autobiography on October 6...

The couple, who shared homes in Bridport and Avignon in the South of France, were celebrating Mrs Martin's 65th birthday. They went home for a siesta, looking forward to watching Floyd on television in an interview with Keith Allen. Floyd died in his sleep before the programme started. Mrs Martin, who says that they had a close but platonic relationship, said: "It was my 65th birthday yesterday and we started off by going to see the specialist to do with his cancer. He had some very good news and he was very optimistic of his chances of beating it. We then went to have a pub lunch in Lyme Regis. He said, 'I have not felt this well for ages.' He had a very good last day."

The couple watched University Challenge while waiting for the documentary Keith Meets Keith to begin on Channel 4. Mrs Martin said: "He had already seen the TV programme because they had sent us the DVD. He liked it very much. He thought it was so brilliantly made and so truthful. He said it was an award-winning programme. He lay down on the sofa and I thought he went to sleep. Then suddenly his breathing became erratic"...

Hugh Fearnley-Whittingstall, a fellow television chef who lives nearby in Lyme Regis, paid tribute to Floyd as his inspiration. He said: "Keith was a force of nature, certainly the first TV cook to really grab my attention. I followed his shows addictively as a student and decided I wanted cooking to be a big part of my life, largely because of him... The chef Marco

Pierre White said: "Keith, in my opinion, was an exceptional human being. He had great qualities. His ability to inspire people to cook just with his words and the way he did things was extraordinary. If you look at TV chefs today, they don't have his magic. It's a very, very, very sad day for my industry and secondly for a nation ... He was a beautiful man. Rick Stein, who made his first television appearance in Floyd on Fish – during which Floyd called him Nick – said: "I first met Keith in the early Eighties. At a time when I was experimenting with Provençal dishes like bouillabaisse and bourride he was a Gauloises-smoking, red wine-drinking hero who had actually owned a restaurant next to the Mediterranean. I never lost that awe of him; he was the first devil-may-care cook on TV who made cooking something that the boys could do too... One thing was certain: he cooked like a dream and loved food and wine with a passion."

There were many other fine obituaries, in many newspapers around the world, containing many warm tributes from celebrity chefs. However, during the funeral I noticed that not one of these so-called celebrity chefs had bothered to attend.

Rick Stein is one of many chefs who owe their career to Keith Floyd. Until Keith discovered him, he was a little-known and relatively unpretentious cook with an enthusiasm for fish, but once he'd tasted media fame, he soon turned into a "personality," complete with a Mummersetshire accent (I wonder which Oxford college he acquired that at?), a glutinously emotional delivery, and that fucking awful scarf-wearing seemingly cutsie prop of a canine cunt named Chalkie – who, according to members of the crew I've met, was halitosis at one end and a wind tunnel at the other. In each of the series that he's made, Stein performs the same unctuous "man o' the people" routine. He is a man whose desperation to be loved by his viewers is so one-dimensional that if he turned around he would briefly disappear. Let's hope not too briefly. Let's make it forever.

RICK STEIN'S FOOD HEROES

BBC2 2002

Call me a finicky orthoepist if you must, but to attempt the correct pronunciation of certain British surnames is to enter a phonetic and psychological minefield. Belvoir must be pronounced "Beaver," Cholmondeley is "Chumley," Bolsover is "Bolesur," and even Diana Dors

TV reviews

used to have problems with the precise articulation of her surname, which was actually Fluck. Indeed, I am reliably informed that when the fat-gutted peroxide actress died, the priest who was to conduct her funeral service was extremely nervous about slipping up on the pronunciation of her real name, so he reinforced his courage with one too many vicarly sherries, before delivering the eulogy, which went thusly: "We are gathered here to celebrate the life of... of Diana Clunt... I mean... er... Jesus Christ... Amen."

Rick Stein (is it "Steen," "Stine," "Shteen," or "Shtine"?) raised a similar problem of pronunciation last night during *Rick Stein's Food Heroes* (BBC2), his "gastronomic pilgrimage around Britain." He was unsure whether to say "scone" or "scon," and I'm not surprised that he was uncertain about which regional emphasis to use, because although he was born, bred, buttered, and educated in Oxfordshire, he nevertheless speaks with a Cornish accent (much to the disgust of many inhabitants of Padstow). It's disingenuousness like that that has made me more suspicious of him than of any other TV chef (and yes, that *does* include Antony Worrall Thompson). Although, to be fair to the man, he does have an excellent way with fish, and I'm told that he recently made a damn good hash. Of his marriage. Well, I'm not one to carp, but dear cod, it's never too brill to shellfishly dump your solemate of thirty years, just for the halibut. I'm sorry. Truly I'm sorry.

While the desire to extol such superb regional delicacies as Waberthwaite ham and Herdwick lamb may be laudable enough, last night's instalment (which looked at food in and around Cornwall) was a mass of contradictions. "Look after your local supplier," he told us, while emptying a bag of frozen supermarket peas into a pan, then derided such "trendy" concepts as "fusion cooking," moments before showing us how to cook Devon skate "with Moroccan flavours," and Atlantic mackerel "with Indian masala." He's also been complaining lately about restaurants that charge exorbitant prices (presumably forgetting that dinner for two with wine in his Padstow gaff can easily exceed £150), but at the heart of all the dissonance and disingenuousness that he's surrounded himself with is his bloody dog. Just as devious street beggars have a mutt on a string in order to evoke unwarranted sympathy in passers-by, so Stein tries to gain our trust and proclaim himself as a man o' the people (even talking about "posh restaurants") by repeatedly whistling up his dog at key moments. Which must make the poor thing's eyes water something rotten.

The small-scale suppliers we encountered were undoubtedly offering fine produce, but what left a funny taste in the mouth were Stein's oily and unctuous comments: "We must applaud the fishermen of Britain," he smarmed; "we've got to look after our game dealers." And he endlessly praised the old, inefficient, (and therefore very expensive),

Ch 1 GASTROTELLY

Cornish practice of handlining for mackerel, while condemning "trawlers that scoop fish from the sea," apparently believing that fish should only be eaten by wealthy people like him, and should be beyond the reach of the poor. Indeed, his whole project seemed reminiscent of Queen Victoria's tours of Britain (during which she would pull down the blinds of her railway carriage whenever the grim truth of ordinary working class life hove into view), because he's just not seeing the reality of rural life in 2002. Yes, there are some thriving and contented corners of excellence, but most farmers are either teetering on the edge of bankruptcy or are desperately cutting corners in order to stay in business, and rates of alcoholism, suicide, crime, repossession, and poverty are all rocketing through the (thatched) roof.

This is not the *real* Britain, nor is it *real* British food, and the sampled Cor anglais that dominated the cheap tinny score unwittingly encapsulated what's wrong with the entire format. As a TV chef, Stein simply cannot compare with Nigel Slater or Delia Smith (the two true culinary geniuses in this country), because they are both consummate technicians who don't require dog-props, nor do they need to utter incessant strings of superlatives to get their message across. Furthermore, he lacks humour, and is starting to look like Keith Floyd during his fourth BBC series, the one when he began to run out of steam (in Stein's case, that's probably because, between takes, he was banging his bit of extra-marital skirt, who should by rights be called Bain-Marie). "Great cooks don't think," Stein once declared, and he's probably right. Sadly, neither do mediocre programme makers.

*Reading that review back, I was rather pleased with myself for including the word orthoepist. For those who wish to drop it in polite conversation, here is a site pointed out to me by a friend – it is called Forvo and promises to deliver correct pronunciation. You can decide for yourself whether it does by clicking on link #7 on the **TV Reviews** page on **www.badastralbooks.com**.*

The same friend tells me "You can put filthy words into the word engine and have posh totty talking dirty at you. For example, you can have "cunt" in 19 different flavours, and even Baskin-Robbins can't do that."

The small-mindedness of Little Britain is shot through the next review of a programme that was made on the eve of the 1997 general election that swept away the old Tory government and ushered in New Labour. Rereading it, I am reminded of Floyd again, because Keith's political views could, on occasion, swing to the right of Genghis Khan. In my experience, that's true of a lot of cooks and chefs. Perhaps there's something inherently fascistic about the profession? That said, and truth to tell, the famous Vietnamese Marxist revolutionary leader Ho Chi Minh – real name Nguyen Sinh Cung – was a cook's helper on a

TV reviews

ship; and when he lived in Crouch End, Hornsey, north London during WWI, he is reported to have worked as a chef at the Drayton Court Hotel, on The Avenue, West Ealing:

http://www.spoonfed.co.uk/london/venue/ealing-25/drayton-court-hotel-1816/

Although the following wasn't strictly a food programme, it was based around a dinner party, and that seems a good enough reason to include it here.

CUTTING EDGE: THE DINNER PARTY

C4 1997

Here are a few medical tips. Never visit a doctor who has dead flowers in his waiting room. Never argue with a surgeon (he has inside information). Never trust a doctor if you see fat women entering his surgery and thin women leaving. And beware if your doctor ever hands you a referral note for a specialist with the abbreviation "NFN" scribbled on it. Inside sources tell me that it stands for "Normal For Norfolk," and it means he reckons your IQ is roughly equivalent to your shoe size.

Last night's *The Dinner Party* (C4) suggested that the abbreviation should be widened to include the whole of East Anglia, since the dimwitted octet who took part came from just across the border in Suffolk. Although no journalist saw the programme until yesterday evening, there's already been a fortnight of intense newspaper interest in this edition of *Cutting Edge*. And for once the speculation proved accurate, as we watched eight well-heeled Conservatives gather round a table to entertain the nation with their wit and wisdom, sounding very much like the contributors to *Stop the Week* might sound if they'd all been involved in a charabanc accident, sustained serious head injuries, and then been booked for one last gig, the other difference being that they all claimed to be loyal *Telegraph* readers. But I'd be furious if I were the *Telegraph's* editor, because the views they regurgitated were unworthy of that newspaper, being mostly taken straight from the crasser pages of the *Daily Mail*, with a few chunks of *Daily Express* thrown in for good measure. Ill-informed yet grossly opinionated, they arrogantly regarded themselves as the *crème de la crème* and so they were, in one sense: they were thick and rich.

Strangers to irony, modesty, and logic, this bunch of fortysomethings addressed the great political problems of our time with curiously sixth form hyperbole. The birching, forcible sterilisation, and execution of criminals had their enthusiastic support (apparently hanging *isn't* too good for them), they were convinced that all homeless people are really rich suburbanites who beg purely for fun, while their incoherent views on blacks and immigration were worthy of the Ku Klux Klan (although, unlike the dinner guests, at least the KKK's hats have a point). In between Rastus jokes and demands for forcible repatriation, one diner smugly recalled how he'd served on a jury full of immigrants who had barely spoken any English, and claimed that he had ended up deciding the verdict for all twelve "because I was the only one who understood what was going on." Maybe so, but if he were half as clever as he claimed, how come he wasn't smart enough to get out of jury service in the first place?

Lambs to the slaughter, all eight participants had been mercilessly cut to ribbons in the editing suite, but the heady combination of arrogance and small-mindedness they displayed throughout made it impossible to feel any sympathy for them. Tales of childhood beatings at Eton were intercut with demands to restore corporal punishment, while the revelation that one diner had a PhD in mediaeval history seemed entirely reasonable, given that she clearly didn't live in the modern world. "Michael Portillo... what a greasy little slimeball... I expect I'll vote for him" said one woman (obviously foreseeing a Beware-the-Ides-of-May situation for Mr Major), while another thought the way forward was to abandon democracy altogether and have a dictator, "Though let's not let the dictator lose touch in the way Thatcher did" (sadly without explaining how one goes about dictating terms to a dictator). By the time pudding arrived, we were onto "No queers in the fucking army... I'm not homophobic but they're all freaks of nature," while someone else asked plaintively "What's wrong with euthanasia anyway?" By this stage in the evening, absolutely nothing whatsoever. Especially in Suffolk.

Paul Watson has plenty of fine documentaries under his belt, but lately he seems determined to become a Todd Browning de nos jours. He's now intent on entertaining his audience with a freak show, and it's not just the aberrations of the middle classes that he exploits – those who say he'd never dare do this with lumpen victims presumably didn't see the Squeegees documentary he made some four years ago. Back in those days, he used to boast that he was "taking the temperature of Britain" and I remember observing what a pity it was that he'd chosen to use a rectal thermometer, and had wiped it all over the screen. Last year, he began urinating on the screen, and now he seems intent on throwing up over it, for good measure. It makes for unedifying viewing, but I hope he at least did the polite thing, and brought up the white wine with the fish.

TV reviews

I do not know why, but after this review appeared, I was on the receiving end of an extraordinary flurry of letters. This included the receipt of my page from the newspaper, including my byline photo, which someone had smeared with shit and drawn Hassidic Jewish sideburns onto, along with various anti-Semitic legends.

If that doesn't leave a funny taste in your mouth, what will? Returning to the subject of gastronomy, whenever a celebrity chef pops up on my television screen, the phrase "Who's minding the store?" comes to mind. Although they're supposed to be running their own restaurants, they've all clearly been desperate for years to get out of the kitchen and into the studio, from all-purpose L.E. show panellists like Brian Turner (the Fred Dibnah of gastronomy) to dish-of-the-day Gary Rhodes, a man so eager to squeeze inside the magic rectangle that I bet he'd agree to appear on Your Life in Their Hands if they'd let him poach his own kidneys in a white wine sauce. But for sheer unadulterated sauce, can anyone match Loyd Grossman, who's used his TV fame to launch a range of pasta dressings? Like Paul Newman, his face is displayed prominently on each jar but, while 100 per cent of Mr Newman's profits go to a children's charity, Mr Grossman (it seems) prefers his earnings to go straight into Loyd's bank.

The only thing worse than one celebrity chef is surely a pair of celebrity chefs. If there was one double act that had me squirming like a salted slug (and still does – endlessly repeated as they are) it was the execrable Two Fat Ladies, a pair of fake "eccentrics" perched atop their vintage motorcycle (the only Triumph in an otherwise appalling show).The programme's intention was to conjure up a fantasy of a brace of Bertie Wooster's Aunt Agathas traversing the British Isles, a heady mixture of Lord Snooty, funny uncles in spats and monocles, tuck boxes with lashings of lemonade, and dancing sprightly until tea o'clock (and therefore total heroes to middle-middle-middle Englanders). Unfortunately, the reality was somewhat different: a pair of corpulent, post-menopausal old boilers, a bulimic Edith Sitwell and Edith Evans who've discovered the joy of lard but forgotten how to throw up. Every time I viewed them, I found myself wondering why homicidal maniacs with misty eyes and Kalashnikov rifles always choose school playgrounds in which to express themselves. Couldn't they have gone after these two instead?

Ch 1 GASTROTELLY

TWO FAT LADIES
BBC2 1996

A sure way of gauging the calibre of a TV programme before transmission is to read between the lines of its billing in the *Radio Times*. If someone is going to "take a sideways look at life," then you know it'll be a comedy without jokes. If they propose to "delve into the archives," then they've simply strung together a few tired old clips that we've all seen eighteen times before which are ready for the knacker's yard, while an "in-depth analysis" will be so shallow that you won't even be able to drown in the boredom it generates. But, above all, beware of programmes whose presenters are "larger than life," because they invariably have personalities so one-dimensional that, if you rotated them through 90 degrees, they'd disappear.

This week's programming has been depressingly full of one-dimensional personalities, though they've been attached to bodies so stoutly three-dimensional that, if you tried to rotate them through 90 degrees, you'd get a hernia (unless you called in Messrs Bovis in to assist). Having endured one fat Italian gastronome on Tuesday, I was greeted last night by the doubly revolting sight of *Two Fat Ladies* (BBC2), a latter-day Miss Buss and Miss Beale who roared across my screen on a Triumph Thunderbird (with Watsonian sidecar), its permanently gleaming chrome making me certain that it was carefully transported from one taping location to the next on a lorry. TV producers have long had an *idée fixe* about the novelty value of eccentric motorcyclists (there was a seemingly endless parade of vicars and dukes during the 60s, followed by the stately George Melly in the 70s), and this tedious series about a pair of itinerant post-menopausal chefs was presumably sold to the network on the mistaken premise that 1,000ccs of raw power would be an adequate alternative to genuine charisma. It isn't.

There was nothing remotely genuine about last night's leadenly quixotic interaction between Jennifer Paterson and Clarissa Dickson Wright, not altogether surprising since they'd only ever met once before the series was mooted. Like a pair of impressionable students who ape the mannerisms of their aged professors, they locked into a sick-makingly unconvincing mock-30s patois, located somewhere between Lord Peter Wimsey and Bertie Wooster's Aunt Agatha ("yummee... I say... chin chin!... perchance... ahoy gentle shepherd... pray do..."), and I cringed at their laboured attempts to deliver the sort of arrogantly twittish one-liners

TV reviews

that only Edith Sitwell could pull off: "I once cooked testicles in Benghazi ya know... I once cooked for Prince Charles. Gave 'im raw fish and called him Your Majesty, arf arf..." Reciting half-remembered snatches from *Macbeth* or *The Wizard of Oz* was no substitute for wit and, just in case a few unreconstructed feminists were loyally pretending to enjoy the show, Clarissa cheerily recalled the old rhyme, "A woman, a dog, and a walnut tree, the more you beat them the better they be," just to alienate them too.

The contrived conceit of a plot involved them, as usual, arriving at a grand location – this week it was Westonburt "Gell's" School in Gloucestershire – and immediately being told in a manner that even Enid Blyton would consider crass that the cook had gone sick: "We haven't a moment to lose, you're the answer to my prayers." They pretended to search for provisions, and prepared food so vile-looking that I'm not surprised they never asked the children for their opinion of it. Clarissa's pan-Asian fillet of beef deserved panning, while Jennifer decided to shape her meat loaf like a hedgehog which was quite a coincidence because, by now, I too had curled up hedgehog-like into a ball, in an attempt to escape from the madness.

I have no problem with uncompromising physical ugliness. Claire Rayner? Vanessa Feltz? I won't have lunch but I'll watch 'em all. But thoroughly ugly personalities are harder to stomach. TV has already had a pair of quarrelsome women chefs who can't cook – they were called Hudson and Halls, and their on-camera joshing and bickering was thoroughly honest, unlike the fake banter of these two (who, I suspect, heartily dislike each other but didn't even have the nous to play on that mutual contempt). Like a pair of magnets, these oh-so-similar eccentric toffs repel each other (not to mention the audience) though Fanny Cradock, a genius of the genre, long ago proved that an upper class accent and assertive demeanour *can* make for fascinating viewing. She, of course, had the tolerant Johnny as her partner, a man famous for his legendary on-air slips. Alcoholic? Put it this way, whisky is a slow poison and he was in no hurry.

*I always thought The Two Fat Ladies were beyond parody, but a couple of Australian comediennes (as I suppose you are not meant to call them anymore)spoofed them something rotten on a 1990s Australian all girl TV sketch show called Something Stupid. I am not sure it was ever aired over here, but the vocal mimicry is spot on, and there are at least 4 episodes on YouTube, which you can see by clicking on link #8 on the **TV Reviews** page on www.badastralbooks.com.*

It was the sheer fakery that lay at the core of this series that made me despise it so. I met their producer, Pat Lewellyn, in the reception area of Channel 4, shortly after Jennifer had opted for the total-cessation-of-life diet. Pat and I were on speaking terms in those days (a situation that ceased a few years later, when I called her a "pernicious bitch" at the launch party of More4), so I said to her: "They hated each other didn't they?" expecting a total denial of what I'd heard on the grapevine. Instead she told me bluntly "Yes they did." It turns out that the one who is still (technically) alive didn't like to be outsmarted by the one who is dead, although frankly it's hard to see how a term like "outsmarting" could reasonably be applied to either of them.

Fakery was at the heart of the Two Fat Ladies, and it's at the heart of The Hairy Bikers too, a sort of feminine version of Clarissa and Jennifer created by the same producer.

THE HAIRY BIKERS' COOKBOOK

BBC2 2004

So intense was the furore when scientists grew a human ear on the back of a mouse during the late 1990s that my own achievements in this field went completely unnoticed. Yet long before that experiment took place, I'd already become the first person to grow a complete live mouse on my own ear, in a highly impressive display of genetic engin-earring. Despite the lack of popular acclaim, I've continued with my experiments, and recent successes include crossing a zebra with a cockerel (to produce a four-legged chicken with its own bar code), and a Barbie doll with the Pilsbury Doughboy, to create a grinning blonde bimbo with a yeast infection. And I'm currently trying to cross a Hell's Angel with a Jehovah's Witness, to produce someone who'll knock on your door on a Sunday morning, shout "praise be," then headbutt you on the chin and tell you to fuck off.

Some boffin at BBC2 has clearly been trying a similar experiment, crossing the *Two Fat Ladies* with the late Hudson and Halls to create the presenters of *The Hairy Bikers' Cookbook*. But something must have gone terribly wrong in the laboratory, because not only do Simon King and Dave Myers have bigger breasts than Clarissa and Jennifer (whose own series ought to have called *The Hairy Dykers*), but they've also turned out to be far camper than La Hudson and La Halls ever were, even at their most fey. Despite the aura of butchness that usually surrounds bearded, burly, leather-clad gentlemen on 1,000cc motorcycles, these culinary wannabe Hell's Angels have proved to be about as menacing as *The Pathetic Sharks*, not at all like the handful of genuine Hell's Angels that I've met over the years.

TV reviews

Believe me, *real* hairy bikers don't ride sedately around the countryside, stopping now and then to admire the scenery and whisk up an omelette. No, they eat furniture for breakfast, they bite the heads off whippets for recreational purposes, and they'll pay good money to see Siamese twins who are joined at the mouth, on the off chance that one of them throws up.

"We're on a quest to find the recipe for the best Irish stew," they told us last night as they rode out of Dublin, attempting to provide their programme with what Alfred Hitchcock used to call "a MacGuffin." But sadly, such a feeble pretext for their journey was never likely to generate much suspense, especially when they began reeling off a Tourist Board-approved list of what they expected to find on their travels – "a land of myths and legends, the blarney gorgeous girls with melting smiles, velvet stout and Irish whiskey" – with no mention whatsoever of those merry, twinkling, clandestine IRA arms dumps that still adorn the green hills of Erin. As with Ant and Dec, I have no idea which of the bikers is which, nor do I have the least inclination to find out, but either Simon or Dave introduced us to a woman with three teeth (two of which I suspect she keeps in her handbag), who proudly displayed a saucepan full of Irish coddle, which she mistakenly described as "a kind of drunken man's supper." I say mistakenly because her sloppy bacon and potato stew was surely the last thing you ought to give to the deeply pissed, being so liquid that the broth would undoubtedly start pouring out of both nostrils simultaneously, as rapidly as it was being spooned into the mouth.

Although the *Two Fat Ladies* also used their motorcycle as a gimmick, they did at least know how to cook. *The Hairy Bikers*, by contrast, simply make statements of the bleeding obvious, such as "I'm trying to get the maximum amount of flavour from the ingredients in the pan" (as if any cook would *ever* do otherwise), and seem to possess no more gastronomic knowledge than the average trainee short-order chef at Wimpy. Having persuaded a resident of Carlingford to shuck a dozen oysters for them, they proceeded to make some deep-fried Louisiana PoBoys with remoulade, but my confidence in their culinary abilities was shaken still further when the one doing the cooking told us that "I have a problem with oysters they make me ill." Anyway, the locally-caught shellfish seemed rather tiny and immature to me, and if the oyster farmer ever tried to palm such undersized specimens off onto me, he'd find himself being taken to the Small *Clams* Court.

The Hairy Bikers may well appeal to the sort of viewers who like Morris dancing and real ale, and think Roger Whittaker is an angry young man, but they don't pass muster with me. Their entire act is a conceit, and because they've never decided if they're making a travel show or a cookery programme, the result is neither Arthur nor Martha, lacking purpose, authority, originality, culinary skill, or even a decent observational script. I never thought I'd find myself pining for the expertise of the *Two Fat Ladies*, but strangely enough I do, uncompromising physical ugliness and all. Which takes me back to genetic engineering, because I'm also trying to cross a hippopotamus with Anne Widdecombe, to produce a widdepotamus, which I'd then cross with a hamster to create a two-ton creature that could run around inside the London Eye.

The bikers really did hack into the grub they made in their programmes. If they keep it up, they'll end up even more seriously overweight than they already are, and probably on a bottle of Milk of Magnesia a day. Incidentally, did I ever tell you that I used to be a dairyman for the Milk of Magnesia company, back in the 60s? Every morning I was up at 6am, calling in our prize herd of Magnesias, then plonking myself down on the milking stool and grabbing their udders, one after another. It was hard work, but honest. Then mechanisation came in, and I was sacked, and that's why I ended up as a television critic. Oh the humanity.

For some reason, thoughts of Hairy Bikers bring me yet again to Fanny Cradock, who once told me as she was sitting on my face, "when it comes to restaurants, trust only your nose and, if the food is lousy, don't return. There is no education in the second kick of a mule." And years of restaurant reviewing have taught me the wisdom of her words. There's probably only one job better than being a restaurant critic, and that is being a friend of a restaurant critic (because you still get the free lunch, and you don't have to write up your notes afterwards). A food critic does have to watch every activity like a hawk when writing about a restaurant. From the moment I walk through the door (extremely significant) to the moment I leave, all my senses are cranked up to eleven. That's the only way to spot what's really going on.

Gordon Ramsay's Kitchen Nightmares was billed as high-octane restaurant criticism on TV, so naturally it caught my eye. I'd written positively about Ramsay when this undoubtedly gifted chef first appeared (sparingly) on television, but by the time he was fronting the show, he'd turned into an f-word-spouting construct, which was why Kitchen Nightmares appalled me.

Unfortunately, I cannot include my review of this programme, since it was the subject of a court order. I had claimed that Ramsay had faked some of the scenes at Bonaparte's restaurant in Silsden, Yorkshire, a claim for which The Evening Standard apologised to the man. After the apology had been read out, Gordon Ramsay told newspapers that he'd had to bring a legal case against the newspaper over what I had written, because the integrity of his programmes

TV reviews

had been attacked. "We have never done anything in a cynical fake way," he told journalists at the time.

So imagine my surprise when, a year later, on 16 July 2007, Channel 4 issued an apology over another Gordon Ramsay programme, which had shown him apparently spearing a live fish in the sea, when in fact he had done no such thing. "The video tape gave viewers an inaccurate impression about Gordon's involvement," said the Channel 4 statement, "We regret that viewers may feel they were let down." Ramsay subsequently appeared on The Jonathan Ross Show, admitted that the scene had been faked, and laughed about it.

Then the US Masterchef, with Ramsay in it, was found to be using CGI to double the size of a crowd to enhance the show's perceived popularity:

The report can be seen by clicking on link #9 on the **TV Reviews** page on **www.badastralbooks.com**.

More recently, he has been exposed for lying about having played for Glasgow Rangers, his loss-making business empire has suffered a series of setbacks, he was revealed to have been having a seven-year-long extra-marital affair, and he admitted to The Observer (14 March 2010) that he "was a crazy fucking psycho..."

The ancient Chinese general Sun Tzu once said, "If you wait by the river long enough, you will see the bodies of all your enemies float by." Not that Ramsay (or indeed anyone that I have ever criticised) was (or is) an enemy. But, while re-reading these fifteen years of television reviews, in preparation for this book, I have seen plenty of metaphorical corpses floating by, and I can honestly say that I felt no joy each time I realised that yet another of the many "personalities" whom I had criticised when they were in their heyday had since met with televisual oblivion. Ramsay has not yet disappeared down the media oubliette, but it would not be unreasonable to point out that he seems to be heading in that direction in a most spectacular fashion.

Ch 1 GASTROTELLY

IF YOU CAN'T STAND THE HEAT

C4 1999

As with adenoids and tonsils, it's become fashionable nowadays to have your definite articles removed. This self-aggrandising operation involves simply amputating the "the" before a noun, and instantly makes the speaker feel more important: "Doctor will see you now Chef proposes Conference has decided" Oddly, down at TV Centre, they buck the trend by insisting that the definite article be put in – "*The* BBC" – but why? After all, nobody says The ITV, The Anglia, or The Channel 4. Still, I once worked at Broadcasting House and can still recall seeing plenty of *definite* articles there – most of them working in senior management.

In the gastronomic world, Michelin star chef and business consultant Patrick McDonald would be fully entitled to bill himself as "*The* Chef." He's as down-to-earth as his food is *haut* (I still remember one of the best dinners I've ever had, at his previous gaffe in Edinburgh), and I'm delighted to see him trying to raise the standards of our nation's restaurants in his current C4 series *If You Can't Stand the Heat*. Far too many chefs are desperate to get out of the kitchen and bask in the glow of the cathode rays instead, but McDonald isn't on our screens to satisfy his ego, rather to act as troubleshooter for ailing businesses, a sort of Sir John Harvey Jones of the catering trade. Certainly, no country needs his services more than this one, for this is the land of "wait to be seated" and "it was lovely, thankyou," a land where the legend "chef's special" usually turns out to be sadly mistaken.

Last night, McDonald had been called in to help a Blackpool restaurant, run by Tony Beswick and his brother-in-law Marco Calle who dreamed of winning a Michelin star even though Marco's sinewy meat was as tough as Michelin tyres. Their establishment was called "Kwizeen," a name which sounds like a cross between an Exhaust Centre and a packet of vegetable lard, and therefore described the place pretty well. Not only did it boast appalling food ("this soup is a horrible colour and lifeless," lamented Patrick, "the fish is horribly overcooked and this little blighter is a hair"), but it also had unfeasibly low prices, though that hardly mattered since it also had pitifully few customers. In desperation, Marco begged Patrick "I hope you're going to tell me which way to go," and I couldn't stop myself shouting out the sad truth at the screen: "go to catering college."

Patrick's reply was equally blunt ("you'll not get the star the food is not up to standard"), but he didn't despair. Instead, he suggested a simpler Mediterranean menu, improved decor, and better wine with

TV reviews

bigger mark-ups, and by the end of the programme his advice seemed to be pulling the restaurant back from the brink. However, Tony and Marco were still muttering darkly that Lancastrians wouldn't want all this foreign-sounding stuff, and I was so intrigued to find out whether they would keep up these standards once Patrick and the cameras disappeared that, yesterday morning, I drove to Blackpool and lunched at Kwizeen (well, interactive television is starting this autumn, so why not interactive TV criticism too?). Sadly, I must report that they've forgotten everything that Patrick McDonald had taught them, standards in the kitchen have plummeted again, and the place still can't decide whether it wants to serve pheasants or peasants, which is probably why hardly anyone was eating there. What could I say? "Thank you, that was execrable" I told the waiter as he cleared away my plate. Trust me, he felt no pain.

If You Can't Stand the Heat is compelling viewing, presented by a man who (unlike most TV chefs) can walk and talk without waving his arms around like a demented windmill, who doesn't suffer from "here's a personality I whisked up earlier" syndrome, and who offers genuinely constructive criticism, without ever pulling his punches. I hope that restaurateurs are watching and learning as the weeks go by, but I somehow doubt it because, as a breed, their arrogance and capacity for self-delusion is quite astonishing, and the bank managers who fund their kamikaze enterprises seldom appreciate the difference between good and bad food. As for the viewing public, the ratings prove that we eat up TV cookery shows, love reading about food in our newspapers and magazines, and are forever telling each other about how wonderful the art of gastronomy is. So how is it that, paradoxically, we are also buying more takeaways and frozen dinners than ever before?

Back in 2002, Gordon Ramsay was one of several TV chefs who lined up to ridicule Delia Smith for being boring, having apparently misunderstood that her technical precision is, in reality, the essence of good cooking. Gastronomy is an art and a science, but what it definitely shouldn't be is a circus.

DELIA'S HOW TO COOK: PART THREE

BBC2 2002

I do not know whether Lorraine Heggessey (Controller of BB Cone Lite©) has been drinking the bong water lately, but she's certainly been doing a lot of laid-back gloating, and all because her station's overall audience share was slightly better in 2001 than that of ITV1. "It is fantastic to see

Ch 1 GASTROTELLY

that Public Service Broadcasting can be so strong," she cooed to the press, which is all very well, but Ms Heggessey has only increased her channel's share by dragging its content relentlessly downmarket, with the licence-fee-funded BB Cone Lite© now being almost indistinguishable from ITV1 (which at least pays for itself). Or, to quote George Orwell's *Animal Farm*: "The creatures outside looked from pig to man, and from man to pig, and from pig to man again; but already it was impossible to say which was which."

However, over on BBC2 last night, it was far easier to distinguish the pig from the human, because Antony Worrall Thompson (the porcine host of *Food and Drink*) was followed at 8:30 by the saintly presenter of *Delia's How to Cook: Part Three*. Whereas Thompson's contrived, boar-ish, and generally pig-ignorant performance would be more at home nowadays on Ms Heggessey's increasingly vulgar channel, Delia Smith has steadfastly resisted all gimmickry, and consequently she remains the best on the block, as this new series succinctly demonstrates. There are no toe-curlingly faked lifestyle glimpses here, no pointless culinary races, and no Ainsley Harriott-like conducting of an invisible orchestra while she works, just an unparalleled expertise in the kitchen, and an undisguised reverence for food in its simplest forms (a reverence that she's displayed throughout a TV career that's now spanned almost three decades). How refreshing. For once, a performer who wants the star of the show to be her egg, not her ego.

Much of last night's course was devoted to the somewhat dry-sounding subject of kitchen equipment, but this wasn't an austere lecture by some pious prude, dear me no. Within minutes, she was shamelessly rolling a joint and beating the meat on TV (as she prepared pepper-crusted fillet of beef), while simultaneously telling us what kind of roasting tray we should buy ("a really solid one"), and also arguing strongly in favour of aluminium saucepans. That surprised me a little, because in the past they've been tentatively linked with Alzheimer's (the great disease that allows you to meet new people every day), and I was also amazed to see a self-confessed vegetarian cooking beef so deliciously and bloodily rare. So perhaps the only hundred-per-cent vegetarian at her table this Christmas was the turkey.

Watching her giving her pastry a damn good forking ("lots of pricks" she enthused), and preparing a wondrously caramelised tarte Tatin with French apples, I was reminded of a famous Gallic chef who once asked me "you can tell me how many pips are in an apple, but can you tell me how many apples are in a pip?" (shortly before I left him lying in a pool of his own blood). Like a Blue Peter presenter, she was obliged to recommend certain makes of casserole dish and frying pan without actually giving us the brand name (surely in these days of

TV reviews

product-placement, the BBC is fighting a long-lost battle?), and rightly insisted that accurate scales, a tape measure, and a timer were three of the most important items in any kitchen. How far away her mixture of expertise and common sense is from the gimmick-obsessed channel run by Ms Heggessey (which trivialises every subject it touches). The sad decline of BB Cone Lite© has caused me to wonder seriously about submitting a spoof proposal, combining history, sport, art, and cooking, and entitled *Mike Tyson's Lobe Cuisine*. In which Mr T travels back in time, talks to Vincent Van Gogh, and asks the seminal question, "Hey man, are you gonna eat that?"

At the close, a variant of the old saying occurred to me: "Too many cooks have their own TV series." Delia is a rare exception, so will someone please persuade her *not* to hang up her pinny, because she's proof of what I have been saying for the past hundred-and-forty-seven years, namely that cooking is an art form, not some branch of Light Entertainment (would *you* permit a comedy juggler to teach your kids how to play the violin?). One classic performer like Delia is worth a million self-obsessed TV chefs, egregiously shallow-frying themselves in the cathode rays, and the only slight let-down last night was the music. There's too much of it, it's too strident, and worse, the voice sounds suspiciously like the dire Lesley Garrett, the soprano who doesn't know the difference between *bel canto* and *can belto*. I'm told that she was recently awarded the CBE. Presumably they're the only three notes she can sing without splitting your head open.

Over the years, I have amused myself by submitting numerous fake proposals to gullible production companies. Such as Candied Camera, where I described "a honey-encrusted lens that will take pictures of birds pecking away at the angelica tripod" (the rejection letter expressed interest, but noted that "we already have several nature programmes in development"). Then there's Alphabetti Spaghetti, a food-programme-cum-game-show where a bulimic presenter would vomit letter-pasta randomly onto the carpet until a well-known phrase or saying appeared ("not suitable for a daytime audience" I was informed). In the early days, the recipient of several such hoaxes was Peter Bazalgette, who went on to be the force behind Big Brother (so powerful did he become as a result that Channel 4 even appointed him to their board).

No section about gastronomy on television could be considered complete if it failed to mention Mr Bazalgette. Having started his career as a researcher on That's Life!, he became the man behind BBC2's Food and Drink, which ran throughout the 1980s and eventually spawned the likes of such gastronomic delights as The Two Fat Ladies and Antony Worrall Thompson. There is a

Ch 1 GASTROTELLY

certain irony in the knowledge that the Bazalgette family achieved fame in Victorian England by pumping excrement out of our major cities, only for Peter to make a career out of pumping it back in again. But the problem runs deeper than that, because in the modern, secular, media-obsessed world we live in, the man behind Big Brother has taken on the role of Mephistopheles in the old Faustian myth. So desperate for fame are many young people (despite their lack of skill, talent, or even pulchritude) that they'll willingly sign away their souls in exchange for a place on any reality show, no matter how tacky or humiliating it is. At least Dr Faustus got twenty-five years of omniscience and the chance to sleep with Helen of Troy as the price for his soul, whereas all today's willing victims receive is fifteen minutes of fame, which are then frittered away on violent arguments about stock cubes.

I regularly criticised his programmes in my column, and his response was to contact the editor, Veronica Wadley, pleading with her to stop me writing about him. In particular, he objected to the phrase "the fearsomely heterosexual Peter Bazalgette." I can't think why. This is one of the paragraphs I wrote about him:

'I thought that the Endemol company couldn't possibly sink any lower, until I opened last Saturday's Times and saw that it could. Apparently, they'll soon be producing Pig Brother, "in which celebrities select animals for the slaughterhouse" and disembowel chickens in the name of light entertainment, and we can only pray that outraged members of the Animal Liberation Front don't discover Mr Bazalgette's home address (readily available at Companies House), and seek revenge on him for presenting killing as recreation. But if they do, I'm sure he won't mind me standing outside his front door with a camera crew, filming what happens, then broadcasting my own hilarious and violent reality show, provisionally entitled "sLaughterhouse."'

The above-mentioned show eventually reached our screens as The Farm, a Channel Five series that is nowadays remembered solely because Rebecca Loos masturbated a pig and collected its semen. Come to think of it, that's the only reason most of us remember Rebecca Loos either.

This is one of the many gastronomic programmes that were produced by Peter Bazalgette, before he discovered that there was even more money to be made from reality television.

TV reviews

ANTONIO CARLUCCIO'S ITALIAN FEAST

BBC2 1996

I have a problem. I know where walnut oil comes from, and I've actually seen olive oil being produced on a Spanish farm, by squeezing thousands of olives in a wooden press. But how the *hell* do they make baby oil? And who supplies the baby crushers? On second thoughts, I'm not sure I really want to know.

There's been so much olive oil flowing each week on *Antonio Carluccio's Italian Feast* (BBC2) that it ought to have been dispensed not from a bottle but through an Esso nozzle. No wonder they say the trouble with Italian food is that five or six days later you're hungry again, since almost every dish we've seen so far has been doused with such liberal quantities of the stuff that it's made the cuisine seem pretty hard to stomach. Not as hard to stomach as Signor Carluccio himself though, a fat jolly man who lives under the curious misapprehension that he's everybody's friend, making grand gestures to complete strangers and generally Uncle Tomming his way through life in a routine that fools some gullible British viewers but clearly doesn't cut much ice with *bona fide* Italians. Despite its nationalist title, his series is actually a tour around Umberto Bossi's mythical Padania, and has never touched the southern half of the country at all (presumably because stroppy Neapolitans wouldn't tolerate Carluccio's patronising *That's Life!* staged comedy routines). He's already visited Umbria, Emilia-Romagna, Piemonte, and Liguria, and last night, he reached Veneto and its capital Venice. And what more suitable city could there be for a programme that regularly dies a death?

Just as I've never heard a real American say "hey bud" or a genuine Yorkshireman say "'appen," so I'd never encountered an Italian muttering "mama mia" until yesterday – although Signor Carluccio doesn't really speak Italian, he speaks a language called Superlative. In the space of a mere half hour, he'd found the perfect description for a seafood salad ("wonderfully moist"), some shrimp ("wonderful"), the company ("wonderful"), the scenery ("wonderful"), not to mention Venetian cuisine in general ("wonderful food"). But he didn't limit himself to that one adjective, dear me no. A shoulder of pork was "fantastic," as was the seafood and the smell, while polenta and boating were both "delicious" (or, for added authenticity, "delicioso"). And now a quiz. Q: What did the eggs, the cream, the saffron (including its smell), the ice cream, the vongole, the peaches (cooked and uncooked), their liquor, the sauce, the

Ch 1 GASTROTELLY

restaurant, the basil, the food at a nearby trattoria, and a bouquet he made in Verona all have in common? A: They were all "wonderful."

"What could be more desirable than eating al fresco in the middle of Venice, wonderful food in wonderful company?" he asked, and it certainly sounded a lot more appealing than watching my TV screen, on which a corpulent presenter was yet again proving that there *is* such a thing as a free lunch. He clearly believes himself to be bilingual, but at times he was barely lingual, talking to a bemused gondolier who'd just won the silver medal in a regatta, and then translating his remarks for us as "so we say between the two what do you say in English?.. between the two the third enjoys it." In between elaborately unfunny skits (the most tedious of which involved a bored Romeo and Juliet, on loan from the Veronese Tourist Board), he knocked up a few dishes in the kitchens of local hotels, using seafood and spices he'd bought in the Rialto market. Shamelessly praising his own cooking, he managed to make a complete doge's dinner of things, especially the tricoloured ice cream which he decorated with expensive, incredible – if inedible – gold leaf. A touch that confirmed what I'd long suspected about Signor Carluccio – the man has absolutely no sense of gilt.

This unfocussed series fails on every level: as a food programme (the recipes are garbled and often seem to have been constructed *ad hoc*), as a travelogue (its portrait of Italy is neither well-observed nor remotely comprehensive), and most of all as entertainment. Apart from the narration's worryingly frequent lapses into near-incomprehensibility, the listen-and-translate method of presentation burns up minute after minute of airtime (a weakness that the use of captions could have rectified), while the soundtrack is unforgivably cheap and tinny. Presumably, executive producer Peter Bazalgette wouldn't tolerate tinned food on his programmes, so why permit tinned music to accompany them? As for Signor Carluccio, there are so many things about him to dislike, but most of all I just wish he'd rid himself of one terrible habit he's acquired: I wish he wouldn't talk with his mouth open. No. Don't write in. I don't mean *eat*. I mean talk.

Signor Carluccio had a bit of bother in 2008, being rushed to hospital after apparently stabbing himself in the chest with a kitchen knife. There was talk of suicide and so forth, and he checked into The Priory. For my own part, having watched his programmes for some years, I can confirm that it is impossible to commit suicide by holding one's breath. But, God knows, I tried.

My review of another of Bazalgette's programmes – Changing Rooms – provoked a furious letter from him to the editor. Mr Bazalgette specifically

TV reviews

complained about my statement that "a TV crew turns up six weeks before" the shows are recorded, and said that "this is wholly untrue."

Which was odd, because I had obtained that information from the now defunct *News of the World*, which on 22 March 1998 (p15) had printed a quote from a Mr P. Bazalgette saying, "We turn up six weeks beforehand and have other decorators to help because we have to stop to film DIY techniques and the like. This slows everything down."

I found it hard to reconcile Mr Bazalgette's quote in the News of the World with the complaint in his letter, and so presumably did he. Because after I pointed it out to my editor, I heard nothing more on this subject from the fearsomely heterosexual producer.

Here's another review of one of his food-as-game-show programmes.

CELEBRITY READY STEADY COOK

BBC1 2000

It was the middle of the night, and I'd just broken into Gary Glitter's house and was downloading kiddy porn onto his computer (prior to notifying the police with the details and his address the next day), when I suddenly realised that I'd just become the world's first interactive TV critic. Well, I simply couldn't bear the thought of hearing "My Gang" or "Do You Wanna Touch?" on TOTP 2 one more time, and I certainly seem to have got my way. Sorry about that Gary, but it was all for the best, really it was.

Interactive TV critics are always especially delighted when those they write about are so riled by what they read that they lose their composure in front of the cameras. Anthony Worrall Thompson is particularly easy to goad, and I remember seeing him ranting incoherently about me on BBC2 (after a review I'd written had failed to provide him with 750 words of closely argued adulation), little realising that the only way to *really* put a critic in his place is to ignore him. Why a man whose *amour-propre* is so easily wounded (and whose portly demeanour screams out "failed diet" every time I see him) should therefore have risked further opprobrium by appearing on last night's *Celebrity Ready Steady Cook* is quite beyond me, but then I have to admit that there are many things about this show that I'll never fully understand. Not least, why an audience of apparently sane people is prepared to brave gales, downpours, floods, and our collapsing public transport system, to travel to a TV studio and watch a couple of C-list "personalities" slice carrots.

Ch 1 GASTROTELLY

As with sex, the British find it almost impossible to treat food with the respect and seriousness which it deserves, which is presumably why this long-running format has performed well in the ratings by turning the noble art of gastronomy into an undignified game show. Last night, Thompson and fellow chef James Martin (sporting his trademark headband, a hostage to fortune since it is going to look increasingly ridiculous as the present thinning of his hair steadily gives way to outright baldness) proposed to cook not well but quickly, using ingredients supplied by their guests to prepare twenty-minute two-course dinners that were fit only for the bin. Many years ago, the Frenchman Edouard de Pomiane proved that excellent *three*-course dinners could be prepared in *ten* minutes, if time was short, but I suppose that's because he concentrated on cooking, rather than shouting out carefully-rehearsed ad-libs, indulging in low-level comedy schtick, and generally conducting himself at the level of a prep school bunfight. What a pity that Thompson and Martin's mothers didn't tell them what my granny told me: "Don't play with your food dear."

As for the celebrity guests, cricketer Dominic Cork came on clutching some beef and announced "I don't like spicy food or herbs," whereupon Thompson decided to cook him a pepper steak with parsley. Meanwhile, Anne Robinson appeared in black plastic trousers, and performed an "impersonation" of Mrs Thatcher which was not only dreadful, but unnecessary too, because her normal TV behaviour nowadays is so rude and haughty that she's increasingly resembling the Ironing Lady anyway. And as the quartet grated lemons, potatoes, and my nerves, my mind wandered off to a deeply inspiring culinary conversation which I'd once had with Christian Willer (one of France's greatest chefs, who inexplicably prefers to practise his art at the Hotel Martinez in Cannes, rather than don a red nose and run about on TV), and by the time I'd regained concentration, Anne had been declared the winner and had donated her £1,000 cheque to the Alzheimer's Society. What a fine organization that is. And a fine illness. And a fine organization. What is?

Unlike Dominic Cork, I love most herbs and spices, but I am becoming increasingly allergic to Bazal. From *Big Brother* and *Changing Rooms* to *You Can't Take It With You* and this insipid pap, Peter Bazalgette's production company is pumping our screens full of televisual idiocy that is both degraded and degrading.

I am including the following review because it outlines one of the most outrageous abuses of gastronomic power that I encountered during my years as a food and television critic.

TV reviews

AIRPORT

BBC1 2000

Congratulations to Egon Ronay and his *Guide to Eating at the Airport*. Published and distributed free by the British Airports Authority, its contents must make the author eligible for the *Guinness Book of Records*, as the first gastronome ever to get the words "Kentucky Fried Chicken" and "quite excellent" into the same sentence. A few years ago, I saw Mr Ronay on BBC2's *Food and Drink* programme, rightly complaining about the terrible quality of food on sale at Heathrow, and using phrases like "I would not give it to a dog" and "this is simply not edible." We can all bear witness that standards have not greatly improved since then, so how can it be that Mr Ronay's guide (for which he's paid handsomely by BAA) contains *not one word* of criticism of any of the 127 listed outlets? Indeed, he scatters his "chef's hat" symbols around like confetti, giving two of them to the "excellent" Pizza Hut, and another two to Garfunkel's. Think about it. *Two* chef's hats to establishments that don't employ chefs, just somebody to reheat food. I'm an experienced restaurant critic, and when I ate at both these places recently, I thought the food was terrible; but I'll happily bow to Mr Ronay's superior wisdom, because he clearly knows one or two things about food. Well, he certainly knows which side his bread is buttered.

What with Mr Ronay's topsy-turvy guide, officious little Englanders running about with clipboards, and TV crews constantly thrusting microphones into their faces, it's no wonder that passengers at Heathrow always seem bemused. Perhaps Gerard and Paul (the paramedics who featured on BBC1's *Airport* last night) were suffering from irritable bowel syndrome after lunching at Burger King (one chef's hat), but they seemed to take a positive delight in telling exhausted and bewildered passengers on a newly-landed 747 from Tokyo that "we're going to have to impound the plane." The law was on their side, because a suspected case of meningitis was on board, but the ghastly glee they seemed to take in depriving people of their liberty suggested that they ought to consider careers as high court judges. All of which goes to prove that, although the Germans invented the word *Schadenfreude*, it's the British who are its expert practitioners.

It wasn't really meningitis at all, but making a drama out of a non-crisis is one of the regular weekly strands on this increasingly formulaic series, along with a "race against time," a comic vignette, and

Ch 1 GASTROTELLY

a confrontation between foreigners and the authorities, all held together by pitifully weak links. Last night's race featured Donatella Versace, who lost some luggage as she transferred from Concorde to her private jet, although the mishap seemed almost inevitable, given that her escort was someone that even Will Hay would have reprimanded for incompetence. "Missing *people* can also be a problem at Heathrow" chirped the voice-over, introducing us to the comic turn, a bewildered old woman who'd lost her relatives, and "roving troubleshooter" Karen, who laughed openly at the customer's predicament, and collapsed with mirth after spilling her baggage onto the pavement. It didn't seem very funny to me, though I confess that I did roar with laughter when Donatella's luggage was officially declared lost, and the Versace bag had to get onto her jet without her Versace bag.

But it was the confrontation between three young French Canadian tourists and the immigration authorities that wiped the smile off my face for good. The trio had been bumming around Europe for months, and clearly hoped to earn a little cash-in-hand while they were here, but was that any reason to humiliate them, rummage through their private diaries, and then rudely refuse them entry into this country? The sight of customs officer Eric admonishing them for not being able to pronounce "Bournemouth" properly was grotesque, particularly as he himself was barely comprehensible, due to his thick Liverpudlian vowels. The three smiled sadly and caught the next plane back to Paris (where they'll doubtless tell their friends about Britain's fabled "generosity"), but they should look on the bright side. As they weren't allowed in, they'll never have to sample the "superior burgers and chips" at the Shakespeare Ale House in Terminal Two (two chef's hats).

The missing Versace bag finally turned up as the jet stood on the runway, so even that small pleasure was denied me, which was a pity because (apart from Mr Ronay's guide) there are precious few laughs to be had at Heathrow. The one blessing was that the tedious Jeremy Spake has vanished, but if this is how the authorities behave when the BBC cameras are around, God knows what they're like when they get you alone in a little room during the rest of the year. Still, despite its manifest imperfections, we all need to visit Heathrow once in a while, and if you're wondering whether it's time for a holiday, then here's a tip. Simply look at your passport photograph and, if you vaguely resemble it, then get yourself down to Thos Cook *tout de suite*.

CHAPTER 2

SANK WITHOUT TRACE

By the turn of the last millennium, multi-channel television had firmly established itself in the UK, with the inevitable dilution of finite resources that I (and others) had predicted when it first arrived here at the end of the 1980s. Even when Britain had had only three or four channels, most of the programmes were lousy, so if the limited supply of televisual talent and money was now to be spread out over 300 or 400 channels, surely a precipitous decline in standards was inevitable? The situation was as absurd as opening thirty theatres in a town that could just about support one local repertory company. And whereas owning an ITV franchise in the 1960s had rightly been described as "a licence to print money," setting up your own channel on Sky became, for many, a licence to lose money, as plucky individuals fulfilled their lifelong ambition of running their own TV channel, only to see it founder for lack of audience and broadcastable content.

I counted them in, and I counted them out. Within a decade, a combination of prolonged recession and the rise of the internet had killed off many of these stand-alone channels, whose owners had proudly forked out millions of pounds a year, for the privilege of being an unwatched slot on a Sky transponder. Search on the www, and you'll discover that some of them still have websites, but they're frozen in time on the day that the channel itself shut down, like those ghost stations on the London Underground that I remember from my childhood, complete with advertisements for now-obsolete products, but no longer serving any useful purpose, because trains no longer stopped there. We still have hundreds of channels on our digital TV sets, of course, but most of them are now owned by a handful of global media players (who can cross-promote their output), or are offshoots of the UK's five terrestrial channels. As in so many areas of modern life, there's no room for the plucky outsider, whose wisest (and least financially hazardous) choice nowadays is to set up a website, and promote it via social networking sites.

This chapter celebrates the best and the worst of those satellite television stations that started out full of hope and low-interest bank loans, only to receive a sharp slap in the face from the wet fish of reality when the first viewing figures came through from BARB.

Ch 2 SANK WITHOUT TRACE

The Baby Channel started out with a viable business model, based around a website with sensibly low overheads. But like too many upstarts, it developed delusions of grandeur and forked out enormous sums for a slot on the Sky platform (272) in 2005, shortly after I reviewed it. It presumably hoped to gather a regular audience of expectant mothers, but – pregnancy being a temporary condition – it predictably failed to build the loyal permanent viewership that any channel needs if it is to pay its way long-term in the digital marketplace.

THE BABY CHANNEL 2005

How I detest the greetings card industry. Like pharmaceutical companies with their "tell them they stink then sell them deodorants" approach to the public, the likes of Hallmark plaster posters everywhere telling us to celebrate an endless succession of days (Valentine's, Mother's, Father's, New Year, Christmas, not to mention driving tests, exam results, new jobs, new houses, birthdays, and anniversaries), so they can sell us cacky, gaudy bits of card at 1000 per cent mark-up, with sentiments so sickly sweet and sugary that only a massive shot of insulin can prevent us from slipping into a fatal (but nevertheless welcome) hyperglycaemic coma. They're so shameless about exploiting every aspect of our existence for commercial gain (even illnesses and funerals) that I once wrote to one of them, suggesting that their fine range of Mothering Sunday cards should be accompanied by a black-edged range of *Smothering Sunday* cards, to be sent to parents who have stifled their babies in their cribs. "They don't all need to be sombre," I added, "you could do some amusing ones too, saying 'it's twelve inches long and stiff in the morning it's cot death!'" Still no reply.

How to minimise the nightmarish possibility of Sudden Infant Death Syndrome is one of the topics dealt with on *The Baby Channel*. Set up a year ago by former CNN presenter Leon Hawthorne, this on-demand subscription service is one of many channels now using broadband to provide high-quality television over the telephone lines (although it will shortly also be available on Sky), and it's cleverly tapping into a market that magazines have been servicing for years, but which television has been slow to address (though TV is never slow to steal from itself, so watch out for doppelgangers). "It's the world's first television channel exclusively for pregnant women and parents of pre-school children," is its watchcry, but anyone can log in and access their library of well-edited and technically flawless mini-programmes for £4.99 a month. And even though I'm not

TV reviews

pregnant (according to my one-fingered gynaecologist), and don't have any small children around the house (I leave that to Michael Jackson), I was fascinated by what I saw, especially in the "Breast *vs.* Bottle" section. Well, where else is a chap going to see gigantic nipples with areolae the size of hubcaps, except in innocent footage of lactating women?

Being an on-demand service, viewers simply select topics from a drop-down menu, and watch them in real time. So after a short general introduction by a man who sounded exactly like the great fiction writer Jeffrey Archer (well, Jeffrey's CV was great fiction), I watched some sensible advice about car safety for small children (no idiotic "Baby on Board" signs for them, just clear instructions about suitable straps and chairs), before alighting on a short programme presented by Wendy Turner. "Posh Spice has one," began Wendy (so she clearly wasn't talking about careers), and the strand turned out to be a review of All Terrain Buggies, those three-chunky-wheeled numbers that I see in supermarkets on Saturdays, going in every direction but straight, and cunningly designed to collide with unwary shoppers at shin height. And inside, there's always a miniature Winston Churchill with a klaxon voice, whose sole purpose in life is to ruin my day, thus confirming my belief that small children aren't precious gifts from Mother Nature at all, they're just irritating little people who won't share the chores and don't pay rent.

Using a mixture of authoritative interviews with professionals, and reminiscences from mothers with first-hand experience, the channel covered everything from potty training and labour pains to the problems of childproofing your house. I learned what it's like to give birth in prison (a surprisingly common occurrence, it seems), and how to resuscitate a very small child (cover their mouth and nose with your mouth, but don't blow too hard, or they'll burst), but I confess that my mouse kept luring me back to that breast-feeding programme. "Always give it at least two weeks before you give up on breast-feeding," said an expert to a mother whose baby "wouldn't latch on or stay on." But if a baby does prefer the bottle, what happens to all that excess milk? That's where my idea of "lady cheese" comes in, a niche market product for which I'd do the milking (personally, by hand), while the consumers could meet the producers and their grizzling mewling offspring at one of our regular whine-and-cheese parties.

I was intrigued by the breadth and depth of knowledge on this channel, so pregnant women (and their partners) will doubtless drink it down like mother's milk. The oddest discovery I made was that Peggy is now a fashionable name for baby girls, which means that in 2080 Britain will be full of zimmer-framed Peggies for whom the very idea of scheduled programmes on conventional TV channels will be but a distant memory, the likes of BBC and ITV having been superseded long ago by niche on-demand

Ch 2 SANK WITHOUT TRACE

services like this. Of course, the information they learned from *The Baby Channel* when they watched it while pregnant in the 2030s will come in handy once again, because the tips about what you can eat with no teeth and how to fit elasticated nappies are just as helpful in old age as they are in infancy. So they'll have a sense of déjà vu to go with their senility-induced amnesia, which means that they'll not only forget things, they'll think they've forgotten them before.

*Sudden Infant Death Syndrome (that's cot death to you and me) struck in 2008. Lady Cheese became a reality in 2010 which can be seen by clicking on link #10 on the **TV Reviews** page on **www.badastralbooks.com.***

From Whine TV to Wine TV. Wine TV was an ambitious worldwide channel, based in Toronto and San Francisco. Launched in 2004, its early programmes gave viewers an intelligent, informative, and practical view of the wine industry and its produce, and at one point it was being shown in 22 countries. However, much of its subsequent output (such as the programme I reviewed in 2006) was almost as pointless as the absurd "I'm getting wet leaves... Marmite on toast... unleaded petrol... newspapers on a Sunday morning" nonsense spouted by the likes of Oz Clarke and Jilly Goolden. I always used to take the precaution of going to the cellar and getting blind drunk in charge of a review once every four years (The General Election) and nobody noticed. Reviewing Wine TV nearly turned me to the bottle. There is a reference in the following to Michael Winner in the days when he was so fat, if he fell down, he wouldn't know. On 1 January 2007, Winner acquired the bacterial infection, Vibrio vulnificus from an oyster meal in Barbados. He almost had to have a leg amputated and was on the brink of death on several occasions, even managing to catch the "hospital superbug," MRSA. As a consequence he lost a vast amount of weight. Never one to miss an opportunity he had photos taken and published The Fat Pig Diet: Michael Winner's Guide to Getting Thin.

You can see before and after pictures here. You may need a couple of bottles of red before you alight on it:

*Once fortified you take the risk of clicking on link #10a on the **TV Reviews** page on **www.badastralbooks.com.***

TV reviews

WINE TV

SKY 281 2006

Given our national fondness for consuming large quantities of booze, it's curious how embarrassed we Brits are about discussing one of its inevitable side-effects. The euphemisms for vomiting are endless (from "psychedelic breakfast," "decorate the pavement," "liquidate your assets," and "call for Ralph on the big white telephone," to "have a liquid laugh," "deliver street pizza," "shout at your shoes" and "make a Technicolor tribute to Disney"), because we hate to confront the subject head-on, whereas the ancient Greeks and Romans saw retching as a natural and wholesome act, and had it in its correct perspective. For them, a quick trip to the vomitorium was part of the thrill of gorging themselves on enormous quantities of drink and food, and it's sad that nowadays only a few plucky bulimiacs are upholding the noble traditions of the founders of Western Civilisation. The rest of us, meanwhile, have to forego the gastronomic luxury of twenty-course alcoholic lunches – except for celebrity endomorph Michael Winner, of course, and he clearly doesn't bother to throw up afterwards.

The regurgitative effect of alcohol is an aspect of oenophilia that's seldom if ever mentioned on *Wine TV*. The mere existence of this Toronto-based channel must ease the consciences of many domestic drinkers each evening, by convincing them that their hobby is a profoundly aesthetic and educational undertaking, when we all secretly know that wine-tasting is really just an excuse to get pissed as quickly as possible (something that's even easier now that screw tops are starting to replace those pesky corks). As the final part of my week-long exploration of obscure digital channels, I tuned in yesterday to hear a North-American voice introducing "a presentation of Greek wines," and I instantly recalled lying on Kavos beach some fifteen years ago, when a passing, intoxicated, representative of the British lumpenproletariat (an Estuary girl who looked as though she only wore knickers to keep her ankles warm) suddenly threw up a bottle-and-a-half of retsina all over me, to the great amusement of her equally drunken friends. That I could still tell it was retsina, even after it had mingled with her gastric juices, may give you some idea of why I've never touched a drop of the stuff since.

"Greek wine producers would like you to think of you got it the wines of Greece," continued the announcer, who explained that *Wine TV* had recently visited one of that country's leading producers. After which came a programme apparently shot in an Athenian garage on a 1980s

Ch 2 SANK WITHOUT TRACE

camcorder, featuring a Greek vintner who looked as though he regularly enjoyed a glass or twelve, and whose name I cannot reproduce here (even though it appeared on screen), because my computer keyboard has almost none of the letters necessary to spell it. As his wife miserably handed out glasses of wine to a small invited audience, he nervously pointed on a map to the traditional wine-growing areas ("er Macedonia er Crete er Samos er Attica, where we er have the er well-known retsina"), proving in the process that to er is human. Frankly, his level of discussion was so basic that, if he'd given me a glass and asked me "what year is it?" I'd have been tempted to reply "it's 2006, it says so on the tops of all the newspapers. I'm surprised you haven't noticed."

As the sampling continued, I marvelled at the utter pointlessness of most TV wine-tastings (or "presentations"). Until Smellyvision is invented, viewers won't be able to savour the "nose" of the wines, nor are we likely to find these little-known vintages in our local stores; and anyway, we all know that the Mediterranean atmosphere enhances the flavour of mediocre wines, which is why that wondrous bottle of Demestica you shared on a sun-drenched hilltop in Patros tastes like piss when you get a caseful back to cold wet Blighty. Furthermore, the vintner's comments during the degustation were a masterpiece of uselessness, telling us that a retsina was "full of taste," that a 1999 Mantineia red "goes with every food you want," and that a 1998 cabernet "speaks for itself. I could not say anything about this wine." Even after downing several glasses, his tongue remained unloosened, and eventually he just dried up (though, sadly, not *out*) altogether.

Moving away from the dull but dependable main channels this week has been a learning experience for me. The programme quality on the digital channels is far more variable than on the terrestrials, but once you learn how to avoid the acres of garbage (or occasionally to revel in it), there are plenty of obscure gems to be uncovered, more than enough to repay your search time. The intellectual standards of the best programmes can be surprisingly high too, so much so that I'm thinking of founding a Graeco-Roman digital channel, devoted exclusively to the reintroduction of ancient classical words, to describe phenomena in the modern world. It'll be called *Hippocratic Oaf TV*, and will inform viewers that a Fallopian tube is part of a television set, Scrotum is a small planet near Uranus, testicles are found on an octopus, genitals are people of non-Jewish origin, Phallus was a city on the Nile, and masturbate is used to catch very large fish.

The channel was ultimately doomed, because sensible people prefer to drink wine, rather than hear about it, and there proved to be only so much oeno-babble that the audience could tolerate. Wine TV closed, largely unlamented,

TV reviews

in the UK in January 2009. At the time of writing, Michael Winner continues to live and remind us all of an old adage, often muttered by members of the British film industry: "If you're playing dice, you're shooting crap, and if you're shooting crap, you're Michael Winner directing a film."

I have always been fascinated by those who perpetrate scams, particularly on the well-off elderly. How I detest greedy pensioners on Watchdog, complaining about having been conned into investing in dodgy offshore tax-avoidance schemes, the thick and greedy TV presenters becoming pointlessly affronted on their behalf.

I reviewed some financial goings-on on the now defunct ITV PLAY. Alright, that's not strictly speaking a TV channel, but it took so much of ITV's schedule in the middle of the night, it almost became one.

QUIZMANIA

ITV PLAY 2006

Even though my solar-powered torch has proved less useful than expected (it only works in bright sunlight), seldom a day goes by without my miniature solar-powered pocket calculator coming in handy. Admittedly, I already had a pretty good idea of how many pockets I possessed, but the device came free inside a Christmas Cracker, and its tiny keyboard soon enabled me to discover many fascinating arithmetical facts, such as that 111,111,111 × 111,111,111 equals 12,345,678,987,654,321. I've also solved the conundrum of "how many beans make five?" (the answer's nine), and worked out that as a £131.50 colour TV licence permits the purchaser to watch the five main channels for one year, each fee payer is legally entitled to view an annual total of 43,800 hours of terrestrial viewing. I therefore estimate that I am paying 0.00354p for the right to watch a fifty-minute edition of Alan Yentob's *Imagine*, and do you know something? I *still* feel robbed.

    I've also calculated that, with odds of 25,000,000 to 1 against winning the jackpot, the survival of the National Lottery remains unrivalled as a triumph of hope over logic (although the Chancellor must be delighted to see half the nation still queueing up each week to pay an entirely voluntary tax). But the chances of winning are still better than on many of the quizzes that infest the late-night digital schedules, such as *Big Game TV*, whose Grays Inn Road premises were actually raided last week by police, investigating the alleged defrauding of viewers. According

Ch 2 SANK WITHOUT TRACE

to a report on Radio 4, almost all of the 75p calls made to the channel by hopeful viewers are simply routed to a pre-recorded "sorry you haven't been selected – please try later" message, and when the on-screen question is particularly easy (and call volumes are consequently very high), the one human telephonist is sent on a tea break lasting up to two-and-a-half hours, so no calls at all can get through to the presenter. And as the channel has received up to 70,000 calls in a fifteen-hour period, is *Big Game TV* getting money for a) old soap, b) old dope, or c) old rope? Send your answer to this column, enclosing a £10 note (sorry if your reply isn't selected – please try again later).

The Evening Standard lawyers tell me that I'm sure ITV Play would never stoop to such tactics when transmitting late-night shows like *Quizmania*. However, this newly born station does warn viewers (in a font so small it's on the verge of illegibility) that "every call costs 60p, whether selected or not," and as the presenters frequently blather for a full five minutes between each phone-in contestant getting through, the chances of winning are obviously much smaller than they might first appear. Last time I tuned in, the show was using the *Family Fortunes* format (right down to the "uh-uh" buzzer) to encourage viewers to call in and "name movie funnymen," but although numerous cash prizes were on offer (including a tempting "bonus"), not a single one was paid out while I watched. "Remember, you must be over 18 to take part," warned a caption, presumably referring to the caller's minimum IQ requirement, although surely if your IQ is over 18, you'd be smart enough to smell a rat and save your money?

My reason for watching was to endure a character-building masochistic dose of presenter Greg Scott, ex-Butlins Redcoat, ex-host of *Price Drop*, and a man *just* clever enough to know he's not clever enough. Known affectionately (to himself) as "Greggles," this human oil slick must surely suffer from an appallingly severe case of low self-esteem (and rightly so), which he overcomes by denigrating the occasional poor sod who is not only naive enough to phone in and pay his wages, but also manages to get through. "You know about pubs though, don't you Mary?" he smirked at a caller from Stockport (who sounded slightly sloshed, but equally might have been recovering from a stroke), then told another defeated caller "Gavin, that's a good answer for somebody in your condition what can I say apart from 'hic'?" To be fair, he did essay a fifth-rate impersonation of every "funnyman" whose name was mentioned (Benny Hill, John Cleese, Norman Wisdom), but to be fairer, there was one impression that was clearly beyond him. He couldn't impersonate a likeable or even competent host of *Quizmania*.

The terrestrial television industry knew what it was doing when

TV reviews

it consigned Greg Scott to the role of perennial warm-up man (chiefly for *Wogan* and *Countdown*), and were it not for the multi-channel era, he'd still be known only to studio audiences. But the insatiable demand for presenters on digital channels has opened the Pandora's box of his ego, and he's now leaving a tidemark on my screen on an almost nightly basis, a revolting personality fronting a revolting and exploitative type of show which the government urgently needs to regulate, because viewers *think* they're gambling at reasonable odds, but are actually being fleeced. "Charlie Drake is a great answer, but not correct," said Greggles paradoxically as I finally gave up and changed channels, and I recalled a (probably apocryphal) story about that diminutive and randy comic, who was once appearing in panto in *Aladdin*, when he espied a very tall and pneumatic young actress standing in the wings. Ever the gigolo, he sidled up to her and whispered in her knee, "I'd like to have sex with you." And without missing a beat, she replied "if you do and I find out, I'll be *very* annoyed."

I discovered (from a mole at ITV) that, partly as a result of that review, Greggles got sacked. It seemed harsh to me that a lone presenter should have carried the can for what had been occurring behind the scenes at ITV Play, until a fellow Soho-ite called Robert Windsor told me more about what had (in his informed opinion) been going on. "Six thousand calls a minute could be taken by Big Game, simulcasting on ITV, and the callers were charged at a premium rate, whether or not they got through," he told me. "Often, all calls were ignored for hours at a time. Tempting jackpot answers were always impossible – Q: Name something you find in a living room? A: A commode; How many wheels does a car have? A: 174." Bob estimates that a total of over £200 million might have been extracted from the public by these methods. On Channel 4 News, Michael Grade publicly promised refunds to all ITV viewers who had been misled by such phone-in quizzes, yet no refunds were forthcoming for the victims of Big Game TV simulcasts on ITV. Big Game TV quietly closed down in 2007.

Greggles is still extant. On his website he says:

"Nowadays, of course, the memory of the whole genre has been blighted by all the nasty business involving Call TV in general – But I need you to wipe all that from your brain / mind / cranial lobe. I genuinely loved working on this show. I wish that we could have a major broadcaster revive it." Somehow, I don't think that will ever happen. But weirder things have happened in TV. Indeed, I believe the BBC's Political Editor, Nick Robinson, is on the brink of taking over as the host of Later With Jools Holland.

For an update of Greggle's career go to his website by clicking on link #11 on the

/ Ch 2 SANK WITHOUT TRACE

TV Reviews page on www.badastralbooks.com.

I have been having the occasional lunch with Mark Thompson since long before he became the BBC Director General. For all that I knew him well and regarded him as a friend, the day he turned up to lunch AS the DG, I found myself slightly starry-eyed (it happens to all those who have worked for the Corporation apparently).

Our conversations always became heated when I raised the issue of the lamentable lack of pure music programmes on the BBC I remember from my childhood (and which were responsible for me studying music at university). Not a lunch went by without me repeating the mantra that one of the dependable joys of my childhood was being able to watch great musicians at work on television. Although there were only three channels available at the time, BBC2 in particular used to feature solo instrumental recitals on a weekly basis (and often more frequently than that), and budding musicians could learn a great deal from being able to see skilful and experienced violinists, pianists, and classical guitarists in close-up.

Now, in our multi-channel era, it's almost impossible to find extended performances from solo instrumentalists on television (except on Sky Arts 1 and 2 who are taking the BBC to the cleaners), and the musicality of the generation that's growing up now will suffer as a result. So despite its manifest inadequacies, I mourn the disappearance of the following channel, which set out in 2004 with the best of intentions (but presumably also with insufficient funding).

THE MUSICIANS CHANNEL 2004

Flicking through the satellite channels this week, I saw the words "music by Wally Stott" in the credits of an old British movie, and remembered a story I once heard about the legendary musical director of *The Goon Show*. For decades, Wally had secretly longed to be a woman, so he finally had a sex change in the early 70s, and arrived to direct the next orchestral rehearsal in full make-up, wig, skirt, twinset and pearls. Standing before the dumbstruck all-male band, the conductor realised that an explanation was necessary, so eloquently addressed them thus: "Gentlemen, forgive me for shocking you. As you can see, I am now a woman and have changed my name to Angela Morley. But, you are all mature professional men, and

TV reviews

as far as I am concerned, this should not affect our working relationship. It is an honour to lead this excellent band, and I hope our mutual respect will be unaffected. Now, before we continue, are there any questions?" There was a long pause, before a hand went up from the brass section: "Er I suppose a fuck is out of the question?"

Playing music is a serious business, of course, so it's hardly surprising that performers often develop an irreverent sense of humour as an antidote. But most are wise enough to keep a straight face in public, and reserve their jokes for the pub afterwards, unlike many of the presenters on *The Musicians Channel*, who unfortunately seek to combine the two. Given the disgraceful cutbacks in music education in schools over the past two decades, I'd like to be able to applaud the setting up of a free-to-air digital channel that seeks to "encourage, inspire, and educate all people with an interest in musical activity," but having watched the output of this Maidstone-based outfit in recent weeks, I can only offer a slow handclap. Because many of the teachers offering tuition don't seem overly competent as performers, and behave like wannabee children's TV presenters, which means that their music makes you want to laugh, and their jokes make you want to cry.

Take the *MTuition – Vocals* course that's transmitted each evening, hosted by the appropriately-named Adam Pain. A grown-up schoolroom idiot cross between Paul Ross and Mark Thomas, he's supposed to play the piano and receive vocal coaching from singing tutor Samira Rankin, but the pair spent much of the edition I saw indulging in witless private banter that made the viewer feel like an intruder, not a potential student. "I like your T shirt great, I've got apricot flapjacks at the back we deserve a break cos it's like getting into that thing of singing making the words legible it's mind-blowing wot you gotta fink about innit?" they rambled, and I soon found myself concentrating almost entirely on the sultry Ms Rankin's attractive bare legs, though that's not simply because I'm a sad man of a certain age. No, it was because they took up a full 70 per cent of the screen, on account of the cameraman shamelessly targeting his lens not at her face, but directly *between* her thighs.

Admittedly, I've had an aversion to singing lessons ever since I was forced to attend them when I was a music undergraduate, only to be told that my voice sounded like a crumhorn (for the uninitiated, think of a mediaeval saxophone in the nude, with a tone resembling a cat chewing a bee). But this wasn't tuition at all, it was simply Samira saying "we're stood properly, our breathing's okay" (they were seated, and she ran out of breath midway through her first long note), and singing "Amazing Grace" in five different styles (pop, rock, music theatre, and so on), all of which sounded exactly like soul. Their attempt at jazz was absurd, mainly

Ch 2 SANK WITHOUT TRACE

because Mr Pain didn't appear to know any jazz chords, while their Dolly Parton version featured both of my least-favourite types of music (country *and* western), and they barely seemed to know what they were doing themselves, so how on earth did they propose to teach anyone? "I'm flying by the seat of my brains here," confided the pianist at one point, but it wasn't just his brains that were located in his seat. He was talking out of it too.

"You just made a complete fool of yourself," laughed Samira after talking Pain into singing *falsetto* (that's an Italian musical term for "with dentures"), which is the last thing a teacher should ever do. But then, having just observed her sing an appalling bum note, pull a face, and excuse herself by saying "well, I don't listen to a lot of country and western," it was obvious by now that the educational content of the show was about as advanced as the Christmas-cracker level of jokes. Of course, singers are vulnerable in this respect, because they really only have themselves to blame when they miss a note (unlike instrumentalists who can point to a leaking keypad or faulty fret), and have to hide behind the dubious claim that "it's not me that's sharp, it's the orchestra that's flat." But what I heard here reminded me of how you can tell when there's a singer at your front door. They can't find the key, and they don't know when to come in.

You may think that being a television critic involves nothing more arduous than rolling out of bed in the morning, then sitting on a sofa eating biscuits and scribbling on a notepad, but you would be wrong (in my case a strict regime of animal strangulation and rigorous masturbation would start the day BEFORE the bicuits). In truth, I spent most of my time seeking out programmes to review in the unlikeliest places, including my local petrol station, which was where I conducted my research for the following review.

FORECOURT TELEVISION 2002

Call me pedantic if you will (although, strictly speaking, a more accurate linguistic formulation would be "excessively sesquipedalian"), but isn't it time that the Oxford English Dictionary belatedly brought itself up to date? For example, Siamese twins should have been listed as Thai twins since 1949, Persian cats ought to have been renamed Iranian cats in 1935, and Ceylon Tea should have been called Sri Lankan Tea since

TV reviews

1972. Furthermore, "Bohemian Rhapsody" should have been rechristened "Czech Republic Rhapsody" in 1993 (okay, the lyrics would sound ridiculous, but no more so than Ben Elton's absurd script for *We Will Rock You*), and such a reference book should surely also have entries for Zimbabwean ridgebacks (formerly Rhodesian ridgebacks) and Zaïrian eels (formerly Congo eels), although over exactly what the Old Phlegmish Masters should now be called, I prefer to draw a discreet veil.

Upon glimpsing DIY expert Handy Andy at my local petrol station yesterday, I found myself wondering if any reference books have yet noted that his German equivalent is called Bastl Wastl. Handrew Andrew wasn't actually on the premises when I saw him, I should explain, but the place has recently installed *Forecourt Television*, complete with 52" screens and BOSE speakers, and I felt that it was my professional obligation to watch what they were showing. Well, this telly reviewing lark is more than just a job to me, it's a vocation, and I'm fully prepared to risk verbal abuse, gobbing, Glasgow kisses, and even the occasional lynching while conducting research for this column. And considering that I occupied Pump 7 for nearly twenty-five minutes (with the petrol gun on minimum squirt, so I could watch for longer), while a queue of increasingly angry motorists behind kept honking, revving their engines, shouting at me to hurry up, and suggesting that I stick my head in an anatomically improbable location (a place where, incidentally, the sun doesn't shine – I checked), you'll realise that I very nearly qualified for the George Cross (posthumous), for bravery above and beyond the call of duty.

If your experience of television in the marketplace has been confined to those wretched little screens in post office queues, then FTV will come as something of a revelation. It's a bonsai satellite channel that's currently received at over 330 petrol stations, and its output can be customised on site, and tailored to suit local conditions. The result is narrowcasting in its broadest sense (or should that be broadcasting in its narrowest sense?), because the target audience is, by definition, confined to car owners, and those who watch it tend to be young, employed, male, and upmarket. The screen springs into life as you drive past an infrared sensor, and while the output probably won't win any Baftas (at the moment), it's certainly a damn sight more interesting than concentrating on trying to hit the £20 mark precisely on the petrol meter (something that I believe to be impossible, because the final droplet always tips it over to £20.01).

Being an unashamedly commercial enterprise, the bulk of FTV's output is well, commercials, but what held my attention was the specially commissioned grouting between the ads. Which brings us back to Handy Andy, who showed us how to fill a crack or two (and frankly guys, some

Ch 2 SANK WITHOUT TRACE

of us need all the advice we can get in that area), followed by a sudden, sobering shot of missing schoolgirl Milly Dowler in the Public Information section. But most entertaining of the dozen-or-so strands I saw were the dozen-or-so strands belonging to Bobby Charlton in 1966, as *A History of World Cup Hairstyles* drew attention to the way middle-aged men skilfully disguise their balding pates by growing their remaining hair very long, then combing it across. Current practitioners of the genre include Tony Parsons and Ann Widdecombe, but I wonder why they do it, because bald people have one great advantage over the rest of us. They're the only people who ever get to hear snowflakes.

In case you're wondering, I don't have any shares in FTV, but I almost wish I did, because it's an advertiser's wet dream of a concept, capturing the attention of a steady stream of A, B, and C1 consumers, whose subsequent recollection of commercials is far higher than for ads viewed domestically. Unlike some other satellite stations I can mention, nothing outstays its welcome, and given that forecourts are just about the ugliest places that most of us ever visit, during refuelling I'm pleased to have a screen distract me from all the grim grey concrete and grubby plastic trim. Now that the problem of boredom at petrol stations has been cracked, maybe it's time for me to implement my plan to banish ennui from another nexus of transport tedium, the bus stop. Under my scheme, bored and world-weary pensioners who are waiting for buses will be invited to keep warm by turning little handles built into the wall of the shelter, which are connected to generators, and thence to the National Grid. As they turn, they'll produce enough wattage to power a town the size of Cleethorpes, and the activity will distract them from dwelling upon the greatest conundrum that faces the elderly. At what age do you stop being too young to die of old age?

I have been meaning to find out precisely what happened to Forecourt TV. It seemed like an excellent idea at the time, and still does; but it never caught on, and soon disappeared in the UK, whereas similar ventures have thrived in parts of the US.

I managed to track down Mike Gull, the boss of Forecourt TV, not long after I wrote the review (April 2003). He told me the business had suffered financial difficulties, and had had to close down, but that he was planning to install a radio version instead. As far as I am aware, this has never happened yet, but I still think there's a future in Forecourt TV, if the right financial model can be devised.

TV reviews

The last I heard of Mike he was working for the African Broadcasting Network and there's no mention of FTV anywhere. So it looks like I will have to go on looking at the depressing fuel counter as I fill up. Indeed, perhaps it was the much higher fuel prices that we Brits have to pay that was responsible for the failure of FTV. Each trip to the pump is so expensive for us that we feel far too skint to be seduced by the advertisers' wares, and the commercial model therefore fell at the first hurdle.

BBC Choice launched in 1998, and was the first British channel to be broadcast exclusively in digital format (previous satellite channels had all been either partially or wholly analogue). At the time, no digital TV receivers were available to the public, so nobody could watch it, but then that's the sort of forward-thinking that we have come to expect from the BBC, advance planning that makes the licence fee seem cheap at the price.

JAPANORAMA
BBC CHOICE 2004

It's said that 90 per cent of Brits who arrive at Orlando airport go straight to Disney World, and once you discover how violently insane life can be elsewhere in Florida, it's not hard to see why. When I flew there a few years ago (on behalf of a glossy magazine), the first news story I heard upon landing was about a Miami man who'd accidentally chain-sawed his own hand off, then immediately shot a dozen three-inch nails into his head "to take away the pain," and I was only too willing to avoid meeting such people by immediately climbing aboard the nearest Disney courtesy bus I could find (although the driver was rather brusque, so it was actually more of a *discourtesy* bus). So it was that I spent the next three days ensnared within a people trap designed by the world's most famous mouse, and it occurred to me that just about every part of the planet nowadays has a Disney theme park within a couple of hours flying distance, except for Tokyo, where the concept has never caught on. You see, nobody in Japan would be tall enough to be let onto the really good rides.

Of course, the Japanese aren't missing much, because most of Disney's "really good rides" turn out to be not unlike having sex with Vanessa Feltz (damp, uncomfortable, over in two minutes, and leaving you with the urge to throw up). They're perfectly content with their own excellent theme parks (based mostly around stylised representations of the natural world), and so was Jonathan Ross, who presented last night's *Japanorama* (BBC Choice) while seated atop an animatronic panda. With

Ch 2 SANK WITHOUT TRACE

the World Cup stimulating global interest in East Asia, the scheduling of this series is timely, and the programmes are also wisely avoiding any crass "funny foreigner" routines of the Jeremy Clarkson variety, but unfortunately Ross gives every appearance of having recently undergone a head-nailing experience of his own. Certainly, he didn't so much present this programme as simply shout at the camera, alternating between Woganesque whimsy and sheer verbosity, and never letting two or three words suffice when a couple of thousand would easily do.

"This week we're going to be looking at Japan's obsession with youth" he promised, but the evidence he'd mustered simply didn't support his thesis that the cult of youth is greater there than in Western countries. "Musical Svengalis who produce disposable pop stars like The Morning Girls" exist in all countries with a strong consumer base, and references to the group's "*unique* Logan's Run-inspired retirement system" (members are periodically replaced by younger singers) seemed bizarre, because that's exactly how the famous Menudo group from Puerto Rico kept regenerating itself back in the 80s. The random appropriation of Western icons and artefacts seemed no different from the vogue for "cultural shopping" amongst US stars like Madonna, nor was I persuaded that the interest which some middle-aged men display in young schoolgirls is unique to Japan. Sadly, the phenomenon of youthful innocence being corrupted by money and power can be observed the whole world over, and the programme's obsession with "compensation dating" and the sale of used schoolgirl uniforms (and even phials of urine) said as much about Occidental prurience as it did about Oriental perversion.

Nevertheless, there were some fascinating reports here, and it's a pity that the entire programme couldn't have been devoted to the extraordinary animations of Hayao Miyazaki, a man whose work has (much to his displeasure) been compared to that of Walt Disney. Clips from the movie *Battle Royale* were equally arresting, mainly because this Japanese version of *Lord of the Flies* took the idea of a fight to the death literally, and made *Fight Club* look as tame as a bout of professional wrestling. *Water Boys*, a weird adventure series based around the antics of a male synchronised swimming team, had me dozing off and I found myself, in a half-dream, wondering how such things are organised at the Paralympics. Do they hold synchronised drowning competitions, where wheelchair-bound competitors hit the pool floor simultaneously? And are there special reserved spaces in the stadium car park for non-disabled people?

Sorry, but when I want to see TV travel journalism done properly, I'll pull out an archive tape of Robert Robinson or Clive James, and enjoy the beautifully-crafted phrases of writers with the wit to observe and condense. Ross's main gift is verbosity, and while that can work to

TV reviews

his advantage on radio (where there's little pressure of time), television requires verbal economy, and needs far pithier and sharper lines than he's able to deliver. Why the executive producer (Jonathan Ross) decided on Jonathan Ross as presenter is something that perhaps only he can explain (though maybe the runner, James Ross, also has some idea), and I was only glad that at least Paul Ross didn't turn up on my screen as well, because he's got an even more severe cathode-ray addiction than his brother. If only the Rosses could follow Samuel Beckett's wise example, and refuse to speak on television. After all, it's surely better to stay silent and be thought a fool, than to open your mouth and remove all doubt.

As we know, Mr Ross had a little bit of difficulty with the BBC after leaving puerile filthy messages on Andrew Sach's answerphone machine. To be frank, I cannot bear the sight of his smug face on my TV screen. He is a man who is living proof that evolution can go into reverse and can be summed up by the phrase "That's enough about me, let's talk about you what do you think of me?.." Some years ago, I had a huge row with him at The Groucho Club when I'd accused him of making lazy travel shows – in particular The American Trip that seemed to have been produced and written by U.S PR companies for tourist boards. As we shouted "talentless cunt" "fucking critic you fucking failure" and so on at each other, a breeze passed under us (we are both about 6 feet tall, I assume) that was created by the surprisingly short Princess Margaret.

*As for BBC Choice, it is remembered today (if at all) solely for having made a minor star out of Christopher Price, the fat, bald, camp, gay presenter of Liquid News, who died (aged 34) of a rare meningitis-like infection, a year before BBC Choice itself finally expired. See him by clicking on link #12 on the **TV Reviews** page on www.badastralbooks.com.*

Given the nostalgia that many of us feel for the TV commercials of our youth, and the excellence of the production values that many of those thirty-second masterpieces embodied, I'd long thought that a channel devoted entirely to advertisements would do well. Vince Stanzione clearly also thought so, but the Advert channel (which began in 2004) soon ran into difficulties with OFCOM (for the reasons I predicted in the final paragraph of this review), and the parent company eventually ceased its TV operations in the UK.

Ch 2 SANK WITHOUT TRACE

THE ADVERT CHANNEL
SKY 694 2004

Necessity may be the mother of invention, but peculiarity frequently seems to be the father. John Logie Baird not only came up with the daydream machine for automatic time-wasting (*aka* television), but also wasted his own time by patenting the electric sock to prevent smelly feet (I wonder if he tried to patent leather shoes too?). A few decades earlier, Armand Murat founded a company the sole purpose of which was to project advertisements through the air and onto the clouds above Paris, but unfortunately, it was a cloudless summer that year, and he went bust. And back in 1851, clothier Elias Howe invented the zip fastener which, to his astonishment, became world-famous after the male side of the British Royal Family adopted it, and began wearing them all year round. Except at Yuletide, of course, when they all went to Scotland and donned kilts, presumably because they didn't want the sheep to hear the zip (well, a sheep never says no, nor can it kiss and tell to the News of the World).

When ITV was created almost fifty years ago, those three diverse inventions started to merge together into one interconnected whole, as television began beaming advertisements for fashionable clothing through the air, and into our houses. Most of the TV industry is still funded by advertising, but modern technology increasingly allows viewers to wind through them at high speed, thereby placing the traditional commercial break in serious jeopardy. Nevertheless, people tend to become nostalgic when reminiscing about old commercials, which is presumably why The Advert Channel was launched, and began broadcasting on digital satellite earlier this year. Twenty-four hours a day, seven days a week, it pumps out a mixture of old ads and vacuous new chat to celebrate the world of TV advertising or, to give it its proper description, the art of arresting human intelligence for long enough to extract money from it.

"Allo, I'm tryin' on dees cloves and I caught me airs in me zip," said a gentleman called Mike when I tuned in recently, to watch a strand in the Home Zone section, apparently labelled *Fashion Cuts*. He and Kath were not so much presenters as human kapok, filling space and uttering lightweight banalities to eke out their meagre supply of old commercials for Diesel and Levi jeans, some of them half-remembered British ones, others from the Indian subcontinent, and all framed inside a rudimentary TV screen. Watching the slow oscillation between show and commercial, it struck me that the old saying about ads being better than the programmes was being disproved before my very eyes as I watched, and here's how I can

TV reviews

prove it. If you liked this ad-filled programme, then logically, that saying must therefore be wrong; and if you loathed it, then logically, it must *still* be wrong. Isn't philosophy wonderful?

While a channel devoted exclusively to archive commercials could be fascinating (especially pre-colour ads, which can be as effective as Proust's madeleines in evoking the atmosphere of a long-gone era), the ones shown on this channel simply aren't old enough, they're just stale. They're mostly the sort that you see on your home-recorded videotapes of ITV programmes from the late 90s, and the presenters lack the wit, knowledge, and insight to tell us anything meaningful about them, beyond informing us that "I liked that one," or "I didn't like that one." Indeed, the whole channel seems to exist for no other purpose than to tempt viewers into contacting them on an 0906 number to enter asinine competitions that cost almost £5 per call, a huge charge that isn't always indicated on the screen, which seems to me to be a somewhat unethical form of advertising. And just in case you didn't know that there were different forms of morality in this field, kindly allow me to explain: unethical advertising uses falsehoods to deceive the public; ethical advertising uses truth to deceive the public.

Wondering who was behind the channel, I did some research, and discovered that the owners are Chelsea Baker (a former lingerie model) and Vince Stanzione, author of a tome entitled *How To Make Money From Financial Spread Trading*. Apparently, that book outlines a foolproof method for beating the markets, yet instead of quietly making billions from it, Vince prefers to sell the system to others (for a hefty fee), which surely makes him a saint. I confess that I'd be more interested to see the financial books and paperwork for his TV station, and check whether he's actually cleared all the ads he's currently showing. I know from personal experience that you cannot rely on the protection of the fair dealing clause in the Copyright Designs and Patents Act 1988 if you're showing old commercials without comment, or framing them inside a TV screen graphic (curiously, this has been done at Ofcom's insistence); and if those ads have not been individually cleared with the actors, the Musicians Union, and the PRS, then the station could soon find itself the subject of the first class action ever taken against a satellite TV channel. Damn. Having written that, I bet there'll be a promo running on the channel by tomorrow, with the words " 'first class action' says the *Evening Standard*" on it. Well, these are advertising people we're dealing with, after all.

Vince Stanzione: the investment doc looked vaguely familiar. I may have received one in the post from him. He seems to me to be a modern-day Horace Batchelor, who (during the 1950s and early 1960s) selflessly shared his famous "Infra-Draw Method" of winning the football pools with millions of listeners of

Ch 2 SANK WITHOUT TRACE

Radio Luxembourg, instead of keeping the secret to himself and scooping the jackpot alone each week. Another saintly, yet misunderstood, figure.

London TV bounced onto the capital's screens in 2004, full of optimism and enthusiasm, and flush with lots of lovely free money from the London Tourist Board. There were grand plans afoot to have it piped into every hotel room in the city, and it boasted that it would appeal equally to both Londoners and visitors alike.

LONDON TV 2004

Not long ago, the results of my three-year survey of first-class flights were published in this August newspaper (to keep our circulation department happy, I should mention that we publish during the other eleven months as well). Despite my having flown on Concorde, the supersonic plane wasn't mentioned in the final article, because by then it had been grounded, but my journey on it remains an unforgettable experience. Although I'd paid thousands for my ticket, I had less seat space than on Easyjet, the hours I saved on the flight to New York were lost again while sitting on the airport tarmac (because nobody could find the right part to open the doors), nor could I cheat those ultimate levellers of class, namely jet lag, Immigration Control, and Baggage Reclaim. But most curious of all was the disproportionately high number of asymmetrical people on board, and I eventually came to the conclusion that Concorde flights were largely funded by big insurance companies and charity appeals, because I've never before seen so many missing eyes, artificial limbs, and bald terminally-ill children off to Florida to wave the world goodbye via Mickey and Donald. Worse still, I couldn't help smirking at them, that wasn't because I was openly mocking the afflicted, dear me no. It was just the G force at MkII.

Concorde's one compensating feature was its speed, which meant it didn't have time to play those appalling in-flight tourist videos shown on slower Transatlantic flights, that reduce London to images which nobody who lives here would recognise. Smiling beefeaters serving half-timbered jellied eels to pearly kings, the Equerry Poursuivant presenting a butt of sack to the Right Royal Bird Turglar, that sort of thing, all fronted by the likes of Roland Rivron, displaying the same ghastly enthusiasm formerly evinced by Roy Castle on *Record Breakers*. When I tuned into London TV yesterday, its first day of transmission, I initially feared that this Tourist Board-funded channel would also portray a non-existent "heritage" city,

TV reviews

so I was pleasantly surprised to see a fairly realistic depiction of what the capital has to offer to residents and visitors alike. It's a sort of listings magazine of the air, offering sneak previews of some of the hundreds of shows, exhibitions, and events that take place each day, and which most Londoners won't ever see, because they're too knackered after work to do anything except go home, watch the television, and feel guilty about why they never go up West.

Fronting the hourly What's On strand throughout the channel's debut was the undeniably voluptuous Georgie Palmer. True, her grin was remorselessly huge (yet another woman with child-bearing lips), and the backdrop was the too-obvious Tower Bridge, but her script was sharp and informative, and full of mini-reports about events I could actually imagine myself attending. The San Francisco Ballet at Sadler's Wells, British Art Week at Tate Britain, Rolf Harris painting in Trafalgar Square, and a compelling and chilling exhibition of photographs of Hell's Angels at the National Theatre.

Given that most American cities have had such dedicated channels for decades, I began wondering why the idea is only now catching on over here. Many provincial British cities simply wouldn't have enough going on to sustain such a service, I suppose (I've stayed in Northern towns where "watching the traffic lights change" counts as top-rank entertainment), but London is another country, increasingly separate from the rest of Britain, and overflowing with places to spend money, some of them more worthwhile than others. For example, I wasn't overly impressed by one reporter's insistence that "Bali Bali in Shaftsbury Avenue is a great place to eat" (great, but only if you like warm beer and gut-wrenching food), nor will I be forking out to see Geordie Ross Noble. Funny he may be, but for my liking he sounds too much like the Big Brother voice that C4 occasionally uses as a continuity announcer, and who now elongates his syllables to such a ludicrous extent (as in "Krishnan Guuruu-Muuuuuurthy") that he's become a Tyneside Uncle Tom.

As I gazed lustfully at Georgie (sorry, as I viewed her with professional detachment), and read the electronic tickertape running across the bottom of the screen, I realised that I was starting to warm to London TV. It'll never replace the refreshing cynicism of the excellent *Time Out*, but the sheer quantity of info in *some* events magazines can give you listings-blindness, and turning to this channel will then prove a welcome antidote. Unlike most digital stations, the hourly What's On segment is varied each time it recurs (I'll be keeping an eye on it as the weeks pass, to see if standards slip), and when the channel has found its feet, I hope it'll foster an occasional streak of anarchy, to keep tourists on their feet. For example, it could start telling visiting Americans that "London

Ch 2 SANK WITHOUT TRACE

cabbies should be addressed as 'Queerboys' – it's an ancient ecclesiastical tradition." Or informing them that "the streets in London are paved with gold," which of course they are. They're called double yellow lines.

Within a couple of years, London TV's key presenters had left, as had its audience, and its purpose and funding had become compromised. It had closed altogether by the time the first whiff of oncoming recession was detected in 2007.

*Will I ever cease to be amazed at the ease with which apparently decent people allow themselves to become involved in vile and squalid enterprises? Recently, while reading about Zyklon B (the lethal vapour used in Nazi gas chambers), I began to wonder about Zyklon A, and what it had been used for. It turned out to be an insecticide to protect fruit trees, invented by the same chemist, a man for whom it was but a short step from germicide to genocide. Information about Zyklon A can be read here on German Wikipedia, which can accessed by clicking on link #13 on the **TV Reviews** page on **www.badastralbooks.com.***

In a similar way, seduced by greed, previously respectable people willingly enter the most loathsome professions, some becoming libel lawyers, bankers, while a few lost souls (perhaps the most grotesque and dispossessed of all) get themselves involved in the selling of houses.

Nobody should ever feel sorry for estate agents, so why therefore should we mourn the disappearance of the short-lived Real Estate TV? No reason at all. Indeed, given the number of aimless property shows that terrestrial stations broadcast each day (and the number of online websites devoted to the buying and selling of houses in particular locations), what further purpose could realistically be served by an entire channel devoted to simply gawping at other people's houses? None.

HEAD FOR THE MED
REAL ESTATE TV SKY 279, 2006

Don't get your hopes up yet, but if my latest money-making scheme pans out, I'll soon be an ex-hack, sunning himself in contented retirement on the Côte d'Azur. My scheme is simple. First, I'll buy a computer capable of dialling a million random phone numbers an hour, and programme it to give each number a single ring, before hanging up. Nobody will be able to lift the receiver in time (so my million hourly calls will cost me nothing),

TV reviews

but some will wonder who the caller was, dial 1471 out of curiosity, and be given my number. Unbeknown to them, it'll be a premium rate number (charged at £5 per minute or part thereof), and when they phone it, they'll hear a recording of a stuttering man saying "th th this is St St Stammerers UK (pause 5"), s s s s orry you were d d d d d dialled in error, but er... (pause 10"), er... th th thank you for c c c calling anyway." Nobody can accuse a stutterer of deliberately lengthening a call, so I'll be free to run my scam for years, and I reckon I'll gross at least a million quid a week. If it all works out, do feel free to drop by and see me in Antibes. If I'm not in my villa, I'll be on my yacht."

I've wanted to live on the Côte d'Azur ever since my first visit there, when I walked head-first into Graham Greene in the old part of Antibes, and he called me (I paraphrase, this being a family newspaper) "a clumsy See You Next Tuesday." Consequently, while continuing this week's exploration of obscure digital channels, I was naturally attracted to the Provence edition of a series called *Head for the Med*, broadcast daily on the Real Estate TV channel (Sky 279). However, the opening titles didn't inspire much confidence, mainly because half of the listed destinations for the series weren't Mediterranean at all, but Adriatic (Venice, Dubrovnik), Aegean (Gallipoli), or Atlantic (Lisbon, Porto), not to mention Lake Bled, which nestles somewhere close to the Slovenian Alps, near the Austrian border. And once the travel show got underway, I soon began to realise that the production team were (like their programme's sense of geography) hopelessly at sea.

"Nice is a true delight, definitely waiting to be discovered," declared Annie Valiant's mind-numbingly redundant script, at the start of the South of France edition. Empty phrases like "fabulous views," "lavishly-furnished rooms," and "a feast of balcony displays" made Judith Chalmers (*aka* the Peripatetic Lobster) sound like Jack Kerouac in comparison, but what tipped the narrative from mere vacuity into downright imbecility was the voiceover from Roger Tilling (of University Challenge fame), a throwback from the 70s who's living proof that the mediocre are always at their best. Like some Radio 1 DJ during the Simon Bates era, he'd fallen in love with his own elongated vowels, talking smugly about "the Côte d'Azuuuuuur" where "the locals play boooooules," oscillating in pitch between absurdly high and psychotically low, and erraTICally emphaSIsing RANdom sylLABles. Swaggering and smarmy, he aimed at euphony but achieved baryphony, and frankly, if anybody approached you in the street and spoke to you in such a voice, you'd call the police (if you don't believe me, listen to it yourself by going to www.rogertillings.com – it's hilarious).

As for the depiction of the Côte d'Azur, the heady talk of shops, restaurants, and even "a market" simply made Provence seem provincial.

"The cafes in the old town are exquisite," Tillings told us, and many certainly are, but not the one they showed (where I once threw up after watching a dog lay a cable in the road, then eat it), and why pretend that the town of Tourettes-sur-Loup is some kind of artistic Left Bank community, when it's actually full of talentless daubers selling tearful Pierrot paintings to gullible tourists? Their brief tour of Cannes missed everything of importance, with no shots at all of the wondrous Martinez Hotel (where pianist Jimmy McKissic has mesmerised visitors for decades), and barely a mention of the Carlton, that legendary hotel whose twin cupolas are modelled on the breasts of the scandalous Folies Bergère starlet, La Belle Otero. Instead, the programme concentrated on the vastly inferior Negresco down the road, which has but a single cupola, and that's not an erotic ornament, that's an architectural mastectomy.

Provence is one of the world's great destinations for the discriminating and epicurious holidaymaker, but you wouldn't have realised that from this bland and formulaic depiction. Indeed, as the programme insists that Atlantic-facing Portugal is also part of the Mediterranean, I'd be more likely to travel there instead, if only to revisit the walls of Lisbon, dozens of which (last time I was there) had been spray-painted by some existentialist graffiti artist with the phrase "sem a verdade, tu és o perdedor." He'd helpfully provided an English translation too on many of the walls, but each contained one small yet tragic error: "without truth, you are the looser." Frankly, from my experience of holidays in Southern Europe, he'd have been closer to the truth if he'd written "without Diocalm, you are the looser."

Real Estate TV launched on Sky in 2004, and closed on 1 April 2009.

Not so much a channel as an analogue text information service, Ceefax was launched by the BBC in the early 1970s. With a display format of 24 rows and 40 columns, its ability to convey information – let alone graphics – was strictly limited, yet it nevertheless seemed astonishingly futuristic in those far-off pre-www days. ITV and Channel 4 developed a rival Teletext service, which closed in December 2009.

CEEFAX 2002

There are few sadder sights in life than seeing a car-owner with more money than sense giving way to the impulse to acquire a personalised number plate. Americans are at least imaginative in their choices (like

TV reviews

the dental surgeon with CME 4DK, or the urologist with 2PC ME), but we Brits habitually choose the most wretched and obvious ones, such as Paul Daniels with his MAG 1C, or Jimmy Tarbuck with his COM 1C. More pathetic still are the cheapskates who don't want to fork out for the proper number plates, and instead purchase cheap ones with numbers that "look a bit like letters" (i.e. nothing like). For example, the priapic moron I once saw proudly displaying S5XY (sexy) on his shiny red sports car. And even the famous have been known to cut corners, such as Michael Caine, whose old Mercedes supposedly read ZULU (but on closer inspection was actually 2ULU), and Bill Roach (*Coronation Street*'s Ken Barlow) who bought his wife Sarah a number plate that read: S4RA R. Sorry, that's so tight-fisted, it's not so much MAG 1C, as TRAG 1C.

Similar lexicographical and numerological scramblings can often be found on the BBC's superannuated Teletext service, CEEFAX. Unlike the vastly superior BBCi system (available on satellite, and through the Internet), this Luddite relic of an earlier technological era has advanced little since its introduction exactly thirty years ago, which means (among other things) that its terrestrial analogue signal is still frequently affected by the weather. As part of my recovery plan after the excesses of New Year's Eve, I spent yesterday afternoon watching the CEEFAX pages roll silently over my screen (the televisual equivalent of becoming a Trappist monk), but strong winds were blowing outside, so half the pag s had missi g chara ters, and some wo3ds even ha8 err4nt le77ers. However, I didn't notice anything quite so sublime as the headline I remember seeing there a few years ago, "Fans nob Gary Glitter." Presumably, the verb should have been "mob," but knowing what we now do about Mr Gadd, anything is possible.

Television is often accused of dumbing down (usually with good cause), but extreme simplification was built into the CEEFAX system (and its ITV rival Teletext) at the outset by the severe limitations of its technology. Using only about twenty of the 625 lines on the screen, its ability to convey information is therefore sorely restricted, so complex news stories (pages 100–24) have to be reduced to seventy words, and the pages turn over at the torpid pace of a Swiss machine gun (bang – one minute's silence – bang – another minute's silence). Worse, the typeface is crude and antiquated, and the attempt to display a weather map of Britain (page 401) is laughably primitive, so the overall effect is of a cross between a Dymo labeller, a 70s Acorn computer, and a box of Lego. Pretty racy, perhaps, back in the days when the Grandstand Teleprinter was considered to be the cutting edge of TV technology, but hopelessly outdated nowadays, and with a depth of coverage so shallow that even the editor of the Sunday Sport would consider it derisory.

Ch 2 SANK WITHOUT TRACE

Admittedly, there are a few worthwhile services buried away in the nooks and crannies of this journalistic Spruce Goose (sporting friends tell me that the football results pages are useful on Saturday afternoons), but the interminable wait for information means that they are mostly accessed by lethargic types who would otherwise (to paraphrase The League of Gentlemen) be flicking themselves off to Trisha. By comparison, BBCi is rapid and user-friendly, and is already using multi-media technology to great effect, even though it's still in its infancy. And as we reach the stage where roughly half the population has access to digital TV and the Internet, and half does not, that poses a serious problem for our once-cohesive society, which is already becoming more fragmented with every passing year. If such a chasm is allowed to persist and widen (and it may well do, because the poor cannot afford to buy the best technology, and the elderly often won't), we will eventually end up with a well-informed and educated digerati, and an ill-informed and CEEFAX-dependent ignorati.

As we enter 2003, CEEFAX reminds me of those slow and limited Amstrad word processors that everybody used in the 1980s before graduating to proper computers, and its inability to evolve is one more reason why analogue deserves to die. BBCi has everything that CEEFAX can offer (including subtitling), and much more, all at ten times the speed; so does Sky (with its News Active and Customer services), and these systems are also available on Freeview, albeit it in a slightly simplified form. Ultimately, for television to pretend it's a book or a newspaper is a mistake, because its strengths lie in other areas, while an over-reliance on print exposes its weaknesses, although I have to admit that I never get the sort of cheek from my TV set that I encountered recently at Waterstones. Just the other day, I asked an assistant there to show me where the self-help section was, and she replied "If I told you, that would defeat the purpose."

The televisual upstart of its elder and more durable radio-based sibling, Classic FM TV is one of those stations that is forgotten, but not gone. Although it disappeared from Sky Digital and Virgin Media in 2007, it does still technically exist, and even insists that it is still "broadcasting" online. But what does "broadcasting online" actually mean? Simply that there is a website, where promotional MTV-style videos made by record companies for the more photogenic of their classical artistes can be viewed. Isn't that the definition of "narrowcasting," rather than broadcasting?

At the time of writing, Ceefax is still transmitted in those few remaining parts of the UK that have not yet lost their analogue signal, and a slot entitled "Pages from Ceefax" is still broadcast on Saturdays on BBC2, but Ceefax disappeared from the nation's screens forever during 2012. A BBC2 CEEFAX Junction into

TV reviews

*the Testcard transmitted on the 3rd October 1982 can be seen by clicking on link #14 on the **TV Reviews** page on **www.badastralbooks.com**.*

Whoever recorded and (more significantly) saved the sequence is – by now – probably living in a room with no doorknob on the inside and sporting a jacket without arms.

THE TEN COMMANDMENTS

C4 RADIO 2006

I've been involved in some strange legal cases in my time, but the weirdest of all was when I decided to sue the Church of England, and its Managing Director, God. Citing a clause in the company's brochure (The Bible) which clearly stated that "the meek shall inherit the earth," I issued a writ pointing out that I was extremely meek, yet had so far inherited absolutely sod all, and I demanded Benidorm and half of Basildon by way of compensation (though hinted that I'd accept Clacton as an out-of-court settlement). The case was heard at the Royal Courts of Justice, and was unfortunately thrown out by the judge on a technicality, after God's barrister observed that suing the church was an act of deliberate self-assertion on my part, so I therefore no longer qualified as meek. What an appallingly sly legal trick that was, and it's why I still regard the quintessential definition of "waste" as being a busful of lawyers going over a cliff... with two empty seats.

Of course, the Christian church has never had much time for meekness, and most Christians I've met seem to prefer the Old Testament's vengeful "thou shalt not" approach to the forgiveness and passivity espoused by Jesus in the Gospels. So it was deliciously ironic to listen to *The Ten Commandments* on C4 yesterday, and hear John McCririck utter the edict "Thou shalt have no religion," before rightly blaming Sky Gods of all denominations for most of the misery and bloodshed that's occurred on this small blue planet. I use the word "listen" advisedly, by the way, because this was C4 radio, which came into existence earlier this month, and is currently accessible via the channel4radio.com website (although their morning news programme can also be picked up on satellite TV, on the Oneword channel). So instead of being greeted by the sight of an obese Worzel Gummidge after an incident with a letter bomb (which is usually what I see on my screen when McCririck is speaking), I found myself staring

Ch 2 SANK WITHOUT TRACE

at the Real Player on my PC, which displayed patterns so psychedelic that I felt as though I'd just swallowed a canful of Chesswood *Magic* Mushrooms.

The programme asks celebrities what ten laws they would enact if they were ruler of the universe, and McCririck's selection certainly encompassed all aspects of human existence. "Religions are the curse of mankind," he insisted as he justified his first commandment, and was utterly incensed that so many people still feel the need to believe in an afterlife, although I can reassure him that he'll have better luck with his supplementary wish that "when I die... I don't want the nation in mourning." He was equally passionate about his desire to end the whipping of race horses during races, because "the hitting of animals in the name of sport is unacceptable," and also demanded "life imprisonment for murder," with no chance of parole, although he ruled out capital punishment. Why? Many people might regard painless execution as preferable to the living death of perpetual incarceration, and if condemned prisoners were cremated afterwards, their ashes could be used to fill pot holes in the road, thereby allowing them to repay their debt to society.

The programme's format allows the guest to be a petty God, as well as an omnipotent one, and McCririck had plenty of trivial commandments too. "No small cups of coffee at functions" and "banning Muzak" were two of the lesser rules he laid down, while his desire to "ban fat people... they're mentally unstable" seemed a little rich, as anyone who saw him in his vast elasticated trousers on *Celebrity Big Brother* will agree. However, his soccer-related commandment that "goals should be six inches wider and taller" made sense (especially if he ever takes up a career as goalkeeper, because it would be virtually impossible to get the ball past him, given the current dimensions of goalposts), as did his decree that "alimony should be fixed at 1 per cent a year" when couples get divorced. But when he told us about trying to force his long-suffering wife ("The Booby") to sign a "post-nup," so he could dump her for someone younger without financial cost, I found myself wondering why she puts up with him, and remembered an old saying about a woman without a man being like a neck without a pain.

Back in the early 1980s, Channel 4 shook up the staid and sober world of television when it burst onto our screens, and it now intends to make a similar splash in the world of radio. I think it'll succeed too, because BBC radio has been painfully slow to respond to the brave new world of iTunes and iPods (which is where the younger audiences are gravitating), and C4 certainly has the resources and imagination to build a lively and irreverent alternative to R4. Television may have more glamour and money than radio, but the latter has always been the Senior Service, and the new means of communication are leading to ever-greater democratisation of the medium, even though the contractual problems relating to sound archives

TV reviews

are currently causing all sorts of legal problems for the industry. Talking of which, McCririck hinted darkly at Paul McCartney's legal difficulties over his divorce, but I think perhaps he's got that out of proportion. Last thing I heard, as part of the overall settlement (and as a goodwill gesture), Macca had bought Heather a plane. Although I think she still uses a razor for the other leg.

Few people can now remember Channel 4 radio, but back in the middle of the last decade, Horseferry Road was seriously planning to create a radio empire to rival that of the BBC. A raft of stations would soon be available on the Sky platform and on digital radio, the channel boasted hubristically, including a rival to the insufferably smug BBC Radio 4. At the time, senior executives were fully behind it, and we seemed about to be entering a brave new world of radio broadcasting.

But then the money ran out, the entire grandiose scheme was axed, and nowadays the only proof that such plans ever existed are a few "Channel 4 Radio" mugs that were given out to journalists (including me), to persuade us that they were serious about the concept. Somehow, a Channel 4 Radio Mug now seems to be an appropriate memento for anyone who was ever involved in the whole absurd enterprise.

Bravo was one of the first British satellite channels, starting up in the early 1990s on the Astra analogue satellite. At first, it broadcast mainly b&w programmes from the 1960s, but gradually began to aim itself at a certain type of young male audience. Certainly their endless holiday-in-Spain formats featured Argos-gold-wearing, testosterone-fuelled, tattooed "freshers" at the University of Moron, held together with dried vomit, soft drugs, aftershave and booze, staggering around chain-smoking, chain-drinking, chain-screwing, and chain-fighting like maniacs.

When they weren't showing Ibiza nights, they'd go upmarket with sci-fi, Italian football, and lots of low-budget documentaries investigating the sex industry. It did have a few high points, including a plucky attempt to introduce Howard Stern's darkly edgy US show to a British audience (Bravo used my review on their advertising for the show), but most of its output was either undistinguished or imported.

Ch 2 SANK WITHOUT TRACE

SIN CITIES
BRAVO 2002

The Koreans eat dogs, and the Colombians eat ants (they're considered a tasty cinema snack). But as a restaurant critic of many years standing (why the waiters won't let me have a chair I'll never know), I've sampled some of the world's vilest epicuriosities right here in Britain. Particularly loathsome was an incident involving a kiosk outside the Planetarium a few years ago, where I naively ordered a hot dog, and received a Durex-ful of mechanically reclaimed meat (89 per cent gristle, 9 per cent beak, and 2 per cent scrotal sac) crawling with e-coli, squirted with the great taste of yellow and red, and served with some twice-reheated onions in a thrice-reheated soggy bun, dished up by some nose-studded, salmonella-ridden maniac whose knuckles scraped along the floor as he moved. "A drink sir?" he enquired as he proffered the diseased comestible with alacrity, and so it was that I was later able to wash away the nauseating taste of the food with a warm insipid British soft drink called Vimto, which (appropriately) anagrammatises into "Vomit."

But for sheer gastronomic cruelty, it's surely the Italians who take the *biscotto*, because although I don't object to them producing their olive oil by squeezing thousands of olives in a wooden press, how on earth do they produce their baby oil? I thought the sinister answer might emerge when last night's *Sin Cities* (Bravo) visited Rome, but the only baby oil on display wasn't oozing out of a baby-crushing machine, it was being rubbed onto the muscley biceps and hairy torsos of youthful Italians (and that was just the women). A sort of Eurotrash without the wit (if such a thing is possible), this lacklustre programme travels the globe each week to film in some of the world's most fascinating cities, then completely ignores the scenery and culture in favour of endless tedious shots of semi-naked people lethargically licking ice cream off each other's erogenous zones in badly-lit night clubs with interchangeable names like "Champagne" or "Swingers." So it's fitting that the proceedings should be hosted by a shallow gentleman called Grub Smith, who's just a little too old to pass muster as a new lad, and living proof that travel can *narrow* the mind.

"They say that Rome wasn't built in a day" began Professor Grub, who continued his groundbreaking lecture with the news that "Italian stallions" are traditionally reputed to be "Europe's most passionate lovers." Then, with the history and geography lessons over, he moved onto more familiar territory with pornography, but it wasn't even good-quality porn, just prurient, fourth-form, Electric Blue fare, the modern equivalent

TV reviews

of 50s fleshings. In one club after another, bored women stripped down to their underpants during lazy dance routines, while the Prof suggested that perhaps all Roman men were really "just big fat pasta-eating liars." Which seemed pretty rich, coming from someone with a huge beer gut and very tight trousers, a combination that made him look unappealingly like what the Italians call *una mela della caramella* (a toffee apple).

Whenever a presenter tells us that "a recent survey says…" without giving us a reference, there's a 99 per cent chance (according to a recent survey) that what follows will be nonsense. So it was with the claim that "87 per cent of Italians would be happy to cheat on their partner," although if their partners all looked like Jessica Rizzo and her love-in chauffeur, I suppose that figure wouldn't be quite so hard to believe. A porn star who's determined not to let a wholesale delivery of cellulite stuffed into her leotard get in the way of her career, Jessica informed us that a good Italian lover is popularly known as a "trombone" (well, judging from the size of her, a piccolo player would certainly be wasting his time), then showed us a clip from her recent video, entitled *La Postina*. "This Italian postal worker certainly seems to offer a first-class delivery" leered Professor Grub as a naked Ms Rizzo bent obligingly over the bonnet of her Post Office van to help a semi-tumescent colleague empty his sack, but the phrase that passed through my mind was "second-class male."

I've seen some cheap title sequences in my time, but a schoolboy's thumb-propelled flick book would have provided higher-quality animation than the feeble opening montage that vainly attempted to kick-start this shambles into life. Yet it somehow seemed appropriate on Bravo, a channel that appears to be going nowhere, and that lost all idea of how to appeal to the 17-35 male market (its intended audience) on the day that terrestrial stations began to broadcast late-night soft porn. As for Professor Grub, it ill behoves a man who cannot read an autocue properly (and who sounds like a Home Counties train-spotter with a peg on his nose) to mock the vocal and lip-synching abilities of Italian pop singers. As I listened to him talking about the ancient Coliseum (or "this place behind me" as he so eloquently described it), I began to search for a suitable Latin motto for him. With his ego, perhaps it should be *Veni Vidi Vipi*: I came, I saw, I am a very important person.

Bravo closed in January 2011, with its better-imported programmes transferring to Sky. Bravo.

One of the few reasons to be cheerful during the early years of multi-channel television was the emergence of Artsworld, launched by Sir Jeremy Isaacs in 2000. A plucky little station, it had high standards and ambitions, but a wholly

Ch 2 SANK WITHOUT TRACE

inadequate revenue stream, and was perpetually on the verge of disappearance before finally being absorbed into the Sky Arts channel. The name may have vanished, but its ambitions live on in the work of Sky Arts, whose nightly output puts the publicly-funded BBC to shame, and gives us some reason to believe that, although the Barbarians have long been at the broadcasting gate, there are still some corners of television where the chasing of ratings is not the sole criterion by which all programmes are commissioned and scheduled.

POEMS ON THE UNDERGROUND
ARTSWORLD 2007

Every month, the best-seller lists are dominated by diet books, while the great works of English literature are nowhere to be seen. But all that is about to change, because I'll soon be launching (in partnership with a manufacturer of seaside rock) the world's first Edible Book Club, publishing classic novels in confectionery form, with each stick of rock having a single phrase written right through it. Our first publication (in 74,000 peppermint-flavoured volumes) will be *Lady Chatterley's Lover* ("a great read, and a damn good suck too"), so you'll be able to increase your intellectual weight *and* your body weight as you gorge yourself on D. H. Lawrence's delicious prose. As for fashion-conscious women readers, why not try our special low-cal edition with Nutrasweet? Or our range of zero-calorie diet books, that will actually help you to slim as you devour them?

The Edible Book Club will operate on the same Shavian principle of the sugar-coated pill as those bite-size poems that adorn the carriages of our city's Tube system. They've been whetting the literary appetite of Londoners each month since the mid-1980s, and now Artsworld has commissioned *Poems on the Underground* to celebrate the twentieth anniversary of this innovative method of bringing miniature poetic gems to ordinary travellers. I first became an avid reader of these verses during the oppressively humid summer of 1992, when the crowded Central Line train I was travelling in broke down, and I found myself trapped with my face pushed into a tuft of moist ginger hair protruding from the armpit of a strap-hanging bull-dyke lesbian in a tank top with halitosis of the oxters. I looked up despairingly, my eyes alighted on John Skelton's "Merry Margaret," and I was instantly transported to a better place than the sweltering tunnel between Queensway and Lancaster Gate, which is why I've been a grateful fan of the service ever since.

"I wrote to London Underground, suggesting they might like to

TV reviews

put poems up in the empty advertising spaces," recalled Judith Chernaik (the movement's founder), "and to my astonishment, they wrote back and said 'we'll give it a try'." So she selected six of her favourite English verses, arranged for them to be printed, "and magically they got put up on the Tube," in an informal agreement that's continued ever since, to mutual satisfaction. Fittingly, the first poem we heard was by John Betjeman, recalling his childhood adventures on the Underground as he delved into the remotest corners of Metroland, with its exotically named stations and "neo-Tudor shops." Sadly, during my own childhood (around the time when "George Davies is Innocent" was the only graffiti to be found inside carriages), I never got further than guessing at what some of those far-flung places might be like, imagining that Ongar was somewhere in the wild African jungle, and that Bushey would probably be a gateway into Robin Hood's mediaeval Sherwood Forest.

As Tara Fitzgerald read from poems by Wordsworth, Grace Nichols, and Wendy Cope ("I am a poet, I am very fond of bananas"), director Mike Sedgwick found ingenious ways to display the relevant titles and authors. Station destination boards were reprogrammed, cunning post-production techniques projected words onto escalators, trains, and architectural nooks, while graphics replaced station names on the Underground map with those of Blake, Shelley, Dante, and Basho. Sadly, there wasn't time to include anything by my favourite poet, Ron (never heard of him? Course you have. I've got a book here with his name on the spine: *POEMS BY RON*), but they did feature Edward Lear and George Szirtes, and we also heard from John Simmonds, who is the Writer in Residence at Kings Cross Station. Writer in Residence? What a great idea. Maybe next year they'll get a Station Master in Residence too, and then the Northern Line will *really* get motoring.

"We were aiming to offer something that would appeal to the imagination... of people who are oppressed by their working lives," said Judith, and her scheme has certainly succeeded in that. As did this splendid little HD programme from Artsworld, the sort of lovingly crafted and beautifully shot affair that gives me some hope for the future of conventional television, just when I was about to concede that the Barbarians had triumphed, and that it was time to turn to YouTube. Long may Ms Chernaik's vision continue to thrive, and if I ever see a blank space on a Tube train where a poem should be, then I know what I shall do. Just as I have an inner compulsion to pull the emergency lever, so I have an urge to write in the Shakespearean quotation that begins: "Who is Silvia? What is she? Phone Basildon 8433." That's the anarchist in me, that is.

The following channel did not go under. But it deserves to.

Ch 2 SANK WITHOUT TRACE

YOUR DESTINY TV

SKY 694 2005

Is astrology a genuine science? It must be, because its continued existence surely proves one incontrovertible fact: that there's one born every minute. As a teenager, I realised that its ludicrous vocabulary could be used to persuade gullible women to get into a Y shape ("my star sign is Ponti... and it's written in the stars that tonight Ponti will be on the cusp of Uranus"); and more recently, I've been performing on Blackpool's North Pier under my stage name of Madame Proboscis, "the mystic gypsy who tells your fortune by reading the contents of your freshly-blown hankie." However, this summer I intend to change my method of divination, and will advertise myself as Britain's first Chunderpsychic. Just enter my tent, cross my palm with silver, and wait while I eat a tin of alphabetti spaghetti, then vomit it up on the floor in front of you. "Truly, the pasta is the key to the future."

When I reviewed the launch of the Advert Channel last autumn, I predicted (without the aid of my lexicographical pasta) that it wouldn't last long in its existing form. And I've already been proved 50 per cent correct, because from midday until midnight each day, the channel now transmutes into *Your Destiny TV*, which bills itself (with pleonastic hubris) as "the UK's first all-live psychic channel... and the best." Both digital stations are run by TV Commerce plc (owned by Vince Stanzione, a "financial spread trader"), and both raise their revenue by encouraging viewers to phone in on an 0906 premium number at £1.50 per minute ("calls last up to three minutes"), or to text in at a whacking £4.50 per message.

I've often noticed that people who believe in a sixth sense have usually taken leave of the other five, and the callers who contacted Cat Javor to obtain a computerised "astro chart reading" confirmed me in that view. "When will my financial problems cease?" was what Leslie wanted to know (an enquiry that had just added another fiver to her phone bill), while Hazel had forked out to enquire when would be a good time to move house, only to be told that "you're better off waiting because prices are coming down" (information that Cat had apparently obtained not from the planets, but from the property section of the Psychic *Financial Times*). No matter what the enquiry was, the comforting answer was always that the problem would come right in a few months, although surely if these predictions were genuine, some people ought to have been told bluntly that they'd be dead, bankrupt, homeless, or divorced by Christmas. But Cat hadn't even managed to predict that her computer would crash during

TV reviews

the next call, so she had to use Tarot cards to advise the cash-strapped sap "don't be led down the garden path with your finances," which for sheer audacity didn't just take the biscuit, it took the entire Peek Frean Corporation.

To be fair, there must be something in this fortune-telling lark, because when I'd sat down to watch the channel, I'd had a clear premonition that it would be crap – and it was. Also, the station did periodically warn us (presumably to comply with Ofcom's feeble regulations) that it exists "for entertainment purposes only, as differing opinions exist as to the true nature of the psychic world." But if it doesn't even pretend that its predictions are anything more than worthless amusements for bored housewives and unemployed credit-card abusers who find Trisha too intellectually challenging, how can it possibly justify charging so much money for them? However, it must be admitted that print journalism is also infested with a plague of pseudo-scientific horoscopes and mystic forecasts, and that (incredible though this may seem) most newspapers value their resident astrologer far more highly than their reviewers, so may I just make a modest observation at this point? If you bunch of fakes can really see into the future, how about giving us a warning of the next tsunami, or next week's lottery numbers, or better still, a cure for cancer? Then we'll talk.

Of course, I'm a Taurean, and it's well-known that all Taureans are sceptical about astrology, but by the time I'd switched off, I felt close to despair. Half the world nowadays seems to consist of religious zealots of various persuasions demanding censorship of anything that offends their narrow sensibilities, while the other half believe that their lives are governed by the celestial meanderings of distant lumps of rock, and the only real integrity I can detect around me seems to emanate from those few level-headed types who have no time for Sky Gods, and hold themselves responsible for their own actions, rather than Pluto. Frankly, you don't need to consult an overpriced astrologer to be told that you can make money by "turning things you no longer need into cash by putting them on eBay," and if any readers really want to know what the future will be like, I'll tell them now, gratis and for free. It'll be just like the past, only much, much more expensive.

Starting life in November 1997, UK Horizons was part of the UKTV network of channels, showing mainly BBC documentaries. Many programmes were hacked to pieces to fit into a channel with commercial breaks (as are many documentaries the BBC sell abroad). The channel took its name from the BBC series Horizon. It produced extended versions of top BBC brands such as Top Gear and Tomorrow's World. In 2004, the channel was replaced by two new

Ch 2 SANK WITHOUT TRACE

channels, UKTV Documentary (now called Eden) and UKTV People (now called Blighty).

ARE YOU BEING CHEATED?
UK HORIZONS 2002

If you're the sort of gambler who's looking for an exciting, thrill-a-minute, white-knuckle-ride of a wager, then why not try your luck on my latest TV venture, *Guess The Orifice*? It's simple. Every morning, I set up live cameras in the foyer of a well-known London teaching hospital, near to the vending machines, then invite viewers to watch how the various consultants purchase their beverages, and bet on their medical specialities. After observing how skilfully their fingers slip the pound coin into the narrow slot, push the Pepsi Max or Diet Coke button, and rummage around in the "change given" hole to retrieve those fiddly 5p coins, digital viewers can press the red "Orifice Victor-Active"© button on their Sky remote control, and bet on whether the consultant is a gynaecologist (2-1), a proctologist (5-2), an ear nose and throat merchant (11-2 against), or a specialist in open-heart surgery (7-1). But watch out. You don't get anything for a venereologist, not in this game.

It's an unusual form of betting, I grant you, but an honest one, unlike the dubious systems featured on last night's *Are You Being Cheated?* (UK Horizons). Heralded by a burst of thunderingly portentous "serious investigation" music (complete with urgent snare drum), presenter Will Daws promised us several reports about innocent punters who'd been swindled by unscrupulous members of the racing fraternity, as recently as "last year," "six months ago," or even "last month." Yet the stories that followed seemed curiously dated, and one relied so heavily on five-year-old copies of *The Sporting Life* and *Racing Post* newspapers that I resolved to undertake some serious investigation myself after the programme had finished. And guess what? I found out that the series was originally made in 1999 for Channel 5, and that UK Horizons hadn't bothered to update it. So yes, I *was* being cheated.

Nevertheless, some classic scams had been chronicled here, such as the one involving John Batten, a trackside bookie at Epsom on Derby Day 1997. Dozens of punters had placed bets with him as to who the fastest runner would be, but they'd all got it wrong, because the fastest runner turned out to be Mr Batten, last seen cantering briskly towards the car

TV reviews

park with a big bag of money in his hand, shortly after the race began. The oddly-spelt *Navigater System* was another one-way bet (though only for its founder), an audacious variant on the old tipster routine that's been suckering mugs since the days of Prince "I got a 'orse" Monolulu, which required people to pay a £5,000 membership fee, then phone a premium rate phone line each day (doubtless fronted by a man with a stutter) for their randomly chosen tips. "The brochure looked good and plausible" said one swindled idiot (whose birth certificate presumably says 3 July 2002 on it), and he struck me as the sort of man who could probably visit Las Vegas and come away with a small fortune. So long as he'd arrived there with a large fortune, of course.

As one story about fools being rapidly parted from their money gave way to the next, I found myself smiling at these satisfying morality tales of greed getting its just desserts. But that smile was instantly wiped off my face by the sudden appearance of the self-obsessed John McCririck, a man whom I wouldn't trust as far as I could throw him (which is quite a long way, as it happens, since I recently came third in the All-England John McCririck-Tossing Championships at Balmoral). *Making a rare and less-than-entirely successful attempt at coherent thought,* he told us at length about what he'd like to do to jockeys who deliberately lose races to improve their horse's odds for the next outing. Mercifully, there wasn't time for his usual tacky ticktack routine, but his "look at me" attire and constant cry for attention further convinced me that the inscription on his tombstone (as soon as possible, please) should read "If you weren't talking about him, he wasn't listening."

Despite being three years past its "best before" date, this was a clearly explained exposé of archetypal betting scams that reappear in new guises every few years, and it confirmed my long-held opinion that the most reliable way to get lucky at a racetrack is to arrive there and immediately discover that you've left your wallet at home. UK Horizons' impressive schedule is crammed with old yet well-made programmes such as this which deserve more than one broadcast (after all, libraries don't throw books away after just one reading), but it's a pity that the station doesn't spend a little time and money on modest re-edits, to avoid confusion on just how recently the events depicted have actually taken place. Still, that's one of the two big problems facing any small digital station that has to run on a shoestring, I suppose. The other big problem being that, as the shoestring passes over the capstans on the playback machine, it tends to smear boot polish all over the recording heads.

The following programme from the now deceased Wine Channel was quite literally, all Greek to me. Cheers.

CHAPTER 3

SACRED COWS

De mortuis nil nisi bonum? I think not. Not only do I speak ill of the dead, I sue them too, which is why I once took legal action against the late Roy Castle, for injuries that I suffered during the great man's cremation. You may remember that, before he died, Mr Castle lectured us on the evils of secondary smoke inhalation; so it was unfortunate that I happened to be near the crematorium at the time of his funeral, and as his mortal remains turned to smoke and floated out of the chimney, the wind blew them in my direction, just as I was inhaling deeply. How ironic that the man who did so much to warn us all about the dangers of passive smoking should thus have been responsible for filling my lungs with his smoke, thereby giving me a tickly cough, nasty snuffles, and irrefutable grounds for commencing legal action against his estate.

I told myself, on the day that I got the job writing about the Idiot's Lantern, that I would stick to two key rules. The first was that I would never take my own views seriously, and that – for fear of falling into the trap of self-importance – I would value my own opinions at about a halfpenny a ton. And sguide to publishing to kindle from quarkxpress 9.3 at taking a poke at them, if I felt they merited it. Don't get me wrong. My page (more often than not) praised the talented to the rafters, but I am told by readers that those reviews generally made for less entertaining reading than those that damned the vain and the self-deluded (well, those reviews were more entertaining for everyone except the celebrity in question, and their fans).

Take Sir David Attenborough, a man who – inexplicably in my view – is held to be beyond criticism. But why? There are plenty of wildlife presenters who bring gravitas to their subject, but the Whispering Attenbore (as I dubbed him long ago) has always brought frivitas to his natural history films (aka snuff movies), which generally consist of a load of tigers, giraffes, elephants, and wildebeest having sex and eating each other, accompanied by a fatuous narrative about the circle of life.

Here is one of the many reviews I wrote about Attenborough, whose increasingly portentous series were a fixture in the schedules throughout my time as a TV critic, mainly because their worldwide sales generated vast income for the BBC (Natural History – along with Period Drama and Situation Comedy – being

TV reviews

one of the things that British television supposedly does well, despite manifest evidence to the contrary).

THE LIFE OF MAMMALS
BBC1 2002

I'm no Mr Micawber, even at the best of times, but this week the light at the end of the tunnel really *has* been an approaching train. Seeing my Hotpoint dishwasher being offered as a prize on a 1985 archive edition of Bullseye didn't exactly give me a lift on Monday, nor was I thrilled when the car windscreen wipers fell off and began wiping the bonnet on Tuesday, and yesterday I spent an hour attempting to make Provencal grand aioli, only to end up with what looked like a bowlful of snot. Things are no better today, because I've just got my clothes back from the dry cleaners and they're *still* dirty (only now they're covered in plastic and stink of chemicals, and I'm £40 lighter), but luckily I can still cheer myself up by thinking of others who might be in an even worse situation than me. Such as wondering what it must be like to be a Siamese twin with a brother who is gay, while you are not. He has a date tonight, and you only have one anus between the two of you.

But for an example of true Micawberism, look no further than the Whispering Attenbore (or *Attenbor susurrus*, for the telethropologists among you). For fifty years, he's strolled majestically around the Bush (Shepherd's Bush), telling himself that something will turn up, and his optimism has always been well-founded, because he keeps being given bigger and bigger budgets to make the same damn programme, over and over again. His latest £8,000,000 series, *The Life of Mammals*, started on BBC1 last night, and he began by telling us proudly that "we will travel the world to discover just how varied and how astonishing mammals are" (the "we" in that sentence meaning, of course, "I"). But we already knew how varied they are, and the only truly astonishing thing about what followed was how devoid of intelligence and how dependent on received wisdom the entire project was, because beneath all the hype and the preening that heralded this series, it's just *Tales of the Riverbank* with a GCSE.

As usual, what the Attenbore provided was the televisual equivalent of an offer from one of those Great Classics Book Clubs ("the complete works of Shakespeare in fourteen leather-bound volumes, fine literature hand-tooled by craftsmen"), which are bought by people who want to impress others with their love of culture, and who put them on shelves where they remain forever unread. The production values were undeniably lavish, with sumptuous aerial shots and the sort of John-Williams-meets-Aaron-Copland lush orchestral score that accompanies Imax films, yet there was no original thought at the centre, just a recitation of the history of natural selection in layman's terms. Typical of the Attenbore's portentousness was his frequent addition of a lengthy silence between the first and second words of a sentence – "This... (2") ... is an arctic dog" "Here... (3") ... is one of the most remarkable places in the world..." – which served no purpose other than to remind that *he* was the alpha male here, who wielded supreme power, even when pausing. As for his assertion that "This... (4") ... is a marsupial leaf-eater, nothing like it lives today," he clearly has never seen Eamonn Holmes at trough in the GMTV canteen.

The bulk of last night's episode was devoted to Australia, a land where (would you believe it?) there are kangaroos, wallabies, koalas, wombats, and possums. "Some... (2") ... are miniature, others are massive," he declared, as the usual litany of birth, sex, eating, and killing unfolded, the sort of thing one can see on satellite channels at any time of the day or night, only made on a fraction of the budget and without all the PR. So delighted was he with some up-close-and-personal filming of a duckbill platypus that he added a ten-minute coda of self-congratulatory backslapping for himself and his team, after which we were encouraged to turn to BBC4, where an extended hagiography of the great man was getting underway. I declined, and although I briefly perked up when he said "We... (2") ... have bored..." even that transpired not to be a rare outbreak of self-critical honesty, just a reference to the cameraman drilling a miniature camera into a subterranean nest.

Yes, I know nature is wonderful, but there's something fundamentally absurd about urbanised *homo sapiens* sitting in a darkened room, staring at recorded images of the outside world, instead of going out into the garden and experiencing it directly. Anyway, I only have to hear the word "wildebeest" and I'm halfway to the land of nod. Despite the undoubted skill and energy of the cameramen, there's something intellectually lazy about the construction of the series (not least in the re-using of footage which I'm *certain* I've seen in previous David Attenborough programmes), and as for the Disneyfied anthropomorphism of mammals ("fortunately... (3") ... this little one still has mother to see off the neighbourhood bully"), frankly... (7") ... it stinks. If we're going to compare ourselves with the rest of the animal kingdom, then how about drawing some *really* interesting parallels, by pointing out that a pig's orgasm lasts for thirty minutes, or that the male praying mantis cannot copulate while its head is still attached to its body? Apparently, the female initiates sex by ripping his head off, which

TV reviews

is really rather thoughtful of her. Well, it means that he won't be put off his stride if she's a bit ugly.

I've been told by people in the business that some nature programme directors have gone so far as to throw birds out of planes in a bid to get the best shots. Fakery and television go hand in hand, it seems, yet whenever I have written about this, it's generated an amount of hate mail exceeded only by my pieces about sufferers from M.E.

Computer trickery is nothing new. Indeed, the head of BBC's Natural History Unit in Bristol used to be proud of the fact, telling readers of New Scientist back in 1988 that his TV crews regularly used tricks, and defending such practices on the grounds that "actuality can be rather dull":

A report on this may be viewed by clicking on link #15 on the **TV Reviews** *page on* ***www.badastralbooks.com.***

The highest amount of hate mail I ever received came from newspaper readers who claimed to be suffering from M.E. (or Chronic Fatigue Syndrome as it's now become known). The medical profession remains divided as to whether or not M.E. is a genuine illness, but letters flooded in by the sackful when I pointed out that this pernicious disease seems overwhelmingly to afflict the well-to-do middle classes in prosperous countries (who can rely on welfare payments to support them) but rarely seems to strike, say, subsistence farmers in the poorer parts of Africa or Third World peasants, who would simply die if they couldn't work.

I don't like to boast, but I would like to point out that my column had miraculous healing powers. Whenever I wrote about this much-hyped disease (which supposedly robs its victims of the strength to walk, write, or even speak), I invariably received thousands of lengthy protest letters from sufferers, usually enclosing bulky research documents which they'd photocopied down the local library, en route to the post office. A few words from me, it seemed, and the sick not only took up their beds and walked – they positively leaped to their word processors and fax machines. Why, ladies and gentlemen, it was a miracle, and I'm still waiting for a letter of thanks from a grateful NHS.

Emily Wilcox was one M.E. sufferer who wrote in the press about her condition, and I had some sympathy for her articles, firstly because they were rational and reasonable, and secondly because the poor woman had surely suffered enough already, simply by being the daughter of Esther Rantzen. If there ever

Ch 3 SACRED COWS

was a Sacred Cow that needed poking, then surely St Esther (Our Lady of Root Vegetables that look like Willies) is one.

In recent years, I have been deeply moved to read about the fall of the House of Rantzen. First, husband Des had a heart attack (only minutes after the transmission of one of my C4 TV shows, in which I had robustly criticised his wife's entire career – but I'm sure the timing was pure coincidence). Then Esther herself collapsed during the taping of one of her shows, and announced that she would be greatly reducing her future TV appearances. Who knows, perhaps the moral contradiction inherent in her work had finally proved too much for her? I am a staunch atheist, but my prayers go out to her.

In 2010, Shergar in a Frock attempted to bounce back by standing for Parliament, and I was devastated to find that she not only failed to win the Luton seat, but lost her deposit. Perhaps the good burghers of Luton were uneasy about certain questions that need an answer. Such as: can the woman who publicly campaigns against bullying, and makes serious programmes about the tragedy of obese children who are cruelly ridiculed by an unthinking society be the same Esther Rantzen who spent decades unthinkingly ridiculing fat people on That's Life, and turning their misery into Light Entertainment? The same Esther who once used BBC money to dump tons of bricks outside the house of a tradesman who'd annoyed her (an irresponsible act that led to an ignominious apology)? The same Esther who unilaterally labelled businessmen as "con men" and harassed them without giving them any right of reply, yet automatically referred to her viewers as "innocent victims," no matter how stupid or greedy they'd been? The same Esther who expected the masses to demean themselves by taking out their teeth for her cameras, or eating snails and bat stew while blatantly fake crowd reaction shots were intercut? The same Esther whose long-running show was simply a feeble copy of the format created by her former boss, Bernard Braden, whose job she took over after Braden was unceremoniously booted out of the BBC for simply voicing a margarine commercial? I rather think she can.

I once sent a letter as an experiment to the Old Bag, addressed simply to: "Teeth, London." The letter arrived.

What follows is not a TV review. I was occasionally asked to write book reviews at the Standard, and when Esther published her autobiography, I was delighted to provide the following piece. A week later, Stephen Fry came up to me at The Groucho Club and told me that the piece had affected him greatly. "It's hard to imagine how anyone could recover from such an unremitting evisceration," he said. You might think that I'd be purring at Stephen's opinion of my review, but

TV reviews

it wasn't my intention to eviscerate her, simply to correct her misremembering of her own history. Anyway, I stopped trusting Stephen's opinions on the day I read that he considered Prince Charles to be "one of the most brilliant minds I have ever encountered."

Evisceration or not, she recovered. She always does. And despite my review, she continues to appear on our screens with grim regularity.

ESTHER RANTZEN: ESTHER

REVIEW OF ESTHER RANTZEN AUTOBIOGRAPHY

I first became aware of the duality of television on the day I first entered a TV studio. Not of duality in a Cartesian sense, but rather as a form of cultural apartheid, separating the professionals from what TV people derisively call the "punters" (who form the unglamorous but necessary ballast for every "people" show). Everybody may be greeted as an equal on set and on camera, but behind the scenes it's only the celebs who are treated to Chablis (the plebs are just treated *chablis*), and the professionals' total disregard for the public is epitomised for me in a story once told to me by someone who worked in the *Hearts of Gold* office. According to this researcher (surely it cannot be true?), Esther Rantzen walked into the office on the first day of production, clapped her hands, and cheerfully shouted "right, what bunch of cripples have you got for me this week?"

I've found myself repeating the phrase "surely this cannot be true?" a good deal this week, as I've worked my way through *Esther*, an autobiography with shameless ambitions to become an autohagiography. My own knowledge of the inner workings of the TV industry forces me to regard the book primarily as a work of fiction, yet until Ms Rantzen meets her definitive biographical Nemesis (as Jeffrey Archer did in the shape of Michael Crick), her vapid mixture of schmaltz, half-truth, delusion, and omission will doubtless be taken at face value by those who regard her as nothing short of a saint. As a TV critic, I've always been irked more by duplicity than by lack of talent, and throughout her career there's always been a yawning chasm between the image she presents to her public, and what appears to be a deep-seated private contempt for them. When her husband Des Wilcox was alive, he would surely have warned her against the risky business of rewriting her own history in a quest for wider sympathy

Ch 3 SACRED COWS

and veneration and, if she did, then at least to be more artful. But he's gone, and she's gone and done it, and it's in her book's many contradictions that (so it seems to me) Esther stands revealed by her own pen as a twenty-four-carat, dyed-in-the-wool hypocrite.

Take her description of herself as a touchingly pure and innocent twentysomething, blissfully unaware of sex or even of what the word "prick" meant. How angelic, you might think, except that elsewhere she boasts of having written a sketch at university about the sexual innuendo in *Peter Pan*, and tells us that "far too many scoundrels joked their way into my bed" during those years, and the book positively groans with similar dissonances. "Nobody could accuse me of owing my success to my love affair with the boss," she states defiantly on p150, yet a later chapter outlines how Wilcox (her BBC boss) was involved in the removal of Bernard Braden from *Braden's Week*, and the commissioning of a replacement show called *That's Life!*, hosted by Esther (with whom Des was having an adulterous affair). "I admired and respected Bernie, and was devastated," she wails after hearing that he'd made a commercial for Stork margarine (which, as a freelance, he was perfectly entitled to do, yet that became the convenient pretext for his dismissal), whereas her leading role in ousting both Braden, and Wilcox's wife, from their rightful places apparently caused her no devastation whatsoever.

But, of course, double standards were at the very heart of the popular success of *That's Life!*, and of its presenter. Who else could display mawkish concern over the way that overweight girls are teased and bullied at school, yet also spend decades hosting a show which thrived on joke after joke about the intrinsic hilarity of fat women? Who else could tearfully inform the nation about the miserable plight of small children with bone marrow disease, then (a nanosecond later) invite us to roar with laughter at a selection of root vegetables that looked like penises, or a dog that could say "sausages"? And who else could misunderstand the principle of organ donation so completely that she thought baby Ben Hardwick was donating his diseased liver to her show, in a bid to boost her ratings? From that standpoint, the transplant was successful, because her audience figures shot up. What a pity Ben died.

As I turned the pages, I tried to set this account of the resistible rise of Esther Rantzen against the not-so-rosy picture painted by former colleagues, many of whom still spit blood at the mere mention of her name. Grant Baynham has attacked her vociferously in print, while Paul Heiney's wife once told me that her husband would run out of the room vomiting if he so much as heard the show's theme tune. And I once made the mistake of mentioning Esther to Barbara Kelly (Braden's widow), who snarled "don't ever talk about that woman again," and denounced the way she'd usurped

TV reviews

Bernard's role in BBC consumer affairs, as ruthlessly as any character in a Greek tragedy. And I could quote dozens more, if personal confidences had not sealed my lips.

But, of course, there's the charity work, the gleaming armour of virtue which she proudly wears to deflect all criticism. Yet millions of people in this country do good work without needing to be seen doing it, and a list of people that Esther most admires was instructive, because it turned out to be a list of some of the people I least admire. Andrew Lloyd Webber, Nicholas Fairbairn, Peter Bazalgette, and above all Margaret Thatcher. Still, that last name seems logical, because the similarities between the two women are striking, and one might even argue that, at her zenith, the old German bag (yes, her surname is German for "an old bag") was the Lady Thatcher of British television. Like the Iron Lady, she was surrounded by catamites (do they hang from the ceiling?), trembling, feeble apologies for men whom she could easily tyrannise, and she mercilessly kept all other females (especially young and attractive ones) well away from the centre of power. Like Mrs T, she believed in dictatorship, not collaboration, and would tolerate no argument. And both women dominated all our lives during the 1980s, not because we liked them, or admired them, but simply because there seemed to be no alternative.

Ultimately, the book reeks of score-settling, from laying into her "sadistic nanny" and "child-hating sadistic headmistress," to a patronising contempt for Wilcox's first wife, who "took great satisfaction in loathing me... she was inconsolable and remained angry and bitter until the day she died" (perhaps in part because she'd been chucked out of the opulent family house to make way for Esther, and had thereafter had to live in a small flat). Unusually for an autobiography, I found myself liking its subject less and less the more I read, and I thought how fine it would be if an unofficial biographer were to meticulously research the story of her life, and unearth the large parts which she has conveniently left buried (why, for two pins, I'd do it myself, and probably for free). Fortunately, her stepdaughter, Cassandra Wilcox, *did* speak out last month, alleging that Esther is a "heartless and calculating" woman who delighted in the destruction of Wilcox's first wife, made jokes about her cremation, and simply invented large parts of this book. Of course, Esther denied all those allegations, and at present this is simply one woman's word against another, yet I find myself recalling the life of the original Cassandra. In Greek mythology, she was the daughter of King Priam, and always spoke the truth, yet was not believed. Esther must be fervently hoping that the present-day public will be equally distrustful, but do you know what? This time round, I suspect that many people *want* to believe the words of Cassandra.

Ch 3 SACRED COWS

Shortly after this was published I received an email from a quite famous person. I will not reveal his identity, because the message was so crass and insensitive that I have no option but to repeat it here:

> Hi Victor. What's the difference between Esther Rantzen and a Walrus?
> One has a moustache and smells of fish, the other lives in the sea. See you at the Groucho, you cunt.

He also pointed me to this link, an excellent "That's Life!" spoof from Not The Nine O'Clock News, which can be viewed by clicking on link #16 on the **TV Reviews** page on **www.badastralbooks.com**.

They really nailed the show with this skit that parodies the arch and unfunny scripts, the catamite presenters primping and writhing in camera hunger, and even the queer old dean Mr "Odd Odes" with his coda.

I have to admit that I know precious little about pop music, although I do know what I don't like. Indeed, when I worked for a pop music radio station (Radio1) I would frequently announce this fact to listeners, much to the distress of the management. One day, while wondering whether human dog whistle Maurice Gibb continued producing a monotonous high-pitched whine right to the very end (the flatlining squeal on his cardiac monitor would surely have been more musical than the falsetto backing vocals of "Night Fever"), I realised what a tragedy it is whenever a great partnership breaks up. Who can forget Morecambe and Mindy, Mike and Bernie Cribbins, Little and Ball, or Cannon and Large? And who can forget Sonny Bono, the other half of Cher, who hit a Yew tree and perished (as prophesied decades earlier in the duo's greatest hit "I Got Yew Babe")? How typical it was of this impetuous man that, while Cher spent decades painstakingly rearranging her features one at a time, Sonny did it all in a single second. And yet, strange as it may seem, Sonny nevertheless still ended up looking better than Cher.

Being ill-informed about pop music, for years I had no idea that nowadays there is an even more famous Bono than Sonny. I learned of his existence while reviewing the following programme, and soon discovered that not only is he a younger version of Bob Geldof, but that he is also (like his role model) a prize wanker.

Speaking of Sir Bob reminds me that the strangest people win awards. Henry Kissinger, Yasser Arafat, and Theodore Roosevelt all won the prestigious

TV reviews

Nobel Peace Prize after dedicating the best years of their lives to waging war, Hitler was a serious contender for it in 1938, and Alfred Nobel himself funded the prize with the money he made from the invention of dynamite. It's even rumoured that the Mother Teresa of pop, Sir Bob Geldof, is now being considered as a future recipient (of the Nobel Prize not dynamite – although that's not a bad idea.)

BAND AID:
THE SONG THAT ROCKED THE WORLD
BBC2 2004

If only we could click on a box and unsubscribe to Christmas. That way we could be spared the horrors of the oncoming month, as grey-suited humourless office bores stick paper hats on their heads and are instantly transformed into grey-suited humourless paper-hat-wearing office bores, people who don't really like each other shop for presents that nobody will really like, amateur drunks pebbledash the pavements with Asti Spewmanti, and Yuletide anthems blare out of every shop doorway on the high street, from Noddy Holder singing "look to the future now it's only just beg-uh-uh-un" to St Cliff (Our Lady of A Cappella) warbling about Mistletoe and Wine. Personally, the only Christmas song I've ever liked is that carol inspired by Good King Wenceslas, who apparently got bored by the mince pies and turkey on the palace menu for St Stephen's Day, and phoned his local Italian restaurant for a takeaway pizza. "Certainly, your Majesty," said the manager, "would you like your usual?" "Yes please," replied the King, "same as always – deep pan, crisp and even." And thus a song was born.

Apocryphal or not, that story makes more sense than the lyrics to "Do They Know It's Christmas?" Even posing such a question about the inhabitants of Ethiopia (almost half of whom are Muslim) displays a breathtaking mixture of arrogance and ignorance, while the description of Africa as a place "where nothing ever grows, no rain nor rivers flow" is a travesty of life on that rich and varied continent; but back in 1984 we were all expected to suspend our critical and aesthetic faculties and fork out for a copy of what surely remains the worst Christmas record ever recorded (and that includes "Mistletoe and Wine"). Saturday night's *Band Aid: the Song That Rocked the World* recalled how Sir Bob Geldof raised money for victims of the Ethiopian famine (and revitalised his own flagging career) by persuading pop musicians to get together and use their celebrity status in a good cause. There was nothing new in that, of course, because the Variety Club of Great Britain had been doing the same thing for decades, but this time the stars were rockers, led by a man who'd gone from Boomtown Rat to Water Rat in a single bound.

"It's more than a song, it's almost a hymn for our time," declared Midge Ure, who (despite being the joint composer of this appalling single) clearly regarded himself as an impartial judge of its artistic stature. Co-writer Sir Bob was even less self-effacing, telling us fervently that "it's just like Silent Night, like O Come All Ye Faithful, it's just Christmas," then weeping on camera as he recalled the TV news report that had touched his heart and revived his ailing fortunes (well, it's always feast or famine in showbusiness, but not usually both at the same time). The nausea induced by that lachrymose spectacle was equalled only by shots of a dreadfully tinny and clangy Yamaha DX7 (I know, because I used to own one, and it regularly attracted all the local cats on heat), and by my revulsion at the line "where the only water flowing is the bitter sting of tears." If that's true, then *j'accuse* Biddy Baxter, because back in 1983, I personally collected eight tons of dried dog crap (or whatever it was that year) for the Blue Peter "Dig a Well in Africa" Appeal, and posted it in. Apparently, I might as well have not have bothered. I won't this year.

As I watched the bouffant-haired pop stars gathering for the original recording, I recalled the wise words of Oscar Wilde, that "philanthropy seems to have become simply the refuge of people who wish to annoy their fellow creatures." Because instead of quietly and unostentatiously donating a slice of their vast fortunes to the worthy cause of feeding the poor, they were all determined to be photographed as often as possible during their brief stint of charity work, thus ensuring that they'd all do well out of doing good. "Maybe every generation should have a version of this song," suggested Ure modestly as he attended this year's re-record, then played us a slow and intimate version of the tune, and I confess that I suddenly realised something about it that had never occurred to me before. Whether it's performed as a sad ballad or a joyous chorus, with just a singer and piano or with a full rock band, as a mournful downbeat song or a vibrant up-tempo number, one quality always remains the same. It's always crap.

You may think I'm being too hard on a record that meant well, and did at least raise several million pounds, but just consider its dreadful legacy. Thanks to the St. Geldof effect, we've now had two decades of organised celebrity showing-off for charity, from Comic Relief and Children in Need to that bunch of C-list nonentities who are currently out in the Australian rainforest, ostensibly to raise money for good causes, but actually in a shameless attempt to get back onto prime-time terrestrial

TV reviews

telly, at any cost. And all because of a trite little song which Bob and Midge talked about magniloquently, as though it were an acknowledged work of artistic genius, on a level with Bach's masterpiece, *The Art Of The Fugue*. The telltale sign of that work's genius, by the way, is that it doesn't end, it simply trails away into serene nothingness at the end. And although I could never hope to match such consummate artistry, I too have on occasion left my work unf

The vanity of the man was captured in a programme where he turned up in Africa like the Messiah. I can only presume that two airplanes had been charted for the trip. One to transport him and his crew, the other to transport his massive ego. I am sorry, but the man is a cunt, and that's an end to it.

GELDOF IN AFRICA
BBC1 2005

Television has always had an ambiguous attitude towards nuns. It's fascinated by the eccentric ones (be they flying, singing, or toothily art-appreciating), but feels distinctly uneasy about the religious variety, with the solitary exception of the late Mother Teresa, who didn't fly, sing, or discuss Botticelli, yet always received uncritical praise from the media. Personally, I didn't trust Agnes (her real name) further than I could throw her (which was quite a long way, actually, as witness the silver medal for nun-throwing that I won back in '64 at the Tokyo Olympics), because whenever there was a flood, famine, drought, or plague anywhere on the planet, who was always the first person there on the scene, taking credit for the relief work before anyone else had arrived? And who was therefore the main suspect for having caused the disasters in the first place? Precisely. I rest my case.

The shrivelled brown nun's joyful wallowing in the suffering of others convinced me long ago that there's no such thing as altruism, and that everything we do in life is ultimately for our own self-gratification. So whenever St Bob Geldof (the Mother Teresa of pop) steps inside the magic rectangle to point and scream at me yet again about how I must give all my dosh to his latest pet project for helping the starving kiddies in Africa, I let my money stay deep in my pocket until I can get to the beer shop and spend it all on myself. Sorry, but the man is a failed pop singer fuelled by the same concomitant rage and need for adulation that seems to drive the failed footballer-turned-tellychef Gordon Ramsay, who's also

Ch 3 SACRED COWS

become more famous for his foul mouth and temper than for anything else he's ever done. But whereas Ramsay is (underneath the froth) a genuinely gifted chef, there's something about the furious zabaglione that Geldof has whipped up to bulk out his otherwise empty career that leaves a decidedly funny taste in my mouth.

Not content with trying to take the credit for the financial sleight-of-hand otherwise known as debt relief, St Bob embarked last night on *Geldof in Africa*. For this six-part tour round the one continent that stands between him and total media obscurity, he's attempted to reinvent himself as the Jacob Bronowski *de nos jours*, but his initial observations (delivered in a portentous voice oozing with fake gravitas) instantly confirmed that he had sadly forgotten to equip himself with a Bronowski brain before opening his mouth. "The first thing you notice is the light, brightness everywhere," he pontificated, "it's not the dark continent at all," but perhaps that's because he was speaking in the middle of the day when the sun was overhead, whereas people who arrive there at nighttime tend to notice something very different indeed. Still, what can one expect from the author of "Do They Know It's Christmas?" a patronising ditty that managed simultaneously to be arrogant and ignorant, given that almost half of the inhabitants of Ethiopia are Muslims, and are therefore unlikely to know or care about a Christian festival.

Like Rousseau praising the noble savage, he strolled amongst the people of the internationally unrecognised state of Somaliland, blaming all the ills of Africa on modern western influences, and nodding deferentially when the exclusively male tribal elders extolled their own ancient traditions. Admittedly, the West does have a lot to answer for (having spent centuries trying to "improve" the continent, yet succeeding only in plundering its mineral wealth and oppressing its people), but why did the famously mouthy Bob have nothing to say about such ancient Somali traditions as forced female genital mutilation, an obscene practice which has ruined the lives of millions of women? The endless shots of him walking through a heat haze in the arid landscape were as banal as most of his observations ("what other continent has this emptiness?" he asked, presumably having never heard of Australia, Antarctica, Canada, or central Asia), and I found myself wondering why he'd ever agreed to write and present such a series in the first place, when he clearly lacks the historical, geographical, anthropological, and philosophical knowledge to do it justice. Okay, all performers are natural show-offs, myself included (I mean, nobody at the *Evening Standard* holds a gun to my head and forces me to do this little daily turn), but it's ignominious to see a former anarchic rock star now trying to get the public to love him for his compassion and his charity work.

TV reviews

Far from challenging our simplistic assumptions about Africa, this first episode only reinforced them. Everything about it, from Geldof in his carefully titivated Gucci Oxfam "gone bush" clothes (and his suspicious efforts to ensure that his chin stubble is *always* exactly the same length) to the emotive slo-mo shots of starving children, smacked of a modern-day reinterpretation of the old colonial canard about the continent being "the white man's burden," a place that continually needs our help when I suspect it would probably have been damaged far less over the centuries by our benign neglect. Geldof doubtless thinks he's well-intentioned, but I have been greatly unimpressed by the cultural apartheid he's imposed on his forthcoming Live8 concerts, consigning African musicians to a cultural ghetto in Cornwall, while the big Western (and overwhelmingly white) rock stars play the prestigious televised venues. Ah well, at least he's doing his work on a *Pro Bono* basis. That is, for the benefit of U2's lead singer, and his other powerful friends.

Post Band Aid, one couldn't attend any award ceremony without Bono or Geldof picking up a gong, which they always did with humility. Or, to put it another way: "Forgive me.. I was so utterly astonished to be getting this award, I nearly dropped my 10-page acceptance speech…"

Terry Wogan is another celebrity who, for decades, was deemed to be above criticism. Yet while his laid-back Irish whimsy did undeniably attract a loyal following on radio – including the Queen Mother – his television work (especially his thrice-weekly prime-time BBC1 chat show) always struck me as lazy and ill-researched. Years after it was axed, I caught him attempting to relive his glory years on a satellite channel.

WOGAN: NOW AND THEN

UKTV GOLD 2006

After decades of systematic research, science has now proved conclusively that *homo sapiens* is born with a gullibility gene. The historical evidence is overwhelming, from mediaeval monks selling bogus relics to credulous pilgrims ("this is the genuine skull of John the Baptist… and that smaller skull over there is when he was a boy"), to the vast numbers of holy prophets making unholy profits by repeatedly predicting Armageddon. I particularly enjoy gloating at those idiot survivalists who spent thousands of pounds in the late 1990s, installing nuclear fall-out shelters in their back

Ch 3 SACRED COWS

gardens in the certain knowledge that civilisation would be destroyed by the millennium bug, and are still miserably chomping their way through thousands of packets of dried food whose contents expired in December 2002, but it's the Jehovah's Witnesses who really take the biscuit. They first forecast that the world would end in 1914, and when I recently asked a pair why their organisation had got its prediction so badly wrong, they just smiled and said "well, it was a *pretty* bad year, there was a war, you know," and tried to sell me a copy of *The Watchtower*. Typical. I reckon they were just in it for the bread, and should by rights have been called Je-Hovis Witnesses.

The gullibility gene clearly rules down at UKTV Gold, where credulous executives have unwisely allowed Terry Wogan to clamber back inside the magic rectangle. Despite a CV that includes a long list of terrestrial Armageddons (*Terry Wogan's Friday Night*, *Wogan's Island*, *Wogan's Web*, *Terry and Gaby*), he's been booked to front thirteen shows on the digital channel, rehashing old clips while re-interviewing guests from the dim (I *stress* dim) and distant days when he had a thrice-weekly talk show on BBC. The man remains undeniably popular on radio. Yet, pathetically, he still craves televisual success, a vanity that has led him in the autumn of his years to invest in a series of increasingly implausible toupees, in a preposterous attempt to disguise the ageing process. Frankly, that wig is currently the biggest rip-off in television (apart from the wretchedly feeble format of this show), and it's high time that somebody brought him to his senses by simultaneously pulling the rug from under and *over* him.

Walking into a tiny studio to the accompaniment of a tinny taped pit band, Wigon's pitiful attempt to revive his old show proved that history does indeed repeat itself, first as tragedy, then as farce. Inevitably, the first show's main guest was sports-presenter-turned-Messiah David Icke, who watched clips from his infamous 1991 "I am the Son of God" interview, then attempted to explain his global philosophy in a somewhat more coherent manner than he had managed last time round. "Everywhere I went, people were laughing at me," he recalled to the host (a state of affairs that Michael Barrymore can now only dream of), and curiously, although he still seemed as wild-eyed and truculent as ever, the audience (to Wogan's increasing irritation) openly sympathised with his condemnation of warmongering Americans who plunder the world for personal gain. Fifteen years ago, Wogan had cheerfully crucified a man who was clearly mentally ill, but this time he inadvertently did something far harder: he made David Icke sound statesmanlike.

There's always a fine line between relaxation and torpor, and Wogan's enervating demeanour (which can seem engagingly laid-back

TV reviews

on radio) always looks suspiciously like laziness when viewed through the cameras. Worse, the guest list had been padded out with people who hadn't even appeared on the old BBC1 Wogan show, including a young woman who'd only worked with him on *Children in Need*, and who told us that when she'd met Paul McCartney "I forgot my own name" (there's a coincidence – I can't remember it either). That fine yet dentally-challenged actor, Christopher Lee, performed his legendary impersonation of a human bell jar by deoxygenating the studio in seconds, while Ulrika Jonsson ungraciously ridiculed Sven-Goran Eriksson's sexual technique as "like a rowing boat with one oar." Never mind Sven. Women have often claimed that I'm a lousy lover too, but as I always point out to them, "how can you *possibly* come to a conclusion like that in fifteen seconds?"

Incredibly, the closing credits revealed no fewer than *four* Executive Producers, including Mark Wogan, whose previous job as a chef may explain why he'd made a complete hash of this half-baked and indigestible programme. One Executive Producer and a few more researchers might have improved things a little (so many shows suffer from having too many generals and far too few foot soldiers), but in truth nothing could save this dodo of a presenter with his dodo of a format, which nobody in grown-up terrestrial television was interested in commissioning. Presumably, he hopes to do a Little Britain by starting on a digital channel and ending up on BBC1 by the tradesman's entrance, a stratagem that's as obvious as the paunch that now sits prominently on his lap, suggestive of too may visits to the drive-thru MacDonalds. You won't catch me doing that, not after what happened last time. "Sorry for your wait" said the girl behind the window as she looked down at me and smiled. She and I both knew that what she really meant was "sorry for your weight." The cow.

He was still inviting us to look back over his televisual career when he made this programme, which consisted of little more than clips from his previous series, held together with a few chauvinistic remarks about the inferiority of foreigners, all delivered with what he incorrectly believes to be a redeeming shaft of Irish wit.

Ch 3 SACRED COWS

ONE ON ONE – TERRY WOGAN

BBC1 2002

If I'm not in bed thumbing a leather-bound Trollope, then I like nothing better than browsing through my complete edition of *Who's Who, Past and Present*. It comes as no surprise to see that Joan Collins has a double entry (shouldn't that be listed under hobbies?), or that Jeffrey Archer claims to have been "educated by my wife" (I've long suspected that that woman taught him everything he knows), but what astonished me last time I perused my copy was to find an entry for Adolf Hitler. Originally filed in the 1930s, it's *still* there with all his personal details: "Address – Wilhelmstr, 77, Berlin, W8; Telephone – 11 6191; Education – secondary schools in Linz and Graz, studied painting and architecture in Vienna; Publications – *Mein Kampf* (1925); Work – Chancellor of the German Reich since 1933, Head of the German State by law of 1 August 1934; Hobbies – watercolours, tropical fish, annexing the Sudetenland, and trying to persuade the Zyklon A people to develop a B product. Alright, I lied about the hobbies, but it's still more reliable than Archer's entry.

After watching *One on One – Terry Wogan* on BBC1 last night, I looked up the professional Irishman's entry too, and saw that he describes himself (with nauseating self-effacement) as a "jobbing broadcaster." His list of achievements reads like a Who's Who entry (for Terry Wogan), yet what struck me most wasn't his membership of the Henley-on-Thames Temple golf club, nor his authorship of an impressive number of unread books (have *you* ever heard of Banjaxed, or To Horse, To Horse?), but his uncanny resemblance to the Fuhrer. He's never invaded Poland, of course, nor (to the best of my knowledge) has he ever set fire to the Reichstag, but his annual xenophobic contribution to the Eurovision Song Contest has surely done (in peacetime) for European brotherhood and mutual understanding what the Third Reich only achieved by war. Because beneath his *faux-modeste* demeanour lies a small-minded and utterly indefensible desire to denigrate foreigners, especially those who aren't particularly fluent or witty in English. Of course, they're only being unamusing in their *second* language. So what's Wogan's excuse?

Although this programme claimed to be a "showbiz self-portrait," Wogan dwelt exclusively on his meagre handful of TV ratings successes, while the litany of disasters went unacknowledged (much as the BMW car museum in Bavaria makes no mention of the company's activities between 1939-45). No reference was made to *Do The Right Thing*, *Terry Wogan's Friday Night*, nor to his dire tour of Ireland, and when the dismal

TV reviews

Wogan's Web was briefly alluded to, he hailed it as a pioneering attempt to put radio onto television, rather than as a manifest failure to understand Marshall McLuhan's dictum that what works on a hot medium seldom succeeds on a cold one. A picture soon emerged of a man who feels he has a right to be on television, despite his pitifully small repertoire of gestures (the swagger, the little boy smirk, the raised eyebrows, all delivered to his special cutaway camera), and who apparently regards radio as the poor relation, although that's the only medium on which he's ever shone. And listening to the tired old sludge that nowadays emanates from him on Radio 2 each morning, that station too seems about to disappear down the Swanee, now that Sir Jimmy Young (its one truly great broadcaster) is leaving.

Wogan devoted the bulk of his programme to oft-repeated archive clips from his thrice-weekly talk show, but (puerile though it may seem) I found myself increasingly distracted by the absurd hair-hat perched on his bonce. Call me the Peter Tatchell of the tonsorial world if you will, but I simply have to point out that Radio 1 publicity shots from the early 70s reveal a man almost as smooth as a billiard ball, yet by the end of the decade, the Blankety Blank presenter had somehow acquired a coiffeur resembling President Kennedy's in Dealey Plaza, with the hair seemingly hovering several inches above his skull. During his reminiscences, Wigon boasted about how little research he usually did on his guests (it showed), and even had the temerity to criticise Michael Parkinson (who has always mugged up), but the footage was instructive in this regard. The only memorable clips from the Wigon shows are the ones where something went wrong (George Best drunk, Anne Bancroft mute, David Icke loony), whereas with Parky, what one remembers are the dozens and dozens of interviews that went enthrallingly right.

Executive Producer Caroline Wright has come up with a potentially revealing format, but sadly it was wasted on last night's guest. He's a lazy and self-satisfied broadcaster (with precious little to be self-satisfied about), and the way that a clip of him lethargically warming up his audience was portentously captioned "previously unseen footage" (as though it was a rare outtake of Lenny Bruce) unconsciously revealed the sheer pomposity of the man. For those of you with a thirst for adventure, don't forget my £1,000 reward for the first person to rip off his toupee live during the Children in Need appeal in November (no violence though, just a gentle tug). "Basically, everybody would like to be famous" he told us last night, so what better way to earn yourself instant stardom (and a grand) than by pulling the rug from *over* him?

Ch 3 SACRED COWS

The greatest collection of sacred cows in Britain have been the royal family. Not the minor ones, who are regularly abused in the tabloids, but the senior ones, who are mysteriously exempt from all criticism.

Take the Queen Mother. I was always a bit unlucky when it came to writing about her. Years ago I made a pilot TV programme called The Future Rock and Roll Years, an ingenious and original concept, whose one tiny flaw was that the format (which relied exclusively on captions to deliver the gags) turned out to be about as funny as being born dead with cancer. As you might guess from the title, it took the structure of The Rock and Roll Years, but set the news stories and music just a little in the future. When I screened it, the TV executive actually got into the foetal position in his office as he watched it (in particular a sketch about dead black babies in African Red Nose sequence and a director saying "that one's dead, bung it in the bin and get something fresh"). He said that not only was it unbroadcastable, but it also made him depressed almost to the point of tears. One of the sketches was a song about the Queen Mother, called "When will the Queen Mother Die?" The atmosphere in the studio was mortuary cold as we were shooting it, but worse still, an announcement of the actual death of the Queen Mother was accidentally released on Ceefax during rehearsals, and the morale in the studio was soon hanging slightly below the ankles. Fortunately, by the time we'd finished most of the playback, it became clear that the Queen Mother had not died, and Ceefax apologised for their error.

GREAT ROMANCES
BIOGRAPHY CHANNEL 2003

Having grown tired of this absurd double-barrelled surname (the hyphen was grafted on one night during a drunken visit to a punctuation parlour in Marseille, when I was young and foolish), I recently dropped in at my local deed poll office, to check out the alternatives. First they offered me Riley (because life is, apparently, all fun and games if you adopt that), then showed me how I could become a household name, simply by changing my cognomen to Mr Windolene J Cloth. But best of all was their invitation to alter my name to Mr A Dogshome, and I'd like to take this opportunity to advise all elderly, sentimental, pet-loving readers that they should urgently consider making a generous bequest to a canine charity. Just send the cheque to me, made out to "A Dogshome," and you can then go to join the choir invisible, secure in the knowledge that your money will be put to good use.

TV reviews

The extraordinary number of commercials soliciting money for dogs' homes tells you a good deal about the sort of sentimental (and just plain mental) people who tune into the Biography channel on Thursdays, to view *Great Romances*. Watching the life story of Edward and Mrs Simpson yesterday morning was like taking a swim in a pool of syrup, with the honeyed tones of the narrator reciting a script that positively oozed sucrose ("few men have made a greater sacrifice for love than the Duke of Windsor"), accompanied by library music *so sugary and cloying that any viewers who were suffering from Diabetes mellitus might well have found themselves slipping into a coma.* But by cunningly connecting myself to an intravenous insulin drip, I managed to stay the course through this ludicrously deferential paeon to the son of George V and Queen Mary, an uppity woman who (like our current monarch) always looked as though she'd just trodden in some doggy-do. However, she had no reason to behave in such a superior fashion, because it transpired that her son's full name was Edward Albert Christian George Andrew Patrick David. Presumably, as a mark of respect, she wanted to mention every chap who'd been involved in the gang bang.

At the end of the day, pretty-long-in-the-tooth journalists like me avoid clichés like the plague, and wouldn't touch them with a barge pole for all the tea in China, so I was dismayed to hear a script crammed with such empty and hackneyed phrases as "he was Prince Charming" and "this was no ordinary affair." Odder still were the many euphemisms, because "Wallis had a hard dark beauty and a flat chest" means "it fell out of the ugly tree and hit every branch on the way down" in my book. And while we were told that "she quickly moved into the circle of the Prince of Wales," there was no reference to him moving into *her* circle. Not that he would have entered very far, I suspect, because Edward VIII was reputedly hung like a hamster, and his relationship with Mrs Simpson was primarily that of slave and dominatrix. What he enjoyed above all else was the smack of firm government, and I wasn't surprised to learn that, during the war, Wallis joined the French Women's Ambulance Corps. Somehow, "FWAC" seems the right organisation for a dominatrix, especially because, if she struck him too hard, she'd know how to bandage him up afterwards.

In an attempt to be uncontroversial, the programme largely glossed over the couple's less salubrious activities, especially their notorious fondness for extreme right-wing regimes during WWII. References to stays in "neutral Madrid and Lisbon" made no mention of the gruesome fascist dictators who ruled those countries, while their extended flirtation with Nazi Germany was excused with such disingenuous phrases as "they went there to look at low-cost housing projects," and "he was only expressing the views of many Englishmen of his age and class." Had Britain fallen to Hitler, the Duke and Duchess of Windsor might even have returned home to be puppet monarchs, but just to show that this unpleasant couple didn't have the monopoly on malignity, we were reminded of the letter sent by George VI (at the behest of his wife) to Edward on his wedding day, telling him that the royal title would be denied Wallis. A charming slight that the same woman repeated sixty years later when, as Queen Mother, she un-royaled Diana, Our Lady of Versace, as punishment for getting divorced.

As cheap as chips, this was little more than a collection of well-worn archive clips arranged in chronological order, and loosely connected by an undeservedly hagiographical script about dysfunctional people who frittered away their lives by loafing and sponging (not just the Duke and Duchess, but the entire royal family). Sorry if that sounds harsh, but the programme was too fawning ever to break through the meniscus of royal deference, and I have a knee-jerk reaction to such uncritical and obsequious biographies. I'm speaking literally, by the way, because my knee does actually jerk whenever I see a member of the royal family on the screen. I trained with Galvani, you know, and any documentary about the Windsors causes involuntary movements of my patella, powerful enough to send me ricocheting around the room. "The Bouncing Republican," that's what the neighbours call me.

Did I mention that I am the proud webmaster of hermaj.com/mummy/oldbat@ chokeonfish.com? On this (fictional) site, you can see footage of the Queen Mother's regal plastic hip joints in motion, and continuous live webcam action of the Queen Mother's unblocked oesophagus, while clicking your mouse on an icon of Her yellow teeth will take you to the Her birthday celebrations, where you will hear nothing but cheers and more cheers. Not the roar of the crowds, just Princess Margaret was at the drinks cabinet again.

When she finally expired a few years ago, I spent the mourning period patriotically commemorating Her passing by inserting a quart bottle of Gordon's and a dozen lemons into a hastily modified Teasmaid, so I could be awoken at regular intervals to offer her a fitting twenty-one gin salute.

TV reviews

ROYAL LONDON
LWT 2002

Reviewing television programmes may seem like money for old espadrille, but the cushiest of all newspaper jobs is surely writing the gossip column. It's easy, because you can simply make it all up if you want to (or "lie," to use the technical term), which is why I've decided to graft a gossip column onto my review, thereby filling this page with even more rubbish than usual. Today, I can reveal that Dale Winton is currently auditioning for a film, and is hoping to get a large part in *Twelve Angry Men*. Salman Rushdie has finally plucked up courage to write another book about religion, provisionally entitled *The Life of the Buddha – That Fat F***er*. And the word on the street is that Michael Barrymore's next series is going to combine wordplay with a talent show, and has a title that's an anagram of *Pop Idol*. It's going to be called *Pool Dip*.

When I run out of gossip about genuinely famous people, I can always fall back on tittle-tattle about the Queen and her appalling decorticated tribe, that chinless legion of ninety-third-in-line-to-the-throne drains on the public purse who are constantly having to have Nigel Dempster surgically removed from their lower colons. Recently, television has also begun filling its airwaves with 625-line royal gossip columns masquerading as documentaries (in an attempt to soften us up for the Jubilee, no doubt), the latest being yesterday afternoon's dire, trivial, and absurdly mistitled *Royal London* (LWT). "How we look and how we dress is a topic of endless fascination to the media" declared Prince Michael of Kent (presumably drafted in to supply some much-needed gravitas, but sounding like a Mysteron with the Elgin Marbles in his mouth), after which a motley succession of hangers-on and camp followers (in every sense) explained why being royal is such a dashed difficult profession. "You have to keep your hat on, shake hands, and accept bunches of flowers," confided one, and when you think of all that posing for stamps and detaining people at her own pleasure that Her Majesty also has to do, you suddenly start to realise what damn good value for money the Windsors really are.

Most gossip columns nowadays are more interested in what Cate Blanchett is wearing (and what Kylie *isn't* wearing) than in the royals' uncompromising lack of dress sense, but this documentary nevertheless embarked on a positively narcoleptic tribute to four generations of regal frocks and follies. There was Edward VII's smoking jacket ("the forerunner of today's dinner jackets" enthused one toady), there was the Queen Mother in a delightful "colour combination" (yellow dress with matching teeth), and there was Queen Mary, described as "conservative" although the accompanying picture showed her apparently sporting a trifle on her head. We also saw the Queen herself, travelling around in her favourite black Rolls Royce (the one that looks like a hearse for vertical coffins), and wearing a Freddie Fox pink beekeeper creation on her bonce, a hat in which (according to rumour) Prince Edward has also been seen. Not that he's camp, of course, it was all just a silly misunderstanding. Apparently, he was once told by his mother to go to open a leisure centre in Basildon, whereupon his father barked out "wear the Fox hat." So he did.

To pad out this meagre footage to the requisite half-hour, each news clip was accompanied by pointless stories from self-important flunkeys, most of whom were well into their anecdotage. We heard about inconsequential visits to hotels, how one man had helped the Queen to shorten her curtains, and even how the young Edward VII "on weekend trips to Dover took forty pairs of shoes with him" (so what? My great-great-grandfather did exactly the same thing, though admittedly he was a shoe salesman). Out of respect, there was no sign of the late Princess Margaret (or "Mustique Meg" as she used to be known *chez* Lewis-Smith), not even a clip of her receiving a twenty-one *gin* salute, but we did briefly glimpse Diana, "the greatest fashion icon of all time," relaxing in Paris. Poor girl. The last time she was picked up by a Frenchman, it was with a mop, and given that she died only months after Gianni Versace, I still often wonder if it wasn't all an elaborate way for her to get a sneak preview of his autumn collection.

A brief appearance by the gastronomic genius, chef Michel Bourdin, was the only worthwhile moment in this otherwise woeful documentary, but like most of the contributions we witnessed, it had precious little to do with royalty, London, or image. Sorry, but I just checked my watch and it says it's 2002, which means we're no longer obedient subjects who become childlike at the mere mention of royalty, so why bother to assemble such a servile and anachronistic series? What we want nowadays is gossip, pure and simple, like the sensational news I can now reveal, which is that one of the senior royals is a cross-dresser. Still, who isn't nowadays? You should see me first thing in the morning, trying to get into my romper suit with a hangover. If I can't push my arms through the holes in the jacket first time, I'm not just a cross dresser. I'm a *furious* dresser.

It has always bemused me that, being a London-based family, the Windsors are held up to the rest of us as suitable role models for society. Why? They're a bunch of divorcees, dipsos, drugtakers, philanderers, army dropouts, racists, hypocrites, and deviants, including a father who wants to be reincarnated as a tampon and a bulimic nymphomaniac mother. Frankly, if that lot are supposed

TV reviews

to be a shining example of family values, then I can only assume that the family they've been modelling themselves on is the Addams. Or perhaps the Mansons.

TROOPING THE COLOUR
BBC1 2000

Although I warned them not to do it, the BBC once asked me to try my hand at newsreading. I knew that the combination of hastily typed scripts and my innate dislike of reading aloud without rehearsal was bound to end in tears, but for some reason it was always the royal stories that threw me. "Prince Charles has opened a new school in Bury Street, Edmonds," was my first broadcast mistake. And no, it's not apocryphal. I am the man who once announced that "the Queen Mother has been rushed to hospital, after suddenly feeling a hundred and eleven." Fortunately, however, this was local radio, so there was only one person listening to the bulletin. Me.

The Queen Mother appeared to be anything but ill as her carriage entered the Mall on Saturday morning (although she probably does feel increasingly a hundred and eleven nowadays). She was there to watch the Coldstream Guards *Trooping the Colour* (BBC1), and was therefore officially "resplendent," one of the innumerable battered ornaments that royal commentators wheel out on such occasions while running the full phatic gamut of the regal lexicon. I had hoped that she'd arrive in the high-roofed Rolls Royce (you know, the one that looks like a hearse designed to accommodate vertical coffins), but instead she and Princess Margaret turned up in an eighteenth-century horse-drawn barouche, and all I could hear were cheers, cheers, and more cheers as she passed. Ah well, Princess Margaret always did like a drink or twelve from the secret on-board drinks cabinet, to lubricate herself during her increasingly rare public appearances.

"History, theatre, and national spirit combine" continued Eric Robson, as the Queen emerged from the Palace in her ivory-mounted phaeton and headed for Horseguards Parade. In years gone by, Her Majesty would famously ride her horse, "Sidesaddle," but I suppose that poor old Sidesaddle must have died, because she was now allowing herself to be transported by Iceland and Auckland, four royal colonels, and a postillion, while the commentary described the proceedings in a

Ch 3 SACRED COWS

language tantalisingly close to English. "The drummer's call is the signal that command of the escort of the colour should pass to the subaltern... an orderly moves from the approach road to take the pace stick...," he declared, as hundreds of men wearing bearskins on their heads waved bayonets in the air, marched backwards in the stifling heat, and took over an hour and a half to parade a regimental flag around Whitehall in celebration of the Queen's birthday on a day that wasn't her birthday. And what could be more quintessentially British than that?

When one guardsman fainted in the sweltering heat, the delirium began to affect me too, and at one point I swear that I saw members of the paramilitary wing of the WI lurking in the crowd with their Kalashnikov trifles at the ready. The Bore War ceremony was now approaching its zenith, with "God Save the Queen" being played for the fifth time, although at least Robson had the sensitivity to keep quiet during the set pieces (unlike Des Lynam's yobbish performance last week at the opening ceremony for Euro 2000). Admittedly, he did take one sardonic sideswipe at Peter Mandelson over his recent "chinless wonder" comments ("I don't see him here... perhaps he's keeping his chin down somewhere else"), but the man's speciality is *Gardeners' Question Time*, so he's therefore best qualified to talk about fruits and vegetables. Which makes him admirably suited to discuss the activities of the Coldstream Guards, if rumours about their off-duty antics on Hampstead Heath are anything to go by.

The Guards halted when the ensign was nine paces from the colour, the Royal Bird Turglar released a flock of qualms (or some such nonsense), and I solemnly thought of the fallen – those brave BBC cameramen who'd been trained to yawn with their mouths shut, but who nevertheless must have keeled over unconscious during this epic of unalloyed tediousness. "There is a tendency today to question its relevance" conceded Robson at the close, and rightly so, because the days when a flag was a rallying point in the midst of battle have long gone, and if there's ever going to be a Palace coup, it'll be the Windsors who plan and execute it, not outsiders. There's still a case to be made for continuing with Trooping the Colour as an unashamed tourist spectacle, but the television screen cannot possibly convey the grandeur and pomp on which such ceremonies depend, so why waste hours of airtime on a ritual that proves only one thing? That democracy in this country still works from the top down.

Having read for myself a hastily scribbled "Sorry to hear you are dead" on Princess Diana's Remembrance Board back in 1997, I feel it is my solemn duty to reproduce some of the public's tributes to the late Queen Mother, which were made available to me shortly after her death. "I thought she would never die, she has let us all down very badly." D. Holmes, Somerset. "She was a marvellous

TV reviews

woman, and a wonderful lover." L. J. Worthington, Penrith. "Once again the Queen is not upset enough for my liking. The woman should have a bit more compassion. How would she feel if it was her mother?" W. Waugh, Richmond. "How refreshing to be able to mourn the death of a member of the Royal family without being accused of being homosexual." J. Fletcher, High Wycombe. "Her death should act as a warning to others who think it is cool to experiment with drugs." E. Franks, Cheshire. "She had such a difficult life, always battling against adversity and misfortune. Let us hope that if there is a next time round she is given a life of privilege and comfort." T. D. Wainwright, Hastings. You may consider these quotes to be as apocryphal as the story about two camp quarrelling footmen at Buckingham Palace (to whom a ginless Highness once remarked "when you two old queens have stopped bickering, this old queen wants a drink").

Alright just one more royal review, then I must move on to other sacred cows.

WILLIAM'S WOMEN

FIVE 2004

The owners of llanfairpwllgwyngyllgogerychwyrndrobwllllantysiliogogogoch.com may boast they they possess the world's longest web address, but I have news for them. Another Welsh station called Gorsafawddachaidraigo danheddogleddollonpenrhynareurdraethcere-digion is already planning a dotcom site, residents of the New Zealand town of Taumata-whakatangihan gakoauotamateturipukakapikimaungahoronukupokaiwhenua-kitanatahu are setting up their own web page, and if the city of Bangkok ever decides to use its traditional name, we'll all have to learn to key Krungthepmaha nakornamornratanakosinmahintarayut-thayamahadilokphopnopparatraja thaniburiromudomrajaniwesmahasatharnamornphimarnavatarnsathitsak kattiyavisanukamprasit into our search engines (try typing that in a force 9 gale). In tribute to the late Queen Mother, I recently registered a website that's almost as long (http://hermaj.co.uk/mummy/oldbat@fishbone/now-horizontal.com), and plan to launch it soon, crammed with interactive features, such as an icon reading "click this to hear royal cheers." And when you do, an archive recording will be played of the Queen Mum and Princess Margaret merrily clinking their glasses together, as they enjoy a mid-morning quart or two of gin and tonic.

I had thought of inviting Prince William to record an official interview for my website, but having seen *William's Women* last night on Five, I don't think there's much point in my asking. "He really dislikes the

Ch 3 SACRED COWS

media," we were told at the outset, and by the end of this ill-informed and laughably lightweight documentary, I was starting to think that perhaps he had a point. Despite having no hard information whatsoever about the private life of "the world's most eligible bachelor," the programme intrusively speculated about the flirtations and fidelity of the future king, a question that not only has constitutional implications, but religious ones too, because he will eventually become head of the Church of England. But luckily, he has the shining example of his parents (both devout worshippers) to follow, so he doubtless already understands the vital importance of obeying the Nine Commandments.

Devoid of genuine knowledge, the programme made do with hearsay and supposition, bolstered by lacklustre scenes filmed with lookalikes (in the style of BBC2's Double Take). Models who'd once seen him from a distance in a night club gave us full and frank accounts of their intimate relationship with him, while expert talking heads passed on worthless snippets of royal gossip, most apparently gleaned from the pages of *Hello!* magazine. "He's sexy... gorgeous... very yummy... he has his mother's looks," was the received wisdom among female contributors, which is news to the rest of us, who've seen that notorious equine gene in the Windsor DNA slowly get to work on his face over the years, turning him into a more effeminate version of Princess Anne. If you ask me, someone in that family once loved horses a little *too* much, and as for talk of "movie star looks," I think they refer to Trigger. Where contributors did have first-hand information to pass on, it was invariably about other royals, not William or his women. So although veteran journalist Harry Arnold's recollections of the Duke of Edinburgh were engrossing ("a rude horrible man... we called out 'Happy New Year Sir' and he replied 'bollocks'"), and Ryan Parry's revelations about the Queen's Tupperware were well worth a re-run, none of it shed any light whatsoever on the subject of the documentary.

Indeed, the only people who seemed to have any relevant memories to share were a few acquaintances from school, who remembered that girls would "giggle" whenever he ran onto the Eton sports field in his shorts (so what? I generate giggles to this day). Which reminds me. If you want to tell people truthfully that "the kids are at Eton," but can't afford the fees, then just move to a village in Retfordshire, and – hey presto – they'll be enrolled free at Eaton Junior School.

This was unreconstructed Channel 5 at its very worst, due not least to a dreadful script, which degenerated from crass double entendres ("many a celebrity has been starstruck by the thought of Royal Willy") to desperately repetitive single entendres ("every American star has expressed interest in a little British Willy"). Worse, many of the

TV reviews

"experiments" to judge the effect of the Prince on others didn't just involve a fake William, but fake bystanders too, resulting in yet another mockumentary of a type that's becoming ever more prevalent, and is damaging the credibility of serious film makers. As for the future king, I've no idea how he'll turn out (nor do I care), but his progress through life certainly won't be helped by the acolytes that surround him. Hang on. Are acolytes the ones that hang down from cave ceilings? Or is that catamites? Perhaps I should ask his uncle Edward.

I'm not sure whether Jeremy Clarkson can strictly be classed as a sacred cow, because there is a large percentage of the British public who have long regarded him as a cunt. It comes as a total mystery to me that his books are best sellers, because he seems to possess about as much ability to write as Debussy had to spot weld.

He once telephoned me, and it's one of the few occasions when I wished I had been able to record the call. His tone was (just like his pisspoor writing) bombastic, vapid, and puerile, and his attempts to ingratiate himself with me (this was early in his career) were toe-curlingly embarrassing. II remember that he seemed to be under the impression that I had attended Eton, and when I jokingly explained that I had actually been to Eaton in Retfordshire, he seemed perplexed.

Besides working for the Evening Standard, I also wrote for the Mirror for many years, so I unwillingly had a ringside seat for some of Mr Clarkson's extra-curricular activities. From 2000 to 2006 Clarkson had a public feud with Mirror editor Piers Morgan. On the last-ever Concorde flight, Clarkson threw a glass of water over Morgan during an argument. And at the British Press Awards in March 2004, he swore at Morgan and punched him before being restrained by security; Morgan says it has left him with a scar above his left eyebrow.

Why the feud? Well, it began when Morgan published pictures of Clarkson kissing his BBC producer, Elaine Bedell (or Bedwell, as the more sexist males at Radio 4 used to call her – she and I started at the BBC at the same time, and I believe she got in because of a student radio doc she had made about sewage farming). Elaine Bedell started her career at the BBC as a trainee, and produced Start the Week and You and Yours for BBC Radio 4. She was a high-flyer in radio, but as often happens in the Senior Service, she was lured away by the glamour of television, an industry where she has doubtless made a great deal of money, but at the terrible price of having (on occasion at least) to snog Mr Clarkson.

Ch 3 SACRED COWS

On television, she became Clive James's producer, and wrote to me in 1998, stung by a negative review. I replied:

Elaine Bedell
Watchmaker
London

13. xi. 98

Dear Elaine,

According to the story, when King Midas lost his touch he was much happier and life was much better.
Why don't you work with something less plastic and artificial? Do another one of those excellent series about Bakelite telephones.

Best wishes,

Victor

To return to Clarkson, this is what I wrote in the Mirror when the story broke:

On Thursday, this venerable newspaper published a picture of the Human Toffee Apple groping his former TV producer, Elaine Bedell, in the street, a picture that left a very funny taste in my mouth. Apart from the distress it must have caused his wife and family, the sheer immaturity of his behaviour is astonishing, although it's typical of the man's general conduct. Just as he tries to squeeze his fortysomething paunch into twentysomething denim (an effect that makes him look like Stephen Fry's older sister, only with bigger breasts), and inflicts his trapped-in-the-seventies musical tastes on us in his dire TV programmes, so he thinks he can carry on behaving in public like a teenager on his first snog. It all suggests what I've thought about the man for years: that he's still trying to live out the life he aspired to when he was nineteen.

That's why he's so obsessed with cars, although the Freudian symbolism of an attraction to long sleek red objects and thrusting pistons is probably lost on him. As men get older, they frequently try to compensate for their waning powers by purchasing a Ferrari Testosterone (sorry, that was a Freudian slip, I mean Testarossa), or some other penis substitute, and Clarkson's TV career has allowed him access to an entire fleet of them. Yet far from bringing happiness, all

TV reviews

these vehicles have done is to trap him in his own arrested development. Surely there are few sights more pathetic than a middle-aged man driving a stubby red sports car around town, silently screaming out "Hey girls, look at me!" as he passes by. Yet that's a pretty accurate summary of the Human Toffee Apple's entire career.

As it happens, I am loosely connected to this story, because (due to the success of my Bach organ series) I'd been invited to the very BBC2 celebration party *at which the picture was taken (as guests were leaving)*. Kind though the invitation was, I didn't attend, because celebrity circle jerks have never been my scene (and anyway, I'm currently filming a documentary about the late Idi Amin, of which more next week). But I used to know Elaine very well, because I worked alongside her many years ago, having joined the BBC at exactly the same time as her, both straight from university. Right from the start, I could tell she was far too beautiful for fusty old radio, and would soon be working in the more glamorous milieu of television, and that's how things have turned out. But if I'd known then that she liked being incompetently groped by fat ugly men, I might have suggested a bit of mid-air refuelling (tongues only) in the sixth floor canteen, between the ring donuts and the bananas.

Well, we were in our early twenties back then, and that sort of irresponsible behaviour is forgivable in young people. But we're supposed to attain wisdom and self-control as the years roll by, whereas Clarkson has immatured with age, which is why his public gropings are so distasteful. If he's going to get up to those sort of tricks, couldn't he at least rent a hotel room, so the rest of us don't have to watch? I've heard it suggested that perhaps women are attracted to him because he has a big todger, but the reality is simpler. He *is* a big todger.

And this is what I wrote about the programme for which he has become world-famous.

TOP GEAR
BBC2 1998

I thoroughly enjoy watching dangerous sports, and there's one on every Thursday night at the moment. It's hard to believe, I know, but there are crazy guys who actually strap a huge TV camera to their car windscreen, accelerate to 70mph, then talk directly into it while it's filming them

Ch 3 SACRED COWS

driving. For this reason alone, I watch *Top Gear* (BBC2) – in the hope that, sooner or later, just as one of the presenters turns to the lens and says "she's a nice little mover," there'll be an unexpected bend in the road and he'll go sailing over the edge of a cliff.

There are no presenters on *Top Gear*, just human soap-on-a-rope with Brut aftershave for blood, and the programme atmosphere is so locker-roomy you can almost smell the jockstraps. Jeremy Clarkson would be first for the cliff edge, please. With each series, he looks increasingly as though he might be Stephen Fry's slightly older, simpleton sister, and once he opens his mouth the diagnosis is confirmed. Last night he was drooling over the bodywork of a trio of BAT cars ("it's a little honey... she's a cracker") built in the 50s for Alfa Romeo, and Romeo was certainly the word for our Jeremy, who got so worked up about the sleek curves and smooth ride he was getting that I didn't like to think what he might do to the cars once the cameras had gone. I only hope the petrol tube didn't have any sharp edges.

Russell Bulgin suffered from Tourette syndrome of the hands (five gestures in his first eight words, all quite unconnected to his speech) and, once his review of the new Nissan Jelly Mould got underway, it was clear he was also crippled with *idioglossia Clarksonitis*. There's only one thing sadder than being Mr Clarkson, and that, surely, is *wanting* to be Mr Clarkson. "Chunky but impressively grown up" was his verdict on the car; I only wish I could say the same of him. Then up popped Vicki Butler-Henderson (whom they called "new girl," but I call "token woman"), a presenter so thoroughly prim she made Mother Theresa look like a slut. She tried to speak Laddish "I'm burning rubber..., street legal is the name of the game") but the gist of her report was clearly "Upper-class bint roughs it in a Golf with the oiks." At one point she shouted "I'm coming up your inside," and I could imagine the hearty male guffaws (in her absence) from the guys in the edit suite.

An Andy Kershaw clone, name of Steve Berry, proved to be a bit of a wag, shining on the programme in the same way that not very funny people shine on *Loose Ends*: because the competition is so poor. He visited the parents of world champion motorcyclist Kevin Schwantz, who lived in the widest, longest, slowest mobile home on the planet. It may be pretty hard to overtake Kevin Schwantz on his motorcycle, but it'd be damn near impossible ever to overtake his dad in his Bluebird Wonderlodge, if you got stuck behind him on the B1258. And finally, there was Quentin "2ls" Willson, who thought the Mazda MX5 was "as cute as lace panties." His idea of humour was referring to the sun as "the yellow orb," and I fear that he now regards himself as the Noël Coward of the motoring world. But accents, as we all know, tell you less about where somebody comes from than about where they think they're going and, despite playing the

TV reviews

toff on this show, his Belgravia tones are periodically betrayed by an errant Bermondsey syllable.

Top Gear is the fluffy dice that hangs in the window of BBC2. Admittedly Mr Clarkson (who, at his age, really should stop trying to cram a 40-inch waist into 32-inch trousers) seems to have been demoted to a mere reporter, which is a move in the right direction, but there's so much wrong with the programme that, if you took it to an MOT testing centre, they'd laugh and say "scrap." The presenters may enjoy going on freebies to test drive open-top sports cars on deserted roads in France and Italy, but we're going to have to use them on clogged city roads; so how about test driving them on a rainy day in Oxford Street, and telling us useful things like whether the roof lets the rain in, and whether you can get the piss out of the seats if you park outside a pub at night. As for the music that accompanies the reports, the choice has all the randomness of ERNIE. "The 1950s" began Jeremy last night, and "Moonlight Serenade" struck up. The piece was recorded in 1939, and Glenn Miller was worm food by 1944. Now, that's so stupid it's almost wilful.

To end this savaging of a herd of sacred cows, here is a negative review of someone who, for decades, I myself regarded as beyond criticism. In his heyday, Michael Parkinson was one of the great television interviewers (equalled perhaps only by John Freeman), and my formative years were enriched by his many memorable encounters with Hollywood legends, songwriters from the golden years of the Broadway musical, and unique inspiring characters like Muhammad Ali. When the BBC axed his show in 1982, it was nothing short of an act of vandalism.

When the show was brought back in the late 1990s, the host initially seemed as attentive and well-informed (yet paradoxically relaxed) as ever. But after a couple of seasons, the show lost its edge, and the host's indifference to many of his guests became all too obvious. This review dates from that later, sadder period.

PARKINSON

BBC 2004

Entropy isn't what it used to be. In our increasingly disordered world, we need people, programmes, and products that we can rely upon, and there's something disconcertingly Stalinist about the way so many of them are silently airbrushed out of history one day, never to be mentioned again.

Ch 3 SACRED COWS

Blue Peter's mobile crunchy pie (Fred the Tortoise) has gone, Gary Glitter's hits no longer feature on the soundtrack of *I Love the 1970s*, Nestles no longer rhymes with "wrestles," and Opal Fruits are now called Starburst (although, judging from the size of some of the people who eat them, they should have been renamed Uranus Drops). And no more can impecunious groups of Saturday night drinkers club together to buy a Party Seven, a giant can of cheap beer which, when you punctured the lid, spurted like the ejaculation from the blowhole of a sexually-aroused sperm whale, as six of your seven pints promptly ended up drenching the ceiling and walls of somebody else's kitchen.

But Michael Parkinson has seemingly been a permanent fixture in BBC1's Saturday night schedule ever since 1971, staying there through thick and thin (that's David Beckham and Calista Flockhart, though not on the same show). Well, that's what we were supposed to believe when the final edition of *Parkinson* was broadcast over the weekend, because nobody had the temerity to mention the host's disastrous decision to leave the Corporation in the early 1980s, and squander his talent first at TV-AM, then on a series of trivial ITV game shows. His return to BBC1 in 1997 was universally welcomed, but he's clearly become bored with many of the younger guests he's had to converse with over the past couple of years, so much so that he's sometimes sounded uncharacteristically under-prepared (although how can you research when there's nothing *to* research?), and has even started telling anecdotes himself, rather than listening dutifully to theirs. So perhaps it's as well that the imminent return of *Match of the Day* has persuaded him to try his luck at ITV again, even though I fear the move will prove only one thing: that when history repeats itself, the price always goes up.

How each guest descends those famous stairs has usually given us a fair indication of their enthusiasm at being there, and that was certainly the case on Saturday night. Boris Becker ambled sluggishly down them with all the pizzazz of a jaded celeb who's midway through an extended book-plugging tour, then told us that "Tim Henman could win Wimbledon... he performs well on the grass" in tones so lethargic that he might well have been performing on the grass himself. Patrick Kielty, however, positively raced down the steps in his eagerness to display his uncompromising lack of talent to the nation, and was soon telling us a "true story" about a nun and a dildo (that was a lie when Bob Monkhouse used to tell it thirty years ago), and showing us a clip of himself standing next to starving street children in India, raising money for charridee. These fund-raising ventures are a reciprocal arrangement, of course, because the celebrities' hungry egos are also fed by the uncritical TV coverage.

There was music too, from a novelty act called Jamie Cullum,

TV reviews

which involved a midget in a foetus costume stamping on a piano keyboard and singing in tones suggestive of a strangulated hernia. But just when all hope was gone, on came Bruce Forsyth (pate sponsored by Cyril Lord), and belatedly re-energised the programme, despite being almost as old as the combined ages of all the other guests (including all the Corrs) put together. In braver times, Parkinson would surely have devoted the entire hour to the myriad talents of Britain's greatest all-round entertainer, and it seemed nothing short of tragic that so much time had already been squandered on banal exchanges with Kielty about how "everyone in Ireland is a character," and recycled anecdotes about how hilarious Oliver Reed was when drunk. How true, and I bet Ollie himself had a good laugh when his cirrhotic liver came flying out of his earhole in 1999, moments before he coughed up blood and died.

At its best, Parkinson has consistently proved that all you need for a good chat show is a couple of chairs and two intelligent people with an ability to talk and listen. But of late, the show has frequently lacked guests that the host actually *wanted* to talk to, and when I witnessed his shameful (I'll go further – disgraceful) capitulation to Alistair Campbell earlier this year, I realised it was time for him to go. Maybe he'll be revitalised at ITV, but more probably he'll fall into the same well-paid pre-senescent ennui that has overcome Des Lynam, and will end up half-sleeping through a succession of unwanted guests that has been foisted on him. That was certainly the case with Becker, who made little effort to entertain us, and was presumably there solely on the principle that "all publicity is good publicity, so long as they spell your name right." Who was it who coined that famous apothegm, by the way?

I think it was Betty Gable.

CHAPTER 4

LIVE AND DIRECT

Spare a thought, if you will, for Wolfgang Dircks. Wolfgang has been my hero for many years, although I only got to know of him after he died a noble death. Wolgang was a German who was discovered sitting in front of his TV set with a listings magazine on his lap, having expired five years earlier. His death coincided with the arrival of BBC1 in Germany, and that nation's first exposure to the twelve-hour live marathon that was Children in Need, so you don't need to be Sherlock Holmes to work out what happened. The man died of boredom.

I have always suspected that mammoth live TV productions such as Children in Need are not made primarily for the enjoyment of viewers, but for the benefit of the production staff. Anyone who works in jobbing TV will tell you that it is mostly a slow, arduous, dull, and thankless industry. So what if a piece of equipment fails? You simply replace it, and continue to record. So what if an actor suddenly forgets their lines? You simply stop and do a retake. But when you find yourself producing "live TV," tedious tasks suddenly become unaccountably exciting. Every little fluff and imperfection has to be dealt with in real time, and you suddenly become part of an epic white-knuckle ride of a show, about which you will be able to tell "on a wing and a prayer" stories to envious colleagues for decades to come.

Thirty years ago (as the old song has it) "Video Killed the Radio Star." Nowadays, the internet is killing television, and no amount of technological innovation – HD, Super HD, or 3D – will change that. The almost limitless variety of instantly available material on YouTube is draining viewers away from traditional TV channels, and undermining the ever-deteriorating case for the preservation of the BBC licence fee.

The one big advantage that television can still claim to have over the web is that it can cover big events live, as they happen (and, in some cases, can fund them too). The Eurovision Song Contest, The Lord Mayor of London's Show, Trooping the Colour, Big Brother, talent shows, general elections, pop festivals, and even wars (although the internet increasingly allows anyone in a war zone with access to a mobile phone to provide their own first-hand coverage of armed conflict, and it's usually much better informed and certainly more graphic than the sanitised versions provided by embedded professional journalists). I

TV reviews

therefore expect we will be seeing more live "event" TV over the coming years, with viewers encouraged to vote (at £1.50 per minute) at regular intervals, to help decide the outcome and fund the coverage. However, that won't stop the world wide web destroying old fashioned TV, although it might delay its demise for a little longer.

For those who are interested in the history of television, one of the first big live events on BBC television was on 27 August, 1950. The most exciting that live television got in those days was a static picture (with an enormous amount of static on it) of the Town Hall clock in Calais. Well, it was static except for the continual Dali-esque wobble of the images, and an engineer accidentally running past the camera.

*You can see it by clicking on link #17 on the **TV Reviews** page on **www.badastralbooks.com**.*

Let's begin this exploration of live television with the annual and truly dreadful live extravaganza that is Children in Need.

BBC CHILDREN IN NEED

BBC1 2006

November is the cruellest month for us skinflints. What with Poppy Day, the Blue Peter shoebiz appeal, collections for victims of autumnal floods and famines, and all those unsolicited Christmas begging letters that keep popping through my letterbox (including one last week that allegedly contained "foot paintings by the disabled," although most of them didn't look anything like feet to me), not donating to good causes has become pretty much a full-time occupation of late. But to prove to you that I'm not a tightwad, and that I care deeply about those less fortunate than myself, I've decided to relaunch my annual Ripathon. In previous years, you may recall, I've offered to make a charitable donation of £1,000 to anyone who will rip off Terry Wogan's "hair hat" during the live *BBC Children in Need* transmission, but this year I'm upping my "Give the rug a tug" offer to a staggering *one million pounds*. And what's more, I'll pay up even if Mr Wigon himself removes his toupée live on camera, and exposes his Gadd-like scalp to the nation for a full sixty seconds. Come on Sir Terry: those children are in need,

Ch 3 SACRED COWS

so why not pull the rug from under my feet by pulling the rug from over your head?

Oh dear. I've just realised that this column is appearing in Monday's edition, so the programme has already been and gone, and my million-pound offer is now closed. But I assure you that this was a sincere mistake on my part, and we all know that you've got it made in showbusiness if you can fake sincerity at will, because you can then appear generous in public without it actually costing you a penny. That's presumably why the studio was full of company representatives on Friday night, handing over six-foot cheques and getting a prime-time name check in return (*aka* "advertising on the BBC"), from Boots and Motorola to Lakeland and BT. I even saw Carol Vorderman telling us that "the best internet website for cards is Remind4U.com," forgetting to add that she is also one of that company's main shareholders. Ah well, we all know that charity begins at home.

Otherwise, this was the usual smuggery of pop stars, soap actors, and celebrities (many completely unknown), queueing up to give a small boost to disadvantaged British children, and a large boost to their own careers. McFly set the ball rolling with an indifferent cover of an old Beatles' hit (they should set up their own website at beatleshit.con), but that was musical gold compared to what followed as the evening wore on. Status Quo partnered Kim and Aggie in a spoof clean-up and song performance that somehow managed to demean *all* the participants simultaneously; a ravaged David Cassidy popped up to prove just how cruel a mistress Time can be; and the irritatingly perky Connie Fisher appeared in her new guise of Maria, performing the "Do Re Mi" scene from *The Sound of Music* with the (shut your) Von Trapp stage kids. Not a lot of people know this (and indeed, it may well not be true), but since the filming of the 1965 movie, the original children have been involved in criminal acts involving drugs, sex, rape, robbery, murder, and blackmail. Now that's what *I* call *Children in Need*.

Presiding over this self-congratulatory farrago at TV Centre (and keeping well clear of the Celebrity Scissorhands hairdressing salon just down the corridor) was Sir Terry, cruising on autopilot, swaggering from side to side, and uttering blarney-infested ad libs that contained not even a homeopathic dose of wit or humour. More nauseating still were the newsreaders, flaunting their steamy sexuality in a feeble James Bond spoof, not so much because the solemnity of the news is compromised by the sight of the BBC's Middle East editor cavorting with a female newsreader in a bubble bath (although it is), but because they did it so badly and so eagerly. Meanwhile, Natasha Kaplinsky was advising viewers "to press the red button" to help make the programme even better, but I was watching BBC1 on terrestrial analogue, and the only red button on my handset was

TV reviews

the "off" switch. But guess what? When I pressed it, the screen went blank, and Ms Kaplinsky was proved right, because the programme did indeed get much, much better.

Geldof Disease has spread through television faster than AIDS through Africa over the past twenty years, and still there is no cure. As with the lottery, the words "it's for charity" are supposed to silence all criticism, but why should we have to endure seven hours of insincere, poorly-rehearsed, life-draining mawkishness, when the material needs of disadvantaged children could and should be funded by honest government taxation?

Sadly, nobody ever took up my Wogan Wigoff challenge, which is a pity, because I genuinely had a million pounds waiting for the tugger (offer no longer applies). The rest is silence...

TWO MINUTES' SILENCE

BBC 1 1996

Dear Marje Proops died a couple of days ago, and I have to admit that I get a secret thrill out of writing to dead agony aunts and gratuitously insulting them. Is this normal? If it is, don't bother to reply – just piss off and get yourself down to the bone yard pronto.

Before appalled readers rush for their Basildon Bond, let me assure them that my tasteless opening remark is not intended to shock, but to raise an important philosophical question: when does a tragic event become a fitting subject for humour? It's a conundrum I first pondered when I worked as a BBC producer and discovered that, while jokes about the *Titanic* were deemed perfectly acceptable on Radio 4 (even though there would inevitably be listeners who'd lost loved ones in that awful 1912 disaster), a similar gag about the sinking of the Herald of Free Enterprise in 1987 would not be permitted. But can we define the exact duration of this period of mourning, beyond which death finally loses its sting, and irreverence becomes permissible? In the case of a person's death, the first impious remarks are usually broadcast a few months later (a few hours, in the case of the unloved Robert Maxwell) but, when a large part of an entire nation has died in two wars of unimaginable bravery, horror, and savagery, even seventy-eight years later seems far, far too soon for any thought of levity.

Yet each year there are signs that the reverence with which television treats the *Two Minutes' Silence* is becoming more and more

Ch 4 LIVE AND DIRECT

grudging. Silence is usually the broadcaster's greatest enemy, to be filled at all costs and, although many stations felt honour-bound to be quiet yesterday morning at 11am, the perfunctory nature of the observance reminded me of someone going to a party, nipping next door to a churchyard to watch the body of a scarcely-remembered relative being lowered into the grave, then gratefully rushing back to the fun and games. The solemnity of BBC1's coverage, for example (poignantly accompanied by wartime b&w stills and printed extracts from Sassoon and Housman), was somewhat undermined by the inanely grinning features of Ainsley Harriott which we'd seen only seconds earlier, and it's my guess that the dissonance caused by such disregard for context will increase each year. Like Victorian graveyards which were proudly built for perpetuity but have since been bulldozed flat to make way for supermarkets, it seems only a matter of time until the schedules are cleared and the annual televised two minutes' silence is no more.

In an attempt to break the *Guinness Book of Records* world record for television reviewing, I didn't just watch BBC1 though, dear me no. I set fifty video recorders to record all available terrestrial and satellite channels and spent yesterday afternoon reliving those same two minutes over and over again, watching through the eyes of those who'd observed and those who'd ignored the Armistice commemoration. ITV and Sky News had the bongs of Big Ben (the least silent thing imaginable), followed by the inevitable shot of ten thousand white crosses, and QVC also did the decent thing, mutely displaying a single poppy (though I kept expecting to see the phrase "Order these attractive flowers at our QVC – introductory offer price of..."). But UK Living stayed firmly in the land of the living by broadcasting an episode of a soap, while MTV viewers were noisily entertained by a French rock star (if that's not a contradiction in terms). NBC was examining the Munich Stock Exchange while, touchingly, NHK Japan broadcast a static altar shot, accompanied by the *Missa Solemnis.* Teutonic stations, meanwhile, continued as normal, with one showing a scorpion (my German is poor but I could just make out the phrase "if you touch it, it will kill you"), a shopping channel selling Lebkuchen (gingerbread houses), and ARD featuring a lederhosen-wearing Bavarian oompah group, performing a piece about old songs being better than all this new rubbish, thereby simultaneously positing and disproving their own theory. And that is how the one-eyed monster saw fit to mark the remembrance of the sixty million men who died in two world wars.

As a child, I remember tuning around the radio dial and encountering whole sections of the wavebands where (apart from the crackle of static) there really was nothing but silence. Nowadays, every available frequency is crammed with information, entertainment, and

TV reviews

sheer noise. Silence has been overwhelmed, like a feeble torchlight on a brilliant summer's day. It is right to remember, but natural to forget, and the two world wars are gradually becoming as remote from the younger generation as the Boer War or Bannockburn. In fact, it's a poignant but tragic irony that many of those who lived through these historic events are now suffering from Alzheimer's, and these remembrance services are being held for people, of whom many cannot remember a thing. For those who gave so much so long ago, what crueller motto could there be than *lest we forget*?

Those who think I was somewhat cruel to Marje Proops (born Rebecca Marjorie Israel) might care to look into her life story. She was, by all accounts, a nasty piece of work, and I state that fearlessly, in the full knowledge the dead cannot sue for libel. For example, it was alleged by her fellow newspaper columnist Vernon Coleman that she held racist views, and she was undeniably a hypocrite. Having spent a lifetime advising her Mirror readers never to succumb to an affair, it was discovered that she herself had been having an affair for just as many years. Which is all the more surprising when one considers her unappealing physiognomy, which surely inspired the phrase, "The face that sunk a thousand ships."

The following review also contains a reference to the dead, having been written shortly after Saddam Hussein had been strung up.

*The moments leading up to (but not including) his execution on 30 December 2006 can be seen by clicking on link #18 on the **TV Reviews** page on **www.badastralbooks.com**.*

Years later, I am still appalled by the nature of that execution. During my New Year vacation, the only television I saw was the endlessly repeated footage of him being hanged. I think this endless repetition was intended to prove that "we" had won the Iraq war, but it did not convince me. Nor, more importantly, did it convince the Iraqi people.

I'd been watching live Celebrity Big Brother late at night, while eating 3 lbs of Boursin at a single sitting (you never get fat if you wear elasticated trousers). So I suppose it was no wonder that I had some peculiar dreams that night. Not least a bizarre recurring nightmare, in which Dale Winton and I were cajoled into appearing in a reality TV show, catchily entitled I'm a Celebrity on a Battery Farm. The details are hazy, but I do remember one traumatic scene in which my rooster strayed too close to the jaws of his donkey, and (to the ratings-boosting delight of the programme-makers) had one of his legs bitten off by the beast.

Ch 4 LIVE AND DIRECT

That was bad enough, but things really took a turn for the worse when I had to go to the diary room afterwards, and explain to the viewers that Dale had an entire foot of my cock in his ass.

BIG BROTHER

C4 2005

Although it's technically impossible to perform an operation on the average estate agent (because they're cold-blooded, thick-skinned, hard-nosed, two-faced, spineless, and produce huge amounts of gall), there's a highly effective operation you can perform on your own house, before you ask them to sell it for you. Simply build false plasterboard walls inside each of your real rooms (allowing one body-width between the inner and outer walls), then flog your house to a childless couple who both go out to work each day, and – hey presto – you can secretly carry on living in the house you've just sold to them. As soon as they leave every morning, you can emerge from your hidden cavity and enjoy the run of the entire house, so long as you scurry back behind the false walls at the first sound of approaching footsteps. And by night (with the aid of a few discreet holes drilled into the plasterboard), you can spy on the unsuspecting couple as they eat, wash, sleep, argue, and have sex, unaware that they're providing you with the never-ending dramatic thrill of authentic voyeurism.

Of course, if the couple ever suspected that they were being watched, they'd either become inhibited or exhibitionistic, so you'd no longer be spying on reality. And that's just one of the many problems with *Big Brother*. Dramatically, it's contrived and inauthentic, and it's poor social science too, being nothing more than the runt offspring of BF Skinner's "operant conditioning box" and Erving Goffman's discredited "stand in front of the one-way mirror and act naturally" experiments from the 1960s, tarted up for a modern-day telly audience that thinks it's watching something new and groundbreaking. Despite claims by the show's fearsomely heterosexual puppet-master, Peter Bazalgette, that "what flows from the false premise is real," the participants are knowingly acting out a semi-improvised drama for C4 viewers; and despite prurient talk about "thermal imaging cameras in the bedroom... so we can see if anything's going on under the duvet," there's far too much tease and too little strip for a sad old voyeur like me.

TV reviews

More than ever, this sixth series has a feeling of "sloppy seconds" about it, being peopled largely by half-witted drama school rejects who've always wanted to be on TV and in the tabloids (without knowing why), but failed the auditions for earlier series. The "completely redesigned" house looks almost exactly the same as it always did, and so do the contestants, the usual mixture of pants and bikini models, leavened with a few eccentrics (a failed Tory politician, a white witch, a cross-dressing Turkish bellydancer). Less Orwellian than Sartrean, the show's motto ought to be "l'enfer, c'est les autres," as thirteen small-brained and huge-egoed bipeds vie for attention, the girls boasting about their fake tits and clapped-out vibrators, while the boys discuss "beer and birds," and proudly declare (as did Maxwell) "I've got opinions, though most of them don't make any sense." Their fifteen minutes of fame may be set to last for eleven weeks, but so far they've been living proof of the old showbiz adage that a celebrity is just a nonentity who got lucky.

Last night's preposterously-labelled "highlights" saw Tory Boy Derek (a cross between an effeminate black ET and that Playstation model with eyes a foot apart) become the political leader he'll never be in real life, calling a house meeting to "discuss the way forward" vis-a-vis washing up and putting out the bedroom lights. *Big Brother* ordered the housemates to make portraits of each other, resulting in pictures that looked like Paul Klee (after he'd received a few Cassius Klee-style bashes to the head), and were so universally inept that you'd have sworn even the prettiest girls were no oil paintings. Meanwhile, Kamal was continually bitching about how everyone else was continually bitching, while Makosi (whose task as the "unlucky thirteenth" contestant is to make herself universally despised) had developed such delusions of adequacy that she'd begun speaking about herself in the third person, like Lady Thatcher *c.*1989. Oh, and Craig burst into tears as he started telling everyone that he wasn't getting the attention he deserved, but I don't know what he said after that because, like everyone else, I lost interest.

When the mendaciously-named phenomenon of "reality television" began, Michael Grade (C4's erstwhile Chief Executive) snorted derisively that "they'll burn themselves out... people will rediscover talent." And at the risk of sounding like one of those bewildered critics who (half a century ago) used to insist that rock music would never last, and denounced Elvis for his lewd pelvic thrusts, I'm still convinced that he's right, because the public will eventually tire of the fakeness of *Big Brother* and its myriad offspring, and regain an appetite for crafted, well-written dramas that engage the intellect as well as the emotions. The conversations I heard last night were awash with superficial sentiment, banal to the point of imbecility, and so illiterate that I was reminded of the following conversation which I'm going to pretend that I overheard recently, atop a number 43 bus. "Who wuz that woman I see you wiv last night?" "It's not I see, it's I *saw*." "Oh alright... who wuz that eyesore I see you wiv last night?"

For legal reasons, I cannot include a letter from Peter Bazalgette that he sent to the Editor of the London Evening Standard shortly after the previous review had been published. In it, however, he expressed his "frustration" over my continuous use of the phrase "fearsomely heterosexual" about him. What did it imply? In truth, I really have no idea why I ever used the term. It just seemed to fit the man perfectly.

Of all the many "reality stars" created by Big Brother, only Jade Goody ever really crossed over into full-time media fame. Due largely to her premature death, she was elevated by most of the media to a semi-beatific status, and regarded as a sort of idiot-savant, with her bullying of Shilpa Shetty largely airbrushed out of history.

*Below is a link to the bullying outburst. It makes for ugly viewing but you can see it by clicking on link #19 on the **TV Reviews** page on **www.badastralbooks.com**.*

Shortly after it happened, I wrote this comment piece about Jade Goody and the media.

BIG BROTHER

C4 2007

Schadenfreude may be a German word, but it's clearly a British condition, because nothing warms the cold cold hearts of the Great British Public as the sight of the once-mighty tumbling unceremoniously to earth. Even their unexpected deaths can bring a wan smile to our cruel and bitter countenances (as happened when Hughie turned Green, when Quentin became Crisp, and when Barbara Woodhouse impersonated her favourite animal by going "woof" at her local crematorium); but how much more satisfying it is for us simply to raise a nonentity shoulder high, let them enjoy their fame for a moment, then nonchalantly step aside and watch them fall to the ground with a satisfying splat. How we laughed when we read of John Major's weakness for bedtime Currie (so *that's* what he meant

TV reviews

when he talked about curling up in bed with a leather-bound Trollope). And we positively rubbed our hands with glee (now available in family-size tubs) when our beloved TV funnyman Michael Barrymore began appearing in a real-life sitcom called *Only Pools and Corpses*.

Most of those who have splatted to the ground did at least possess some talent, so there's usually a touch of regret mixed in with our cynical satisfaction. At least Major didn't go around starting needless wars, we recall sagely, while Barrymore was a fine game-show host, and most of us felt genuine regret when the Seinfeld actor Michael Richards wrecked his own career with a racist rant late last year, because in doing so he tarnished his undeniably classic portrayal of Kramer. Not so with Jade Goody though, a woman devoid of talent, education, intelligence, or achievements, whose sole claim to fame was that you could shine a torch into one ear and see the beam emerge from the other side undimmed. She's never had the ability to entertain us with anything except the precipitous arc of her own career, and having been raised aloft for her stupidity, she's now been brought down by her racist outbursts. But her downfall is not high tragedy, just low farce.

Like the old French optical illusion that allows us to see first a beautiful woman, then an old hag, society has suddenly blinked and collectively changed its view of Ms Goody. After she had been victimised inside and outside the *Big Brother* house during the 2002 show (remember all those pig jokes, and the sadistic pleasure taken in stripping her naked on live television?), the media chose to expiate its own guilt by celebrating her idioglossic prattle as though she were the new Oscar Wilde, and treating her comprehensive ignorance as some sort of folk wisdom. Soon she was a millionaire with her own range of perfume, but now all she's famous for is the almighty stink that her spiteful attacks on Shilpa Shetty have caused. The programme that created her has now destroyed her, and the only person for whom this could possibly be good news is Bill Oddie. Why? Because finally, after thirty-five years, he's no longer the least amusing Goody on the planet.

For five years, Jade was hailed by the media as the salt of the earth, fighting the ordinary person's cause. Most of the self-proclaimed intelligentsia treated the girl from Bermondsey as their pet moron, and laughed along with her malapropisms ("why am I always the escape goat? [...] I am the fiftiest most influenzal people in the UK [...] wot's a paragus?"). They even chuckled initially over her mother's equally Prescottian way with words ("there's a lotta blood around that water is thicker than"), which is why they now sound so woefully insincere when they profess themselves to be deeply shocked that racism should have raised its ugly head.

Ch 4 LIVE AND DIRECT

Much of the media laughter was always self-protective (because most journalists are themselves only a university education or a generation away from belonging to Jade's milieu). But it was never entirely honest either, because Ms Goody is frankly not the sort of girl that anyone from *any* class would want their son to bring home. The constant public belching, farting, aggression, and gratuitous obscenity should have been clues enough that she's common in the way that Vicky Pollard is common. And now that she's been put in close proximity with a beautiful, intelligent, dignified, well-educated, and extremely polite Indian woman, is it any wonder that the racism that continually bubbles away just below the surface of our supposedly liberal society has burst into the open too?

But dismissing Jade simply as a "dimwit" (or as "a stupid woman," as Jeremy Paxman described her on Newsnight) only scratches at the surface of what's wrong with *Big Brother* in all its incarnations. A better clue came a week earlier, when Jermaine Jackson was asked to sing, and was happy to oblige. His vocal performance lasted barely a minute, but he sang beautifully and powerfully, and it stopped the housemates and viewers in their tracks, since it suddenly reminded all of us that talent is what used to be on television *all* the time, whereas on reality shows like this it's become an endangered species. He had screen presence, where Jade and her chums only have screen absence, and like Shilpa, he has somehow managed to come through the programme with his dignity intact (in as much as *anyone* who willingly signs a contract to appear on *Big Brother* can be said to have any dignity at all).

So while most viewers and media commentators prattle on about whether or not Danielle is the ringleader, or whether Jade Goody's crass remarks were racist, and what their possible effect on Anglo-Indian relations might be, I'd like to redirect the public's gaze behind the scenes, to where the blame would be far better directed. For the real *éminence grise* of this affair is Peter Bazalgette, the Endemol executive who has played the role of *Big Brother* puppeteer throughout the past seven years, and who apparently regards all the participants as his personal marionettes, to be played with and discarded at will. He must have known perfectly well that putting a sophisticated, conservative, and attractive Indian woman in a confined space with trailer trash would cause some kind of explosion, which is precisely why he did it. Like a spoilt child with a junior chemistry set, he loves pouring volatile and unstable substances into a crucible and holding it over a bunsen burner, confident that something awful is bound to happen, and that he won't be the one who has to clear up the mess afterwards (although he is currently being burned in effigy on the streets of Mumbai, which is justice of a sort).

Years ago, I met the Singing Postman (of "ave yew gotta loite

TV reviews

boy?" fame), who had once been a real postman, cheerfully delivering the mail in Suffolk. He had no real talent, but it amused the pop industry in the mid-1960s to raise this yokel shoulder high, then drop him, and by the time I spoke to him, he was alcoholic, bankrupt, and living (if that is the right word for it) in a Salvation Army hostel in Grimsby. He'd realised too late that his Faustian pact with the media had destroyed his life, and I fear that former dental nurse Jade Goody will come to a similar painful realisation over the next few months (although I doubt if she'll ever be able to pronounce "Faustian pact" correctly). Meanwhile, C4 and Endemol will eventually issue a mealy-mouthed apology, make a token act of contrition, and absolve themselves from all responsibility for this latest Big Brother debacle, having found one final use for Jade Goody: as an escape goat.

Belatedly, Channel 4 admitted that the incident had been racist, that they had covered up for further racist outbursts by Ms Goody and others, and that their response to it all had been inadequate: If you are not convinced go to link #20 on the **TV Reviews** *page on* **www.badastralbooks.com.**

Ms Goody's rise to stardom was largely due to the widespread amusement that her lack of education gave to her slightly more knowledgeable audience. According to her, Cambridge is in "East Angular," Rio de Janeiro is a person (rather than a city), and when one of the (relatively middle-class) housemates asked her to prepare asparagus to accompany her Hollandaise sauce, Jade replied "what's a paragas"?

Of course, British ignorance about food has never been confined to Ms Goody. Over the decades, television has made fitful attempts to improve our gastronomic knowledge (as opposed to simply teaching us to play with our food), and no other programme did as much to combat culinary ignorance as Good Food Live. Not only was it consistently one of the funniest programmes on British TV (as I have said in other chapters), it was also truly educational, and I cannot shout enough about what it did for daytime TV and for standards of gastronomy. (Why was the BBC unable to offer anything of similar integrity in its daytime schedules, given its much, much larger budgets?) It was, live, on the edge, flawless and, often had me on the floor.

Jeni Barnett was and still is a masterful presenter. She can be seen in action at by clicking on link #21 on the **TV Reviews** *page on* **www.badastralbooks.com.**

Ch 4 LIVE AND DIRECT

GREAT FOOD LIVE

UKTV FOOD 2007

Never mind about xylitol, tartrazine, and monosodium glutamate (or stereosodium glutamate if your equipment is fitted with a suitable stylus); when it comes to additives, can anything be less palatable than the linguistic adulterants with which tellychefs pepper their every utterance? I'm not anti-semantic (in fact, some of my best friends are words), but I'm sick to the teeth of the nonsensical phrasal verbs that they keep expecting us to swallow whole, prepositions and all. During the past few days, I've been compiling a list, and have heard such bastardisations as "caramelises out," "steam off," "bake down," "puree up," "cook out," "reduce down," and "plate up," terms exceeded in absurdity only by "stale up" (as in "I've staled this up overnight"). But this reckless addiction to adverbial particles can easily backfire, as is proved by an enlarged copy of the TV listings from a local Cumbrian newspaper that adorns my office wall, blithely announcing a programme called *Ainsly's Big Cock Out*. Really, there's no excuse for such a disgusting and offensive misprint as that. I mean, didn't the sub-editor realise that Mr Harriott's Christian name has an "e" before the "y"?

At the other end of the telly-linguistic spectrum are celebrity chefs who routinely express themselves in vulgar monosyllables. The narcissistic sellout Jamie Sainsbury (nee Oliver) and Gordon Ramsay (who used to berate TV chefs for demeaning their art, but has now become the P.T. Barnum of gastronomy) have little to offer us but their F words and, despite owning several restaurants between them, both spend so much time in TV studios that I'm frequently left wondering "who's minding the store?" Fortunately, there is an oasis of sanity between those two loathsome extremes, in the shape of *Great Food Live*, which has no time for egotistical pretensions or linguistic gimmickry, but has been quietly (and magnificently) celebrating the joys of gastronomy for the past five years on the UKTV Food channel. Unlike most food shows, which contain far too much chat and far too little cookery, it neatly reverses those proportions to create a high-quality daily programme that actually teaches you *how* to cook, rather than simply how to juggle with your food, or abuse your fellow diners.

In an age when public service values are in decline (even at the BBC), this show bucks the trend, and regular long-term viewers like me have been afforded a veritable *Larousse Gastronomique* education on the airwaves. Over the past week alone, I've learned how to cook sweetbreads

TV reviews

(not testicles, as is commonly thought, but the pancreas of a lamb or calf), and how to make your own *moutarde de meaux* from seed (thereby proving that you can cut the mustard in your own kitchen), while a master baker showed us how to bake excellent herb bread (I favour phallic-shaped rolls made from dill dough). Unlike most self-obsessed tellychefs, who seem to labour under the misapprehension that they are the dish of the day, these experts talk about the food far more than about themselves, whether introducing a novel recipe for poached chicken with artichoke puree, or explaining the tiny differences between several varieties of garlic, if that doesn't seem like splitting hares (which, incidentally, we've also learned how to do). In fact, I can only think of one food-related question that they haven't yet addressed: who was the first person to say "see that chicken over there?... I'm going to eat the next thing that pops out of its arse," and why did anyone follow his example?

Ensuring that this informative diet doesn't become too dry is presenter Jeni Barnett, whose daily presence has been central to the show's success. She has energy and pace, is extremely quick-witted, and frequently hilarious too, besides conveying great culinary knowledge. "I never have a twinkle in my eye – it's just my contact lenses," she retorted to one cheeky chef the other day, and she keeps the programme rolling effortlessly along with food-related news items freshly plucked from the morning papers, and occasional impersonations of anyone from Marilyn Monroe to Hughie Green. Nor is she remotely overawed by the medium in which she works, as she demonstrated last Friday when a guest told her that only cockroaches will survive nuclear warfare, and would then start to evolve. "Yes," she replied, "they'll evolve into television executives." I couldn't agree more.

Great Food Live has been easily the best daytime programme on British television over the past five years, and it is now receiving its reward by being taken off air for good at the end of next week by some cretinous half-man-half-desk. Meanwhile, pale imitations like *Saturday Cooks* and *Saturday Kitchen* remain. It's a disgrace, and I'm amazed that someone in terrestrial TV hasn't stepped in to transfer the entire show to become the centrepiece of their weekday morning schedule, because it has a large and loyal following (an estimated million viewers each week, which is impressive for *any* show on a digital channel), and because it has helped to educate culinary neophytes like me (who once used their smoke alarms as egg timers) to appreciate gastronomy as an art form, rather than as a branch of Light Entertainment. It's also taught me that food is central to all human existence, a lesson I first learned from the late Fanny Cradock, who emphasised this point to me with a wise old saying. "Give a man a fish," she told me, "and he will eat for a day. Teach a man *how* to fish, and he will sit in a boat all day and get pissed out of his head on strong lager." I *think* that's what she said, but I'd been on eight pints of Special Brew at the time, so I'm still not quite sure.

As often happens on British television, after several years of consistent excellence, the programme was axed by a new channel controller who was anxious to make his mark. The replacement was pisspoor when it started, and only got slightly better over the years by shamelessly plagiarising more and more aspects of the format and content of the show it had replaced.

MARKET KITCHEN

UKTV FOOD 2007

Hello and welcome to our exciting new TV game show, *Nepotism!* It's a sort of media *Happy Families*, where contestants score one point for a pair (Julia and Nadia Sawalha, Paul and Stella McCartney), two points for a trio (Nigel, Nigella, and Dominic Lawson; Richard, David, and Jonathan Dimbleby), three points for "four of a kind" (Emma, Clement, Esther, and Matthew Freud), and a whopping five points for a full house (the dozens of Rosses, say, or the army of Redgraves). The Corens (Alan, Giles, and Victoria) are particularly easy to collect, because they're often found in the same newspaper, but remember – Edward Windsor doesn't count as part of a set because, despite his family connections, he's never been able to get his media career off the ground. Probably because he comes from a family so dysfunctional that his brother Prince Charles can be Head of the Church of England, despite having admitted adultery, yet still insist that his sons be confirmed, which means that (just like their parents) William and Harry must obey the Nine Commandments.

The Princess Consort (a name which I always think sounds like an old banger from the 1940s) has a son, Tom Parker Bowles, who has also eased his way into a lucrative media career. He's currently one of four hosts of UKTV Food's new daily show, *Market Kitchen*, and alternates with another well-connected presenter, the photogenic but wooden Tana Ramsay (so ligneous that she should be sponsored by Cuprinol), who spent much of the first week referring unashamedly to her famous husband Gordon (the millionaire chef whose complexion suggests that he must have sneezed years ago, while someone was cutting his hair). Some may suggest that she too owes her position to nepotism, but not me, because I recently read her cookbook *Family Kitchen*, which expertly teaches us how to make all manner of exciting new dishes. For example, there's one recipe for canned

TV reviews

peaches and ice cream (open a can of peaches, then add some ice cream), and another for the "full English breakfast" (fry sausages, then eggs), and the advice is perfect in all respects except one. It's bloody hard to swallow.

When Optomen Television won the contract to produce a daily programme (replacing the long-running and highly-regarded *Great Food Live*), their press release promised to broadcast from Borough Market. The titles suggest that is what's happening, but it's not, because the show is actually recorded miles away in Kentish Town, in a studio disguised as a "Borough Market-style cafe," with only a couple of brief genuine inserts from Borough as a fig leaf (available from the Mediterranean vegetable stall) to cover this naked subterfuge. On Friday night's show, co-presenter Matt Tebbutt didn't inspire much confidence when he seemed unsure what suet is (it's not just "grated animal fat," it's specifically the hard waxy fat found around the kidneys), and repeatedly pronounced "restaurateur" with an "n" in it, but he was leagues ahead of Ms Ramsay, who simply cannot read an autocue with even a hint of naturalness. Indeed, her general demeanour is reminiscent of Lady Penelope from *Thunderbirds*, her voice as monotonal as the "Mind the Gap" message at Bank station, and her producers must already know that well-connected though she may be, she's simply not up to the job.

Where *Great Food Live* dealt knowledgeably and naturally with its subject, this show is as forced and stilted as a 1980s' edition of *Food and Drink*. Weak editorial ideas (such as the wearily overdone "is bottled water a con?") weren't thought through, leading to absurd suggestions that all tap water is heavily chlorinated (often true in cities, seldom in the countryside), while the food-tastings recalled the feeble starved vocabulary of Chris Kelly, relying on such empty adjectives as "amazing," "really nice," and "mmm, that's delicious." As for a competition to make the best steamed pudding, one can only despair at such witless interchanges as "I'm making spotted dick," "I'll try not to smile at that," and the pointless Closing Generation Game-style "can you fillet a fish in two minutes?" contest suggested desperation at how to fill the hour. The fish in question, incidentally, was brill, but the programme was anything but.

Given that the best food programme of the decade was axed to make way for *Market Kitchen*, the decision so far seems disastrously misguided. The show looks hastily made (I'm told they record five in two days), the location cameras are "hot" (over-exposed), the editing is appalling, the approach is far too London-centric, the prompted questions from members of the public serve no purpose, and the scores of negative postings on UKTV Food's message boards suggest that the channel has made a very serious mistake indeed. The only time the studio crackled briefly into life was when Matt asked Tana to prick his lemon, and a definite sexual frisson could be detected between them, not that Tana would ever stray from her husband, despite his self-confessed low sperm count. Although, whenever I see Gordon Ramsay flogging his lacklustre F-word routine on the telly, it amazes me to think that, of ten million sperm, he was the quickest.

During the period that Max Hastings edited the Evening Standard, it surprised and delighted me that I was allowed pretty-well free rein to condemn and criticise the British Establishment in my columns. When he was about to join the paper, I checked him out in Who's Who and concluded that I would soon have to make a principled resignation from the paper (probably minutes after he sacked me). In fact, he turned out to be one of the best editors I've worked with (up there with the unjustly maligned Piers Morgan). Although he's something of a High Tory by nature, he was wise enough to understand that a Metropolitan audience had a different outlook on Royalty and the British Establishment from his own, and the newspaper flourished under his aegis.

As he's now Sir Max Hastings, I presume that he approves of the royal family and all the palaver that goes with monarchy, including military parades. But to his credit, he never changed a word of the abuse that I used to regularly hurl in the direction of Buckingham Palace.

*The 2006 Trooping the Colour ceremony can be seen atby clicking on link #22 on the **TV Reviews** page on **www.badastralbooks.com.***

Or you can read about it on the following pages.

TROOPING THE COLOUR

BBC1 BBC2 2007

We debated many issues at the annual Siamese Twin convention in Hove and Brighton last week. Whether to modernise the name ("Thai Twins"), whether to pilot an exchange scheme for British and American twins (so the other one can have a go at driving), and whether to expand our society's interests to include lexicographical Siamese Twins, those curious pairs of words where one can exist only when attached to the other: "halcyon" (days), "squally" (showers), "pyrrhic" (victory),

TV reviews

"betwixt" (between), "fettle" (fine), and "extolled" (virtues). Regrettably, a heated debate amongst delegates as to whether "ill" and "behoves" constituted an acceptable pairing soon degenerated into a brawl, punches were thrown, and a hot-headed Siamese twin from Texas pulled out a gun and fatally wounded an opposing speaker. He then fled back to the US, but was arrested at Houston airport and charged with murder, leaving the judge there with yet another philosophical conundrum: if he's found guilty and sent to the electric chair, must the innocent twin fry with him?

I detected several Siamese twins ("serried ranks" being the most prominent) during BBC1's live coverage of *Trooping the Colour*, along with a couple of archaic and pompous clichés of the type contemptuously referred to by the grammarian Fowler as "battered ornaments." BBC commentaries on state occasions have always employed a quaint vocabulary seldom encountered elsewhere (epitomised by Richard Dimbleby during the 1953 Coronation, with "Her Majesty's Colobium Sindonis resplendent with the lambent magnificence as two pursuivants take seisin of her dominion"). But on Saturday morning, Huw Edwards did at least make some attempt to tone down the phatic pointlessness of the regal lexicon, and to address viewers in a language reasonably close to English. "This is a birthday parade unlike any other since the end of WWII," he told us from an overcast Horseguards Parade, explaining that (for the first time in 60 years) *every* single guards regiment and battalion that this nation possesses is tied up in Middle Eastern wars, and that the 1,700 troops on display would all soon be back in Basra or Helmand, being shot at by grateful residents. As Tony B Liar looked on, he must have felt a swell of pride at this official acknowledgement that he's started more wars than any other Prime Minister in our history, thereby ensuring that (even though he'll be gone within days) his legacy will be with us for many many years to come.

Although the ritual of the military spectacle varies little from year to year, the cast of royal onlookers does, so it was on them that my attention was mainly focused. Amongst the Windsors that I could tick off in my *I-Spy Book of Human Battered Ornaments* were the fast-balding Prince William, the feckless Prince Andrew, his horse-faced sister Anne (reportedly seeking yet another divorce), and I even caught glimpses of Prince Charles and the Duchess of Cornwall, whose nickname – given that her husband has expressed a desire to reincarnate as her sanitary towel – ought to be "Cammy the Tammy" (okay, I know that a sanitary towel is worn outside, whereas a tampon is worn inside, but who's splitting hairs?). As the bearskins of the Streamingcold Guards marched past in close formation (like military Tiller Girls performing a Busby Berkeley routine), the Queen and Prince Philip drove by in their traditional phaeton,

Ch 4 LIVE AND DIRECT

rather than the high-roofed Rolls Royce in which they're more frequently seen. You know, the one that (as I may have mentioned before) looks like a hearse designed to accommodate vertical coffins, and always makes a satisfying sound as it crunches on the grovel. Sorry, gravel. No, on second thoughts, I was right first time.

As Her Majesty took the salute, Prince Philip looked up and grimaced at the inclement weather. Or perhaps he was recalling that stormy period of his life in Germany in the years before WWII, when he was living with his high-ranking Nazi brother-in-law Christoph von Hessen-Kassel, and being educated in the Hitler youth curriculum, a period we're not supposed even to know about in this country, and which is repeatedly airbrushed out of the sanitised patriotic version of royal history that the British are expected to swallow. And swallow it many of them do, thanks to colourful ceremonies like this, which encourage the gullible to wave their Union Flags, stand to attention for the National Anthem, learn nothing from history, and join the Great Forgetting. Thus do we perpetuate the image of this kingdom as a modern-day Ruritania, obsessed with fossilised tradition, while the silent transformation of this once-independent country into America Junior draws ever closer to completion.

For years I've complained that this ceremony is mendaciously named, because one seldom sees a single person of colour amongst row after row of uniformly white troops. However, this year, the screen kept displaying what at first sight looked like an admirably fine example of full multicultural integration; but closer inspection revealed that there was only a tiny handful of black soldiers amongst the 1,700 whites, and that this meagre smattering was being repeatedly picked out by the cameras for close-ups. Was the BBC director ordered to do this, I wonder, and if so, by whom was he instructed? Or perhaps it was all a simple mistake, like the birthday honour I received in the post at the weekend from HRH. A Siamese twin of an honour it was, because she'd made me both an Earl *and* an OBE. So from now on, you will now curtsey and refer to me as an *Earlobe*.

I watched the most recent Trooping the Colour only a matter of days ago, and there's been no change at all. It's still a misnomer, because there's still row upon row of white faces with seldom a person of colour to be seen, and Prince Philip was still grimacing.

And now to other issues of black and white (and colour).

TV reviews

TEST CARD

SKY ARTS HD 2007

Long long ago, back in the days when I was a radio producer, I was once in charge of the live broadcast of a one-act "avant-garde" opera. During the performance (which sounded uncannily like a fire in a pet shop), I sneezed in the control booth and accidentally pressed a button, whereupon a tape of François Couperin's "Le Tic-Toc-Choc" roared out through the tannoy at 130 dBA into the concert hall, blaring on for a full five seconds until I managed to switch it off again. Afterwards, as the audience were leaving, I eavesdropped on their conversations, and heard someone clearly say "wasn't the moment with the baroque harpsichord exquisite? A masterstroke... perfectly timed... it said so much." Which I confess caused me to lose what faith I'd ever had in experimental art of all descriptions, and even to rebel against it by starting to draw pairs of cubes on the lavatory walls of art galleries, accompanied by the legend "balls to Picasso."

Much to the chagrin of the critics (though what the hell do they know about anything?), the best-known and best-appreciated pieces of twentieth-century art aren't avant-garde at all. No, they're the functional design classics that we all take for granted in our everyday lives, like Harry Beck's inspired map of the London Underground, or George Hersee's Television Test Card F, which has been viewed by far more people than anything hanging on the walls of Tate Modern. In these days of twenty-four-hour broadcasting, Test Card F seldom gets aired by the BBC, but we all still instantly recognise the sight of George's daughter Carol playing noughts and crosses with Bubbles the Clown, in the centre of a geometric design that once enabled engineers to check the grey scale, linearity, ghosting, frequency response, corner focus, chrominance and luminance delay error, static, and convergence in the central screen area. Who can forget the anticipation felt while watching it, as we waited patiently for the real programmes to begin? Or the famous afternoon in 1966 when BBC1's transmission of the Test Card drew higher ratings than Election Special over on BBC2?

Test Card F may be rarely seen nowadays, but the Test Card tradition has just been revived on the Sky Arts High Definition channel. And when I tuned in recently, there was classical pianist and star of *The Vagina Monologues* Myleene Klass, seated by the blackboard next to a simulacrum Bubbles, and even dressed in the same headband and frock, though with considerably more cleavage on show than was ever the case with the eight-year-old Ms Hersee. As a child, I was convinced that the Test Card was actually a live broadcast (with director, camera crew, and full orchestra conducted by Eric Coates), and that if I waited long enough, I'd eventually see the moment when they all stopped for a break, and blow me down, that's just what happened here. Because the camera suddenly zoomed in through the central circle, whereupon Ms Klass pulled off the headband, said "thanks boys, I was feeling a little bit too retro there," and started telling us how to adjust the settings on our widescreen HD sets to the 16x9 aspect ratio (introduced especially so that Vanessa Feltz could finally fit inside the screen).

As the tutorial got underway, she and her two gormless assistants (named H and D) showed us how to alter the factory defaults, to conform to the Sky system. Apparently, there should be 1080 lines on the screen, while the Dolby Digital 5.1 Surround Sound needs an HDMI cable for full aural satisfaction, and it was fascinating to see and hear what the pictures and sound would be like if your system was incorrectly wired (although, of course, you could only appreciate the demonstration of errors if your system was set up correctly in the first place). Despite Myleene's frequent exhortations to look at the circles and rectangles in the corners of the screen, I found it hard to tear my eyes away from her tits, so I closed my eyes and thought back to the first programme I ever saw in High Definition. It was the *Trooping of the Colour*, a mendacious name if ever there was one, because the HD screen allowed me to peruse every single one of the hundreds of faces in the regiments, and I failed to notice a single person of colour amongst the row after row of uniformly white troops.

At the end of the demonstration, Myleene resumed her stationary game of noughts and crosses with Bubbles, to the accompaniment of suitable light music. For a gentleman of a certain age, her Test Card is a more satisfying watch than Carol's Test Card F could ever be, but to tell the truth, what I like most about High Definition isn't that it faithfully reproduces female beauty, but that it faithfully reproduces every line and wrinkle on every jumped-up telly celebrity with such stunning accuracy that even the make-up plastered over the time-ravaged faces of older broadcasters is mercilessly visible to viewers. In fact, the best reason for its introduction is that Terry Wigon will never cross over to any HD channel, for fear that everyone will be able to spot the line of his expensive rug, which is just about good enough to avoid immediate detection on 625 lines. Which wasn't the case with 60s Bonanza star Lorne Greene, whose syrup was so unconvincing that it could be spotted even in the days of 405 lines. So much so that he should have had his own show, called *Lorne's Lawn*.

TV reviews

If your organs of nostalgia were aroused by that review, you might like to relive the glorious days of the Test Card (F) and Music from 1978, which you can do by clicking on link #23 on the **TV Reviews** page on **www.badastralbooks.com**.

Or how about this 40th anniversary tribute to Carol Hersee (with a written interview) at, which can be viewed by clicking on link #24 on the **TV Reviews** page on **www.badastralbooks.com**.

Although I never claimed to be infallible as a television critic, readers naturally drew comparisons between me and the current Pope. Not because I was ever a member of the Hitler Youth though, dear me no. I'd like to scotch that rumour here and now, once and for all. No, it's probably because the appointment of a new television critic at the Evening Standard was traditionally announced by a puff of white smoke, emerging from the chimney tops of Northcliffe House.

Here's the white smoke that signalled the appointment of Joseph Ratzinger to the top job, and his first speech as Pope, which can bee seen by clicking on link #25 on the **TV Reviews** page on **www.badastralbooks.com**.

THE INAUGURATION OF POPE BENEDICT XVI

BBC 2005

We're barely halfway through the election campaign, yet already the nation is bored witless by the empty rhetoric of the ineluctably unelectable. "Racism is just a pigment of the imagination," says Grey Party #1, while Grey Party #2 tours the country stirring up apathy, so clearly it's time for my own organisation, The Dinner Party (motto "we drink as we dress – Chablis"), to come to the country's rescue with some fresh thinking. Just last night, over a case or two (each) of Chateau Musar, we devised a foolproof way to alleviate the plight of the homeless, after discovering a loophole in the current electoral system. Apparently, there's no time limit on voting once a constituent has entered the polling station, so a homeless person can enter a cubicle and stay there for weeks, months, even years, shooing away impertinent scrutineers by telling them "I am exercising my democratic right, and I have not yet made up my mind which candidate to vote for." That way, society gets all the homeless off the streets for good, and compared to a cardboard box in a rainswept shop doorway, what vagrant wouldn't prefer a nice cosy voting booth of their own?

Lamentable though our democratic system of choosing leaders might be, I suppose it's marginally preferable to the theocratic methods still in favour at the Vatican. Such is the secrecy enveloping the selection of a new Pope that perhaps the ultra-conservative Joseph Ratzinger simply picked the lucky raffle ticket from a tombola drum, yet a billion Catholics worldwide now have to pretend that his appointment was divinely ordained, and feign delight that God's Rottweiler has become their German Shepherd. Why the "Panzer Pope" was chosen has baffled many commentators, especially as he's pushing eighty and looks decidedly frail, but watching *The Inauguration of Pope Benedict XVI* on BBC1 yesterday morning, I realised that the cardinals who voted for him were perhaps wilier than they first appeared. Because after a decade in which every media story about the Catholic Church has revolved around corruption and paedophile priests, they've suddenly had an entire month of undilutedly reverential coverage on television (as the demise of John Paul II gave way to his lying in state, then the election and inauguration); and if this new Pope goes tits up in a few weeks, they'll soon be enjoying another month of uncritically positive reporting, all over again.

"Benedict XVI is the oldest man to be elected since 1730," said Huw Edwards, greeting us from a studio next door to the Sistine Chapel (Seventeen Chapel, I suppose). And I wondered if perhaps the Match of the Day production team had inadvertently been put in charge of the coverage, because the presenter had been provided with a trio of Big Ron-style pundits to discuss form and tactics ahead of the big event, including the news that the cardinals wouldn't be wearing their familiar all-red strip, but their reserve colours of gold and white (well, they were mostly playing away from home). As a close-up of the Pope's new Fisherman's Ring revealed that it looked alarmingly like the Bling Ring in the current Argos catalogue (page 16, no. 22, cat. no. 232/2566, £9.99), the choir sang "pax vobiscum" and St Peter's Basilica was seen in its full glory, with catamites hanging down from the ceiling. Or is it acolytes that hang down, and stalactites that go up? I can never remember, but I do know that I once got it badly wrong during a guided tour of Rome, and a member of the Swiss Guard threatened to put 18 inches of steel right up me.

The BBC love huge public spectacles of pomp and ceremony, because they get to film a cast of thousands for the cost of a couple of camera crews, and once the inauguration was underway, the tone moved fluently into extreme unctuousness. Visually, the scene resembled a cross

TV reviews

between the Papal fashion show in Fellini's *Roma* and a pop-up *Book of Kells*, while the commentary degenerated into the hushed, phatic, and grandiloquent Corporation-speak known as Dimblebore, as devised by Richard Dimbleby for the 1953 Coronation. "The investiture of the pallium with three ceremonial pins...," whispered Edwards, "he has venerated the altar and incensed it," and I too felt incensed as I thought of the cruel words that have been written about this Pope, just because he was once in the Hitler Youth. So what? The entire Vatican (under Pope Pius XII) actively aided Hitler during the 1930s, so why should he have been any different? A point I trust that Prince Philip (who attended the ceremony, and whose own family included many Nazi sympathisers) made to the Pontiff after the show.

"He's a very humble man... with a deep spiritual faith" said one of the pundits, as though the day might ever dawn when they'd say "this new Pope is a very arrogant man who thinks transubstantiation is a load of superstitious nonsense." And I longed for the days of Pope Victor IV, an alcoholic anti-Pontiff who spectacularly managed to overthrow *himself* in 1138, and is surely just the sort of charismatic telegenic figure that's needed to revitalise the Catholic Church's fortunes. Actually, the logical thing for the Vatican to have done would surely have been to keep the embalmed dead John Paul II in power (thereby getting a direct broadband connection to God), but I suppose it's none of my business whom they choose, because I have no time for spiritual leaders of any faith. Except one. Gandhi. Now *there* was a leader. Apparently, he once walked barefoot across India, subsisting solely upon foul-smelling cacti. Or, to quote the now-thankfully-mute Julie Andrews, he was a super-calloused-fragile-mystic-plagued-with-halitosis.

During his reign so far, the Catholic Church has been exposed as perhaps the most prolific organisation of paedophiles in modern times, and is facing class action law suits around the world from abuse victims that could potentially run into many billions of dollars. So he must be very glad he got the job, considering that it's all turned out so well.

Back in 1983, when I bought my Sperry Rand typewriter, the only hi-tech problem I encountered was aligning the two-colour ribbon correctly on its spools, so that the letter O didn't have a red bottom. Apart from that, it was faultless, and even rewarded me with a Pavlovian ding of its carriage return bell as I completed each line of type, and I often reminisce about the elegant simplicity of its keyboard, especially the pristine @ key. Back in those days, the humble @ sign was seldom used (except by ironmongers, who'd scribble "60 widget bolts @ 6d per dozen = 2/6d" onto invoices with a freshly-licked indelible pencil), but the rise of e-mail has turned it into the most worn-out key on PCs across the planet, yet incredibly, there's still no agreement about its name. English speakers call it the "at," the Danes call it "snabel" (elephant's trunk), the Koreans "dalphaengi" (snail), the Czechs "zavinac" (rollmop), the Hungarians "kukac" (worm), the Turks "kulak" (ear), and in colloquial Portuguese it's "furo da senhora," which is far too filthy to translate here. So let's just call it tw@.

*Tw@.con would serve as an excellent email address for Terry Wogan. Here he is, messing up as he announces the winner of the BBC's 2007 Making Your Mind Up competition to find a UK entrant for the Eurovision contest: just click bon link #26 on the **TV Reviews** page on **www.badastralbooks.com**.*

*And here's a news report, finally announcing that Terry Wogan would be replaced by Graham Norton for the 2009 contest, which can be seen by clicking on link #27 on the **TV Reviews** page on **www.badastralbooks.com**.*

Some of the best radio that I've ever watched has been on the television – now that dozens of radio channels can be received via satellite and cable TV. Yes, I know that I said "watched" and not "listened to." That's because, as the old cliché has it, on radio, you make your own pictures. Although I'm not sure how true that saying really is. I tried it once, making my own pictures during a football commentary on Five Live, and frankly it was a disaster. I'd only just finished my first drawing of both teams and the goalposts (that netting is a bugger to draw), and was still colouring in the faces of the crowds, when the referee blew for half time. It was a farce. No, I have to admit it, the pictures are much better on the telly than on the radio. The music, however, is far better on the radio, especially late night on Radio 3.

LATE JUNCTION
BBC RADIO 3 2006

Notwithstanding Thomas Beecham's celebrated "riposte" when asked if he'd ever conducted any of Stockhausen's music ("no, but I've trodden in some"), it would be crass to describe all modern atonal music as sounding like an aural assault on the audience. Equally, it's absurd for high-minded academics to dismiss all melodic tonal composers as irrelevant anachronisms, yet that's what happened to the great Sir Malcolm Arnold throughout his most creative years. This week's obituaries may have been fulsome in their praise, but for decades he was ignored

TV reviews

by the musical establishment (especially Radio 3 controllers, such as the uncompromisingly modernist William Glock and the appallingly pompous "Lady" John Drummond), simply because he chose to express himself in an accessible and tuneful style. Which reminds me. Sir Malcolm Arnold, Sir Edward Elgar, Sir William Walton, Sir Michael Tippett, but *Lord* Lloyd Webber. What's *that* all about?

Fortunately, Drummond is long since gone, and our nation's premier classical music station is no longer in thrall to a narrow-minded, self-publicising, bitter and twisted old queen (don't worry, *Evening Standard* lawyers – he snuffed it earlier this month, and you can't libel the dead). Indeed, as the *Third Programme* celebrates its sixtieth anniversary, it's never sounded more all-inclusive in its tastes or more confident in its purpose, especially at night when the mesmerisingly eclectic *Late Junction* takes to the air. Superb quality digital radio has been available for some time to satellite television subscribers, and given the increasingly infantile fare pumped out after the watershed by most of the TV channels, I frequently take refuge in this consistently ear-opening programme, which celebrates music from around the world, with soupçons of jazz, mediaeval, and modern classical thrown into the mix. And because I'm a TV critic, I remember the old adage that "on radio, you make your own pictures," and conscientiously sketch a drawing of whatever I'm listening to, which is easy enough when they're playing music for solo Chinese nose flute, but completely exhausted my supply of charcoal pencils on the night they programmed Mahler's Symphony for a Thousand.

The programme succeeds because its producers and presenters are blessed with excellent taste (mine), and aren't afraid to juxtapose great complexity with utter simplicity. So the edition I listened to yesterday (using the Play Again facility on the BBC's website) was happy to place the Brad Mehidau Trio's intricately chromatic jazz piano piece "Alvarado" immediately after Moondog's charmingly repetitive "Wine, Woman and Song" (composed, like many of his madrigals, as a harmonically static round). There was plenty of North European folk music too, including the strident fiddles of JPP (Finland's premier folk band) performing "Järvelä: Köyrinkulma," and I was surprised by how Celtic their traditional music sounded, mainly because the only time I visited the country, the entire population was playing nothing but tango. Although that was admittedly because Helsinki's legendary tango singer, Sauli Lehtonen, had been killed the previous day in a car crash, when (I kid you not) a full-grown elk flipped onto his roof and crushed him. The poor man was really Finnished.

Linked by Verity Sharp's well-informed and huskily-delivered presentation, new releases mingled with archive recordings. A short piece by Davy Graham confirmed why he is now hailed as the pioneering founder of the English folk guitar style, while two soberly titled "Studies for Electric Guitar" by Leo Abrahams displayed an atmospherically original approach to the instrument that often disguised its plucked-string nature. Only the traditional English folk singing failed to delight me, with Lisa Knapp sounding like Bjork on Prozac, and others (whom I shall not name) performing with the sort of Mummersetshire accents beloved of RADA-trained yokels on *The Archers*. Sorry, but something inside me rebels when I encounter middle-class city dwellers in knitted sweaters (with knitted beer guts to match) sticking their fingers in their ears and singing about their poor-but-honest lives as ploughmen or blacksmiths, thereby confirming the widespread urban prejudice about rural people: that they're amusingly unsophisticated and... well... ever-so-slightly simple.

Late Junction is Radio 3 at its best, and much of the credit for its existence must go to the current controller Roger Wright. He's steered a sure path between those siren voices who wanted the station to chase ratings by imitating the bland and unthreatening play lists of Classic FM, and the tiny band of elitists who'd rather that the riff-raff didn't tune in at all, and has thus ensured that R3 (which officially celebrates its sixtieth birthday on Friday) remains a vital part of our national cultural life. As long as TV channels keep churning out a late-night diet of prurient chat shows, crappy porn, and mindless screaming celebrity chefs, I'll keep listening to this gem of a programme. And talking of gems, a haunting Rajasthani folk tune suddenly reminded me of Maharaj Ji, the Indian boy guru with allegedly miraculous powers who came to the West in the early 70s, and developed a great fondness for jewels and gold watches. On one occasion he was even arrested at an airport by customs officials, who reportedly discovered $200,000 of diamonds in his robes, but was he nonplussed? Not a bit of it. "It's another miracle," he declared, and I have to admit, that's chutzpah. But unfortunately for him, it was also smuggling.

I had a few running gags that I used as annual markers during my years with the Standard. Every 5 November, I would remind my readers to put the sprouts on to boil now, so they'd be ready for Christmas dinner. Every Mothering Sunday, I would promote my own rival service of "Smothering Sunday," in which my crack team would arrive at the homes of troublesome infants and smother them with pillows. And once a year, I would play the following trick on psychics.

We supposedly live nowadays in an enlightened and rational society, so why (I would ask) does television stuff its schedules with pseudo-scientific claptrap like haunted houses, astrology, and messages from beyond the grave? Allegedly adult slots seem increasingly obsessed with this infantile stuff, especially on the digital channels, most of it fronted by furtive presenters who insist on telling

TV reviews

us that they're blessed with a sixth sense, but behave as though they've taken leave of the other five. Of course, if you ask them to peer into the future and come up with something that would be genuinely useful to humanity (a cure for cancer, say, or next week's lottery numbers), all you'll get are blank looks, so to demonstrate beyond doubt that believing in ghosts is a load of old ghoulies, I have placed the following advertisement in the Psychic Times: "Millionaire wishes to hire telepath. Will pay £5,000 per day. If you're genuine, you'll know where to apply." Strangely, I've still not had a single reply.

If you've never seen Your Destiny TV, then enlighten yourself by clicking on link #28 on the **TV Reviews** page on **www.badastralbooks.com**.

Furthermore, Mystic Vic predicts that, within minutes, you will fall into a deep deep sleep. Spooky or what?

Along with shopping channels, rolling news channels are the places where just about every broadcast is always live. You might think that having to produce twenty-four hours of live output each day would result in a stream of drivel, and you would be right. Perhaps 9/11 was a legitimate day for extended live news coverage, but little else can justify it.

Most loathsome of all the rolling news channels is Fox News, a Mecca for people who hate Mecca. And perhaps the most loathsome (yet comical) of all their presenters is Bill O'Reilly.

A video of him (made by people who, to be fair, don't think very highly of him) can be seen by clicking on link #29 on the **TV Reviews** page on **www.badastralbooks.com**.

THE O'REILLY FACTOR
FOX NEWS 2005

What with Tony B Liar having no identifiable policies and having lost all trust, Michael Howard having lost the plot, and Robert Kilroy-Silk having fallen flat on his Veritas, I suppose it's up to Vic to lead the nation out of crisis at the next election. That's why I've formed the Dinner Party, whose principles have been carefully drafted during drunken evenings at some of London's premier restaurants, and whose motto is the simple effective: "eschew obfuscation." Our policies are clear. If elected, NHS hospitals will no longer give artificial respiration to patients, they'll give *real* respiration. Millions will be invested in scientific research, to discover where your lap goes to when you stand up. Expensive Brillo pads will be replaced with cheaper alternatives, by injecting pink soap into Shredded Wheats. And we'll deal firmly with the two issues that most concern the electorate, the soaring crime rate and the terrible state of the roads. How? By retrospectively bringing back capital punishment (thereby allowing us to hang the corpses of people we missed out on, like Hindley and West), then cremating their remains and using the ashes to fill in the pot holes in the road.

If the Dinner Party isn't swept into government here, I'm thinking of setting up branches in heartland Middle America, because those Bible Belt states clearly have a highly developed sense of irony. They must have, because not only have they just re-elected a Global Village Idiot to the White House (to the horror of everyone on the East and West coasts), but their favourite current affairs programme is a long-running satirical spoof called *The O'Reilly Factor*, shown nightly on the Fox News channel and available here on satellite and cable. In case you haven't seen this hilarious high-rating show, it's best described as a parody of television news in the tradition of *The Day Today*, lampooning the excesses of the extreme far-right shock-jock style of broadcasting by claiming that its blatantly prejudiced output is "real journalism, fair and balanced." And its star is the unnamed actor who plays the central character of Bill O'Reilly, a xenophobic Archie Bunker-esque loudmouth who insults any "liberals" that venture into the studio, whose ignorance about the outside world is matched only by his belligerence towards it, and who generally behaves like an anchorman with a capital W.

Last night's edition was classic O'Reilly, with the host welcoming us into a "no-spin zone" where the surreal distortion of reality was worthy of Orwell's Ministry of Truth. The Iraq war was top story, with O'Reilly ridiculing Senator Kennedy's call for the US "to start working with other countries" as "nonsense... that would be a disaster," then reducing the complexities of the Middle East to the idiotic jingoism of "these terrorists are Nazis who kill for sport in the name of God." When a "liberal journalist" complained to him that "you insult people," O'Reilly retorted (with perfect comedic timing and a straight face) that he'd never ever done any such thing, even though gratuitous rudeness is his broadcasting trademark, and (last time I watched the show) he called President Chirac "a loathsome weasel." Still, unfamiliarity with the truth is what makes this comic creation so

TV reviews

endearing, as he proved recently when he told viewers that Saddam had been responsible for 9/11, and that America had won the Vietnam War.

Of course, any comedy genius needs a great supporting cast, and O'Reilly is fortunate to have amassed such a fine repertory company of gifted mimics and character actors. From the staring Midwich Cuckoo who read the spoof news items ("McDonalds may be encouraging children to eat fattening foods"), to the televangelist who claimed that "millions of Muslims have never heard of Jesus Christ" (even though Christ is revered by Muslims as a prophet of God), every red-necked imbecility was perfectly understated, so much so that at times you almost felt you were watching a *genuine* news programme. Inevitably, the writers did sometimes overstep the bounds of good taste – such as when they asserted that the colleagues of a psychologically-ill woman (who'd tragically killed herself and her baby) were immoral because they wanted to erect a memorial to her – but offence is bound to be caused from time to time, when you're producing dangerous ground-breaking comedy like this. And anyway, having one's sensibilities affronted now and then is good for you. It's like having a thorough physical workout, and personally, I try to be outraged at least five times each day, just for reasons of health.

Okay. By satirising the far right so mercilessly, the writers and performers of this show reveal themselves to be unrepentant liberals. But as with Alan Partridge, they've created a true comedy original with great depth of character, so much so that they even ran a storyline a few months ago in which O'Reilly, the moralising (and married) presenter was revealed to have been making obscene phone calls to an unwilling and deeply disgusted female employee. They even created a tape of these calls, in which he talked lasciviously to her about masturbating himself with a vibrator while fantasising about doing something to her in the shower with a loofah, a tape that cleverly reveals O'Reilly as an utter hypocrite, because he mercilessly pursued Clinton over his own sexual foibles. Still, I suppose O'Reilly could always claim that he was simply the innocent victim of a vast right-hand conspiracy. Long may his comedic genius be with us.

A further irony for those who are interested. Mr O'Reilly was one of President Clinton's fiercest critics over the Monica Lewinsky affair, claiming that "having sex in the workplace makes it impossible for anyone to maintain their post." Curiously, when it emerged a few years ago that Mr O'Reilly had allegedly been making very lewd (recorded) phone calls to a female producer of his show, and describing how he would like to pleasure her with a loofah while they were in the shower together, he (and his employers) decided that sex in the workplace was not a resigning matter after all.

Fox loudly proclaims the values of the Christian far right, and the next review deals with the views of fundamentalists, the sort of people who believe that the Bible stories about the serpent in the Garden of Eden, and the animals in Noah's ark, were literally true. Over the years, I became increasingly irritated by the absurd animal myths that were being promulgated by television, so I decided it was time that somebody dispelled these fables, and after mammoth research at my local library (don't ask me why they're employing mammoths as researchers there – it must be some government retraining scheme), I can now tell you the unvarnished truth about our fellow creatures. For a start, crocodiles don't shed tears while they're devouring their prey (unless they're chomping on raw onions, I suppose), lemmings don't deliberately commit suicide by jumping off cliffs, and mules are generally rather docile beasts, not at all stubborn. As for dogs being man's best friend, that legend also deserves to become as dead as a dodo, because what canine in its right mind would want to be the best friend of someone who'd just lopped its balls off without permission? Dodos, by the way, actually are dead. That much is true.

*Ostriches do not bury their heads in the sand either, only their eggs, but it must be admitted that there are plenty of human ostriches in the world of religious TV. All of which finally leads me into this review of one of the most pernicious of all religious TV channels, run by Rory and Wendy Alec who can be seen discussing Armageddon prophecies and the Apocalypse if by clicking on link #30 on the **TV Reviews** page on **www.badastralbooks.com**.*

Sounds quite nasty. Still, it's not the end of the world.

GOD TV

SKY 671 2005

I continue to receive letters by the millions (Mr & Mrs Frank Millions of Crouch End), postulating that people with two Christian names and no surname are inherently dodgy. Look at the evidence, they say: Dean Martin (drunk), Ben Elton ("socialist" who consorts with Lords), Elton John (dodgy hair hat), Barry Norman (miserable sod), the end is listless. And I

TV reviews

can add others, such as Tony "shot in the dark" Martin, Barry "I don't like Mondays" George, and Craig Charles, whom I regard as dodgy not because he was once arrested on rape charges (mercifully, he was acquitted of those), but because he once threatened to put me "straight through a plate glass window" after I'd reviewed one of his programmes. From Clive James and Paul Simon to Cliff Richard and Russell Grant, such people are clearly over-compensating in adult life for the childhood trauma of not having a proper surname, which reminds me that the US actor Timothy Bottoms has apparently decided to change *his* highly embarrassing name. From now on, he wishes to be known as Tim Bottoms.

Top of my list are Rory and Wendy Alec, two dodgy Christians, each with two Christian names. Back in 1993, the Lord revealed to these South African Smart Alecs that there's a hell of a lot of dosh to be made from Heavenly broadcasting, and two years later they moved to the UK to found God TV, Europe's first Christian television channel. The pair originally broadcast their shrill evangelical gospel from Tyneside and Wearside, but left Britain four years ago after the ITC rebuked the channel for "offence to human dignity" and "denigration of other beliefs," and fined it thousands (a five-figure amount) for repeatedly denouncing homosexuality as "an abomination." It's now based in Washington, D.C., and Jerusalem, and has an arrangement with the great Sky God himself (Rupert Murdoch) to broadcast its Christian message, largely consisting of homophobic, hate-filled, rabble-rousing, fundamentalist bile, fulminating against everyone who does not share its message. So much for gentle Jesus meek and mild.

However, this week is Mission Week, when the Smart Alecs and their colleagues ask viewers to "sow a seed for Jesus" (in secular terms, they're on the cadge). When I tuned in, a Nigerian preacher was practising a variant of those ludicrously optimistic e-mail scams so beloved of his countrymen, shouting "give your seed, give abundantly... a caller gave £24 to God TV this morning and says 'later in the day, my father on earth gave me £750.' Praise Be!" An obsession with the number 24 underpinned the appeal ("you need a twenty-four-hour miracle... pledge £240, or £24 a month, invest in this ministry"), but when it came to *really* large amounts they weren't quite so concerned about the numerological significance ("businessmen – you could underwrite God TV with £1 million, and your business wouldn't even feel it"). And in return, the names of the donors were tickertaped across the screen, along with the size of their donations, and I wondered whatever happened to good old Christian principles about doing your good deeds in private.

Then Rory and Wendy began appealing (although they've never appealed to me), and I realised something remarkable. They're God's very own Richard and Judy, only they're operating in a parallel universe,

Ch 4 LIVE AND DIRECT

because she's the dim, slim and attractive one, while he's much smarter than her, but has piled on the weight to the point that he looks like one of those rosy-cheeked plastic pigs you see outside a butcher's shop. Although most of the donations came from Britain, the pair couldn't even remember how to pronounce the place names ("Ber-MOND-sea... Biller-ri-KAY... Uttoksatix..."), but even more excruciating to my ears was a musical interlude featuring a Bon Jovi lookalike named Edward John (See? Another dodgy pair of Christian names). You and I have never heard of him, but he's big on God TV, proving yet again that if you can't cut the mustard in the *real* rock world, why not have a convenient religious conversion and let Jesus prop up your flagging career?

I began this week with Papal edicts from the Vatican, and am ending it with another load of religious bull. Not only are these people fleecing the credulous to swell the coffers of their TV station, they're spreading highly dubious propaganda about "God's prophetic agenda for Israel" and "repositioning the European Church to enable it to fulfill its significant end-time role in Europe and the Middle East." I came away wondering what the hell is the point of Ofcom, if it sees no problem with stuff like this getting onto our screens. *Somebody* should at least be investigating its UK operations at Angel House in Sunderland, run by Johnny Woodrow, who is currently boasting about having the co-operation of several British MPs. It's televangelism at its worst, and I can only hope that the careers of these two Smart Alecs will end like those of the Swaggarts and Bakkers before them, in sexual and financial scandal. And hopefully in prison.

William Tainton was, arguably, the most important person in the history of television. You've probably never heard of him, but he claimed to have been the world's first human TV presenter. Admittedly his audience consisted solely of the inventor John Logie Baird, who paid him a buy-out fee of half-a-crown for his services. Apparently he appeared on I've Got a Secret in 1966, which you can see by clicking on link #31 on the **TV Reviews** *page on* ***www.badastralbooks.com.***

I am reminded of Adrian Chiles, a man born with the perfect face for radio. I had a certain sneaking regard for him early on in his career, because there seemed something pluckily defiant about his determination to have a career in television despite his obvious physiognomical disadvantages, rather like a legless man entering an Olympic sprint event in his wheelchair. By clicking on link #32 on the **TV Reviews** *page on* ***www.badastralbooks.com.*** *There you'll see just what a handicap Mr Chiles had to overcome when he began as presenter of Working Lunch.*

TV reviews

However, such is the charisma that repeated appearances inside the magic rectangle can bestow on a face, that people soon became inured to his boat race, and he went on to the dizzy heights of fronting BBC1's The One Show. Sadly, however, he then decided to jump ship and went to GMTV, after which he was never heard of again (but made so much money that he probably doesn't care).

WORKING LUNCH

BBC2 2005

Whenever I hear people complaining that television is obsessed with youth and has never aimed itself at the elderly, I silence their foolish prattle with three simple words: *Mr and Mrs*. In its 70s heyday, this show was a veritable Mecca for geriatrics, not just in its choice of aged and infirm contestants, but also in the toothless crocodile of gumming senility that bussed and Zimmer-framed its way into the studios of Border Television in Carlisle each week, to form the semi-comatose audience. While the septuagenarian husband was consigned to "the soundproof booth" (a needlessly theatrical subterfuge, because most could have been plunged into the abyss of silence simply by disconnecting their deaf aids), Derek Batey would ask "the distaff side" how many sugars her spouse took in his tea, a question she would invariably answer incorrectly, even though they'd lived together in wedded misery since 1923. And each edition commenced with Tony Hatch and Jackie Trent singing "Mr and Mrs, be nice to each other, Mr and Mrs, gotta love one another," advice they clearly took very much to heart. They got divorced soon after recording the song.

"I'm getting married tomorrow," declared Tony Hatch during Friday's edition of *Working Lunch*, BBC2's daily business and financial programme. But the composer (now of pensionable age) gave no further details of his impending nuptials, and as I marvelled at this latest example of the triumph of hope over experience, I recalled another telling characteristic of *Mr and Mrs*, namely that the couples could always remember *where* they got married, but could seldom remember *why*. Although I'd tuned in primarily to hear the songwriter being interviewed about his career, I often watch this programme anyway, not least because it's refreshing to find a show where uncompromising physical ugliness (amongst the male presenters anyway) is regarded as more or less *de rigueur*. And I'm not referring solely to regular anchorman Adrian Chiles (absent from this edition), who always looks as though his head has been jemmied into a goldfish bowl, because the show is peopled by some homely financial consultants; the sort who, if they went to see *The Elephant Man*, would be forced to sign autographs in the foyer after.

Looking dapper and tanned (as though he'd just been sprayed with liquid bronze by the "metaliser" who'd preceded him), Hatch talked absorbingly about how his childhood passion for music had developed into a lucrative career. Starting out as a teaboy in Denmark Street (then known as Tin Pan Alley), he went on to make a fortune by writing some of television's best-known theme tunes, like "Crossroads," "Emmerdale," and "Neighbours" – not many, "but the ones I've been associated with have always been long runners." When presenter Adam Shaw sang a brief snatch of his 1964 hit "Downtown," Hatch encouraged him to continue, then revealed that "the BBC have to pay me some money." They'll have to pay him even more after showing a clip of the definitive version, as performed by Petula Clark. And I recalled a strange experience from my youth when, after drinking a potent mixture of Emva cream sherry and wood polish, I hallucinated a parallel universe in which the charts were topped by a chanteuse called *Petulance Clark* singing "Don't Sleep in the Fucking Subway you Fucking Loafer."

Surrounding this central interview was a mosaic of finance items and consumer news, interspersed with magazine-style reports. There were pre-tax profits galore for Unilever (a company that's made its fortune by telling us we all stink, then selling us deodorant), and redundancies galore for Marconi workers, while a survey showing that house prices have stalled was treated as a calamity (although if you're a potential first-time buyer, it's surely welcome news). When share prices were discussed, I felt much as I do when my eyes stray onto the excellent City pages of this newspaper (I understood all the individual words, yet had no idea what they meant when joined together), but I could understand why fund managers like Nicola Horlick were relieved that the election had resulted in a clear-cut victory. Although now that the Prime Minister has become a Bliarbility, she did reveal nervousness about Gordon Brown taking over, "because he is more socialist than New Labour." True enough, but then again, Genghis Khan was more socialist than New Labour.

Working Lunch is a reliably engrossing daytime watch, at a time when the other terrestrial channels are devoted to teenage soaps and vapid game shows, but sometimes I wonder just whom it's intended for. The target audience presumably never see it, because they're either too busy trading shares or else down at Balls Brothers drinking claret from bottle-sized glasses, and even Mr Hatch presumably switches over to *Neighbours* most days, to hear the sweet sound of cash tumbling into his bank account. As the programme ended, the words "be nice to each other... love one another" rattled in my head, and I thought of Vanessa Feltz, another celebrity whose

TV reviews

apparently perfect marriage ended in divorce. Sadly, her weight has been yo-yoing ever since the separation (slim, then fat, then slim, then fat), so much so that I'm told, whenever she does a gig at Television Centre, they book her into dressing rooms 16, 17, and 18, just to be on the safe side.

Live morning television was dominated for many years (from 1988 onwards, in fact) by those intellectual giants of the airwaves, Richard and Judy, long-time hosts of *This Morning*. Certain cruel critics used to intimate in their columns that, in later years, Judy's hands seemed to shake more than was usual in the mornings, and even suggested that perhaps she had a drink problem, but I would like to scotch all such rumours now, because they all sound pretty rum to me. Absolut nonsense in fact. Although I did hear gossip (in-cider gossip) that the Finnegan household possessed the only corkscrews ever to be diagnosed with metal fatigue.

*You can see the pair by clicking on link #33 on the **TV Reviews** page on **www.badastralbooks.com**.*

reliving highlights of what they touchingly still seem to regard as their triumphant careers. After they transferred to Channel 4, their yawning chasms were partially filled by Philip Schofield and Fern Britton, Holly Willoughby, or – on this occasion – Lorraine Kelly.

THIS MORNING

ITV 2005

What an appalling, anally-retentive nation we British are. Still in denial over the loss of Empire, we sit here on our pinprick of an island off the coast of Western Europe, deeply suspicious of a continent that has open borders and a single currency, still insisting on the need to keep out beastly foreigners (who let those Huguenots in?), and our historic right to "save the pound" (or preferably the groat). In summer, our national dish is the charred-yet-raw salmonella steak, cooked on home-made barbecues by boneheads who've never progressed beyond the Neanderthal caveman's fascination with fire, which is why our national summer sport is visiting Outpatients with second-degree burns and acute food poisoning. And when Mardi Gras approaches, and other nations let rip with three days of carnival and near-naked street dancing, how do we celebrate? By cracking open a Jif plastic lemon and squirting the contents onto a circle of fried batter.

Ch 4 LIVE AND DIRECT

The voluptuous, pouting Nigella Lawson chose to cook pancakes on Friday's edition of *This Morning*, an appropriate metaphor for a programme that is itself as flat as a pancake (or, if you prefer, utter crepe). Sounding out of place on ITV (like Princess Anne but without the pantomime horse's head), this high-class hotty-totty brought a rare dash of glamour to one of the most lacklustre slots on British television (although personally I've found it impossible to fantasise about her since the time her head unexpectedly morphed in my mind into her father Nigel lecturing me sternly about fiscal probity). But why was she here at all, when she'd recently dismissed daytime broadcasting as "plunging into TV rivers of banality"? Simple. She was plugging her new ITV series, along with half-a-dozen more charismatically-challenged micro-celebs who were also pushing theirs, because this daily two-hour show is nowadays little more than a vehicle for channel three to cross-promote its own programmes. Trouble is though, fewer and fewer people are now bothering to watch ITV at all, because the channel is increasingly plunging not merely into the rivers of banality, but sinking 40,000 leagues beneath a sea of dross.

This being Friday, Fern Britton (the only presenter on British television who can wear an army tent as a summer frock) was absent from the studio, and consequently 80 per cent more daylight streamed in through the window to illuminate Lorraine Kelly. With her unflappably friendly demeanour, her merry Scottish twang, and her permanent rictus of a smile, she's becoming increasingly easy to detest with every passing year, agreeing so readily with anything and everything her guests assert that she'd doubtless say "och, Herr Himmler, I take your point about Zyklon B's advantages over Zyklon A," if so required. But even she could pass for an intellectual when standing next to Phillip Schofield. "I am wearing specs due to a moment of stupidity," he announced solemnly, and I wondered why on that basis he hasn't been wearing bottle-bottom goggles for his entire lifetime, until he explained that he'd accidentally got hydrogen peroxide in his eyes, a mistake he attributed to a mix-up with his contact lens solution. Possibly, but I reckon that the bleaching agent got into his eyes after he stood downwind of "celebrity stylist" Wendy Elsmore, because either there's something very wrong with the colour guns on my TV set, or else the woman has more black roots than Kunta Kinte.

What followed was an endless paternoster of "coming up later" promos (to persuade viewers to keep watching), interspersed with blatant publicity for ITV shows (*Emmerdale*, *Coronation Street*, *Ladette to Lady*, *Nigella*, even ITV's own award ceremony) masquerading as features. "The best bottom in Europe" briefly appeared and was made to look like a complete arse, while a tattooed couple were given a desultory makeover, and (as usual) looked worse "after" than "before." A tanned lawyer called

TV reviews

"Mr Loophole," who was well on his way to take Silk (Kilroy, that is), bragged about his ability to ensure that drink-drivers "get off" in court (a proud boast indeed), and there was the inevitable plug for Live8, which will apparently force the world's politicians to stop exploiting Africa and selling arms to corrupt regimes, simply through the power of mass music. Although, curiously, nobody explained why people power in 2005 might persuade politicians to do anything they aren't already intending to do, when the anti-war marches of 2002–03 were contemptuously ignored, nor why we're supposed to regard rock musicians (rather than politicians) as inherently trustworthy, when they're clearly a bunch of self-obsessed egomaniacs, who spend most of their lives powdering their noses and fighting court cases over the ownership of a pair of trousers.

This Morning had passed its sell-by date at the end of the last century, yet ITV not only persists with this moribund format, it has also (for the first time ever) decided to keep it running throughout the summer, when we can usually expect a couple of banality-free months. Such decisions suggest a woeful lack of imagination at the channel, and the responsibility for that (and other recent disasters) must ultimately lie with Nigel Pickard, its director of programmes. A few years ago, when he was first appointed, he vowed to revive the network and I wrote optimistically (in regard to *This Morning*), "thankfully ITV now has a new boss in place, and one of his first tasks must be to end this waste of ten hours of airtime each week." Sadly he didn't axe it, and is now allowing it to expand, and unsurprisingly (as mistake follows mistake) his network increasingly resembles a shambles. The first kick of a mule is education. The second is surely stupidity.

Whatever happened to Mr Loophole (aka Nick Freeman), you may wonder? He still specialises in helping celebrities (especially sporting ones) to get their speeding tickets quashed on a technicality, which sounds pretty unsporting to me.

You can see him on YouTube, defending what he does while being interviewed by Alan Titchmarsh, who attacks him with all the tenacity and effectiveness of a toothless arthritic poodle. This can seen by by clicking on link #34 on the **TV Reviews** *page on www.badastralbooks.com.*

Okay, I'll admit it. I have an almost pathological dislike of Alan Titchmarsh, and it goes back a long way. When I wrote for the excellent Time Out magazine, some twenty years ago, I was the first person to describe him in print as a cunt (they printed the word in full, despite protests from the feminists there, because even those feminists had to agree that it was the mot juste). The man is a media experiment in artificial stupidity, he's life switched off at the mains, he's the acceptable face of television for blue-rinsed ladies who quiver with excitement as they re-read the steamy bits in his devestatingly lightweight novels, his affected delivery is full of phrases like "oh crumbs" and epithets like "bonnie," and to say that his programme is as dull as ditchwater would be grossly unfair to ditchwater. During one programme I saw him in, he stood next to an old charabanc, and told us "I used to go to school on a bus just like this." No wonder it said "Special" on the front.

LAST NIGHT OF THE PROMS

BBC 2004

A friend of mine with odd predilections (they used to be even, but he shot one off, and now has only five) told me recently about a visit he'd made to a sex shop. Having ascertained that they didn't actually sell sex, he asked for the nearest healthy alternative, and was offered a choice of blow-up sex dolls. "Would you prefer the Christian or the Muslim version?" the gentleman behind the counter enquired, whereupon my fictional friend asked "What's the difference?" "Well," replied the shop assistant, "fundamentally they're the same, but the Muslim one blows herself up." Boom boom, as that philosophising canine mammal of the genus Vulpes, Basil Brush, used to say.

My interest in inflatable women and terrorism predates 9/11, because as a student, I invented a radio-controlled, helium-filled, three-hole flying sex doll. My plan was to release it in the Royal Albert Hall during *The Last Night of the Proms*, and I wish I'd had one there on Saturday night, so I could have positioned it in geo-stationary orbit over the head of BBC1 presenter Alan Titchmarsh, then pressed a button and released gallons of KY Jelly over the simple head of that simple man. "It's the greatest music festival in the world," he told us, and he's absolutely right, but with each passing year the eighty-sixth and final concert seems to have less and less connection to the previous eighty-five. Unlike the others, this one isn't primarily about great performances of the classics, it's just an absurd and prolonged ceremony from some pointless ritual that long ago lost whatever meaning it once possessed, fittingly hosted by a man whose artistic credentials are limited to his having Van Gogh's ear for music.

As for the crowd, many of the Promenaders look completely different from the thoughtful and respectful people who attend the other

TV reviews

(usually wonderful) Proms, boorishly behaving as though *they* are the stars of the show, drowning out the quieter solos, and generally giving classical music a bad name (which it could well do without). The prats in hats, Dr Seuss might have called them, geeky men in fancy dress, shouting out their tedious, carefully-rehearsed ad-libs (mostly "heave ho," although I heard one shout "huzzah" this time), honking their horns like performing seals, and enacting their entire Corybantic repertoire (knee bends and arm-locked swaying) for the look-mum cameras at every opportunity.

Do they imagine that the musicians on stage adore their noise? Because they do not. Indeed, several orchestral members have told me over the years that they despise this ill-disciplined and attention-seeking bunch of largo-louts, and wish that the ushers would throw a few of them out, as an example to the rest. Yet, year after year they're allowed to wave their Union flags and St George's crosses, hoping to impress the smattering of equally goofy girls in the arena, most of whom look so frigid that if they opened their legs, the central heating would come on.

Miraculously, the BBC Symphony Orchestra and Chorus nevertheless succeeded in smuggling some noteworthy music past the barbarians in the front row of the auditorium. The Ojai Festival Overture confirmed just how much the once-forbidding style of Peter Maxwell Davies has mellowed (this score sounded like Aaron Copland left out in the rain), while Thomas Allen's version of "I've Got a Little List" (the G&S song, updated by Kit Hesketh-Harvey) took timely sideswipes at Vanessa Mae and Lord Hutton, and was noticeably more tuneful (and funny) than Peter Lilley's infamous rendition at the Tory Party Conference. A live link-up with various Proms in the Park events included an obbligato from James Galway (who no longer seems to be watching a speeded-up tennis match that only he can see), while a rendition of Sousa's "Liberty Bell March" delighted the geeks, who doubtless used it as a pretext for repeating every line of the Dead Parrot sketch for hours afterwards. Better still, the piece (commemorating a cracked bell, forged in London and housed in Philadelphia) symbolised the special relationship between the US and the UK, a flawed yet lasting relationship of whose existence only one side seems to be aware. I suppose that's what makes it so special.

As the "Sailor's Hornpipe" reached its climax, the Promenaders displayed en masse the symptoms of our national disease of *arrhythmia*, the genetic inability of a large group of Brits to clap in time (even the Northern Irish made a complete London derriere of it). Of course, that's part of the reason that so many foreign TV stations take a live feed of *The Last Night*, because it's a great chance to see the once-mighty Brits Uncle Tom-ing themselves for the rest of the world, smugly singing that they will never ever ever be slaves, when the whole world knows that this island has been regularly conquered by others during the past two thousand years. BBC4 has provided excellent coverage of many of this year's concerts, but if Aunty is serious about reviving her Corporation's commitment to the arts, we need to see far more substantial concerts on BBC1, not just this insipid zabaglione presented by Mr "One O Level" (now seemingly with added Botox under his eyes). "It's not jingoism or xenophobia," Titchmarsh told us as "Land of Hope and Glory" faded away, "it's honest-to-goodness national pride," and perhaps he's right. But then again, he once defiantly told us on one of his gardening programmes that "the sun moves around the earth," thereby consigning five hundred years of Copernican theory to the astronomical dustbin so, chances are, he's not.

To be fair to Mr Titchmarsh, even he recognised that there was a problem with him fronting the Proms, and he even gave an interview to The Daily Telegraph (entitled "And just why shouldn't I present the Proms?") to try to appease his critics, which can be read by clicking on link #35 on the **TV Reviews** *page on* **www.badastralbooks.com.**

However, when I read it, the answer to his question seemed obvious: "Because you're a cunt."

Nigella Lawson's attempt at hosting a Titchmarsh-style chat show was judged by most critics (though not me) to be an ignominious failure, and it was axed after a single series. However, unlike Mr Titchmarsh, Ms Lawson is a delightful and universally adored goddess, so she was able to shrug it off and return to what she does best: making the sort of gastroporn that delights sad gentlemen of a certain age, and was brilliantly parodied by Ronnie Ancona. This can be viewed by clicking on link #36 on the **TV Reviews** *page on* **www.badastralbooks.com.**

NIGELLA

ITV1 2005

As I was saying recently to Hans Frei (my German slave who holds the phone for me when I'm driving), if you want to reveal the truth about somebody, make an anagram of their name. Who can disagree, for example, that Ted Heath has become "The Death," that evangelists are "evil's agents," that a mother-in-law is really a "woman Hitler," or that Miss

TV reviews

Esther Rantzen has become an "ersatz thinner mess"? The Spell Checker on my PC also sends me hidden messages about the famous, frequently suggesting improper alternatives for the proper nouns in my text, with no prompting from me. Just last week, it turned Jimmy Savile into "Jimmy Saveloy" (not far off the mark, according to rumour), Kat-o-Meat into "catamite," and Vimto into "vomit," until the entire screen was filled with innuendo. I didn't know where to put myself.

Anagram king Richard Whiteley (*aka* "lecher with diary") received a fond posthumous mention on *Nigella* yesterday afternoon, but the show was fuelled, as ever, by a steady stream of innuendo. "You must lubricate from within," Ms Lawson told us with her trademark faux-innocent smirk as she presented a daily magazine show that could otherwise have been made in the 1950s (right down to her frock), and last week I even heard her declare that "I've been balling all morning," while idly fondling her melons. Being a professional TV critic, of course, I had prepared myself for her inevitable attempts at titillation by donning a pair of Vibranium underpants (guaranteed to accommodate involuntary organ movements in gentlemen of a certain age), but even so it was difficult for me to concentrate purely on the technical side of the programme, because whether she likes it or not, the woman is quite simply sex on a stick. And she's at her most erotic when cooking, whether she's licking molten chocolate off a wooden spoon or simply stuffing citrus fruits up the rear end of a chicken (a process once memorably described by Conan Doyle's meerschaum-smoking sleuth as "lemon entry, my dear Watson").

Fortunately, her chief guest yesterday was the televisual equivalent of bromide in your tea, namely Jo Brand. While Nigella tossed off a feta salad, the woman largely responsible for the development of widescreen television told us that "I hit my children very hard," then added "no, I'm only joking," although I was quite unable to detect even a homeopathic dose of humour in that remark, or in anything else she said during her kitchen interview. Indeed, the duo's smalltalk flatly contradicted Nigella's pre-series protestations that "I don't want to plunge deep into television's rivers of banality," yet the host can get away with a good deal of inanity because (as Brand observed enviously) "everything you do oozes sex." And it's true, because although she only likes to be filmed from the waist up, her eyes, teeth, hair, and cleavage are a devastating combination, especially when accompanied by a husky voice that teeters permanently on the edge of tonsillitis (which is, incidentally, the worst infection it's possible to have, if you're Welsh).

As the pair joined Maria McErlane and Jan Ravens for a pointless discussion about overpriced bikinis (none of which they dared to model), I wondered why ITV had decided to commission what is essentially a remake

Ch 4 LIVE AND DIRECT

of the long-defunct Southern TV's upper-middle-class *House Party*. Nigella is Katie from the Oxo ads, with a dash of Elizabeth Montgomery from *Bewitched* (an allusion cleverly highlighted in Adrian York's cunningly-scored title music), and there's something curiously dissonant about posh totty talking in tones that make the Queen sound like a slut, as she addresses an ITV lunchtime audience consisting mainly of housewives relaxing on the sofa with a postprandial quart of sherry. My suspicion is that she's simply such a figure of lust for middle-aged male ITV executives that they decided to book her anyway, and to hell with the consequences, but what's harder to understand is why *she* is prepared to slum it in a daytime slot, where the viewing figures are only a fraction of what she's used to at primetime. After all, her hubby isn't short of a few hundred million, so maybe Charles Saatchi is simply doing the traditional Jewish thing, and sending his wife out to work.

Although it's been savaged by the critics (who've decided that ITV is to be this year's whipping boy), this is competent lightweight early-afternoon fare. It's true that the ratings have halved since the start of the month, but that's only because the series generated an abnormal amount of interest when it began, and although it is inconsequential stuff, Nigella is a far more agreeable fantasy companion than most of the people who get their faces and personalities inside the magic rectangle. Like Cilla, Oprah, and Esther, she's one of those women who are instantly recognised by their first name alone, and I remarked upon this recently to her father, who is now a much thinner version of the man who used to run the economy back in the 80s. "You've named your daughter Nigella," I pointed out, "and perhaps Salman Rushdie could do something similar. Only his daughter would have to be called... Salmonella." And do you know what? The former Chancellor never even cracked a fucking smile.

The reference to Jimmy Savile reminds me of this entry from my diary, which I had made several years before writing this review:

"Yesterday, I was sitting in a chip shop in Scarborough, when in jogged Jimmy Savile, followed closely by another shell-suited beanpole. Savile talked to some young girls and beckoned them to go upstairs with him, clearly with the acquiescence of the owner, a 30-stone Italian who was himself surrounded by young boys. Savile must have recognised me from my byline picture, because he suddenly stopped, having obviously decided that he'd better come and talk to me, before disappearing upstairs with the girls. He said hello, and noted that I had, several times, referred to him in print as 'Jimmy Saveloy' – an error which, I explained, was due to my spell checker (but which he said was a fairly accurate

TV reviews

description). He pointed to the girls and said 'they're my godchildren', and then pointed to his colleague, saying 'this is my minder, he carries the gun'. And, with perfect timing, the minder opened his jacket, to reveal the handle of a pistol." It wasn't the thought of being shot that concerned me, so much as the possibility of being taken, as a corpse, to a morgue, where Savile was the orderly. I have my pride.

You might be surprised to see the verbal adjective "fucking" at the end of that review. Every so often, I felt one was necessary, albeit that the Evening Standard liked to think of itself as a "family newspaper." Well, so did I, but the family I was thinking of was the Gallagher family from Channel 4's Shameless. Sadly, however, the "fucks" were never printed. I worked on the theory that if I did it often enough, then one day my review would be left in charge of a drunken sub editor who wouldn't even notice it, and that I'd eventually get one in. It never happened.

Had one ever got through, all hell would have broken loose, I suppose, but no matter. I've always been a believer in biting the hand that feeds you (right up to armpit), as in this next review, which took aim at the dubious business practices that exist in the City of London. Until very recently, the Evening Standard depended on the City for much of its circulation (in pre-online days, share dealers and financial houses were willing to buy a new edition of the newspaper every hour, because that was the easiest way for them to obtain the latest stock market prices), but I've always regarded the Square Mile as the most disreputable part of London, and I frequently said so in print.

If you're unfamiliar with the following event, there's an introduction that can be seen by clicking on link #37 on the **TV Reviews** page on **www.badastralbooks.com**.

THE LORD MAYOR'S SHOW

BBC1   2005

Autumn is riddled with ironies. Moving from British Summer Time to Greenwich Mean Time saves us an extra hour, which we are then obliged to spend adjusting the displays on our alarm clocks, watches, videos, cookers, car stereos, and computers. We're supposed to be thrilled by the news that *le Beaujolais nouveau est arrivé*, even though the stuff leaves the

Ch 4 LIVE AND DIRECT

body in much the same condition that it enters. And then there's that "lest we forget" slogan on Poppy Day, which is not only ironic, but deeply cruel too. After all, those to whom this annual ceremony means the most have now reached the age when they're liable to forget pretty much everything, even their names, and before long the rest of us will find it convenient to forget too. Despite the bold pledges about eternal remembrance, amnesia is the handmaiden of progress, and one day somebody with a hard hat and an even harder heart will walk around the disused graveyard where *we* lie buried, utter a cursory "amen," then send in the JCBs to plough up our bones and smash our headstones, as our last resting place is prepared for the erection of yet another Tesco or Sainsbury megastore-cum-necropolis.

At first glance, the annual anachronism of *The Lord Mayor's Show* seems to be the most ironic anomaly of all. When I was a child, nobody could ever quite explain to me the point of the parade that marches through the City on the second Saturday of each November, and now that Londoners have a real live democratically-elected Mayor ensconced in City Hall, the ceremonial one with the floppy hat and the Cinderella coach surely seems more than ever like an ineffectual refugee from a provincial Christmas panto. But as I've grown older, I've realised that that perception is wrong, because despite Ken Livingstone's high-profile battles with Downing Street over transport policy and policing, his budgets are strictly limited and his power largely illusory. Whereas the Lord Mayor is the public face of the freemasonry who've been running the Square Mile like a mediaeval city state for centuries, living amongst us yet apart from us, and quietly carving up the nation's most lucrative business between themselves.

The BBC first covered the show in 1937, and although the picture quality has improved considerably since then, Saturday's ritual remained as Gormen-ghastly as ever in its elaborate pointlessness. To the strains of a discordant fanfare, the golden coach set off towards Aldwych, carrying within it a sword-bearer and a common crier in fancy dress, along with the 678th Lord Mayor, a Peter Bull lookalike whose name hardly matters (though for the record it's David Brewer) because the only one anybody can ever remember is Dick Whittington. Surrounding the horse-drawn buggy were drummers from the Royal Marines playing Russian Roulette with their drumsticks and nostrils, ahead of a giant papier-maché Gog and Magog, followed by Sea Scouts, naval bands, Worshipful Companies, and dozens of charity floats with prominent logos from their corporate sponsors, who know it's a surefire way to advertise cheaply on the BBC. In short, it was a linear ambulant precursor to what we'll be seeing next Friday on *Children in Need*, where the studio will be crammed with sponsored show-offs and managing directors holding gigantic cheques aloft, thereby ensuring free publicity for their company names.

TV reviews

Maybe it was the sound of the gormless Matt Allwright sporting a Madonna cheek microphone and pretending to know about the Magna Carta, or of Clare Balding (imagine a butch Libby Purves who's let herself go) telling the Countess of Chichester and Therese that they were "equally beautiful" (a charming compliment, if only Therese hadn't been a camel). Or maybe it was the polytonal cacophony generated by twenty marching bands playing simultaneously like Charles Ives on amphetamines, but I found that I simply *had* to mute the volume for a while, so I can only describe what I *think* happened thereafter, Members of the Royal Livery and Onions paraded past the Old Lady of Threadneedle Street, followed by the Ancient Guild of Plastic Seaterers, a regiment of convulsing BSE Beefeaters, the Prince of Wales' Own Brigade of Horsefaced Slagbags, lashed by aldermanic lavatory chains, and Matt Lucas playing Daffyd slapping his thigh and shouting "twenty miles from London and still no sign of Dick" (okay, I lied about the last one). And Richard Stilgoe, taking the opportunity to plug his all-wheelchair production of *Starlight Express* (worse, I'm *not* lying about that one).

Like The Last Night of the Proms, this event attracts an almost exclusively white audience, and seems so unwelcoming to ethnic minorities that I half expected to see a police float rolling past, sponsored by "The Worshipful Company of Invisible Bruisers." Only the presence of a few Chinese and Muslim participants indicated an acknowledgement that the world's financial centre of gravity is relocating eastwards, but otherwise the pageant reflected traditional CofE values, especially when the new Lord Mayor stopped to get himself blessed at St Paul's. That vignette reminded me of an old acquaintance (a Bishop at one of our grander cathedrals), who once arranged to meet a hard-drinking friend called Neil (nicknamed the Belisha Deacon, on account of his red nose), and was waiting outside his church as a group of American tourists approached from below. Seeing his friend in the distance, he raised his arm and shouted out "Neil!" whereupon twenty bemused and intimidated Yanks immediately genuflected as instructed, in expectation of a bit of open-air Anglican prayer.

That the television industry manages to cling on in the face of competition from the infinitely more fleet-of-foot internet is due in no small part to the rise of live-and-interactive talent shows such as The X Factor and Britain's Got Talent. Of course, they're all runt sons of the original TV talent format, Opportunity Knocks, but with the added benefit of instant voting by text, a simple idea which can often generate a revenue stream that is greater than the entire programme budget. Some TV critics become obsessed with such shows, and follow them week by week. But I preferred to don asbestos gloves and a face mask, observe them just once, then walk away.

Ch 4 **LIVE AND DIRECT**

THE X FACTOR
ITV 2005

What with Ant and Dec resuscitating ancient game show formats in their new Saturday evening series, how about them trying out one that I've been peddling without success for the past decade? It's called Lottery Buzzle, and ingeniously caters to television's insatiable appetite for big money prizes and sadistic punishments by inviting convicted murderers to sit in the electric chair, and take the ultimate life-or-death challenge by playing the metal-ring-on-a-wiggly-wire game on live television. If the felon keeps his nerve and a steady hand, he'll win a million pounds and freedom, but if he shakes and his ring touches the wire, he'll get a million volts and there will be "frying tonight." But the fun doesn't end with his summary (or wintery) execution, because rolling numbers on the screen will freeze at the precise moment that he takes the juice, so one lucky ticket holder watching at home will get the cash prize that the unlucky lifer was dying to win.

I once proposed that format to a BBC executive, who thought long and hard before replying (in all seriousness) "nice idea, but not for us – try ITV." And perhaps he was right, because it's no more degrading a concept than the gratuitous cruelty of *The X Factor*, which requires the public to submit to character assassination of the most demeaning and humiliating kind, in return for a one-in-a-million chance of becoming "the nation's next singing sensation." The central idea is nothing new, of course, because sadistic dream-crushing verdicts passed by unqualified judges, and intrusive close-ups lingering on the hurt faces of auditioning hopefuls, were also at the core of *New Faces* (or *New Faeces*, as it was unpopularly known back in the 70s), which was the first talent show systematically to ridicule its own contestants. So the current legal spat between Simon Cowell and Simon Fuller over whether *The X Factor* infringes the format of *Pop Idol* is a clear case of Dear Kettle, Yours Sincerely Pot, because both shows are the biggest rip-off in showbiz since the day Paul Daniels finally abandoned his ludicrous wig.

The X in question is presumably a missing chromosome, because what else could explain the parade of mentally and dentally retarded wannabees that traipsed across my screen on Saturday night? Where the likes of *Opportunity Knocks* did at least expect some modicum of variety, skill, and originality from its participants (flexing your shoulder muscles to the strains of "Wheels Cha-Cha," for example, or bashing your head with a tin tray while singing "Mule Train"), this prefers to encourage those with

TV reviews

a severe case of mistaken nonentity to appear on camera, and positively revels in its status as a lack-of-talent show. In general, I'm all for mocking anyone who voluntarily puts their head inside the magic rectangle (if only to ensure that precocity doesn't degenerate into vanity), and when the contestants are simply students making fools of themselves for a bet, or practical jokers having a laugh, there's no damage done. But there are far too many David-Icke-on-Wogan moments in each show, when self-delusion tips over into clinical madness, and laughing at this roll call of the desperate, the demented, the needy, and the empty isn't simply a harmless bit of fun – it's the twenty-first century equivalent of a horse-and-cart trip to Bedlam to jeer at the Mad Toms inside.

Without exception, the acts were derivative (imitations of 90s boy and girl bands, interspersed with melismatic R&B acts and "I-eye-eye weeeeel always lurv you-hoo-hoo"), but then again, so were the judges. Most especially Simon Cowell, reprising Tony Hatch's "hatchet man" role of a generation ago as he sows division amongst groups of friends ("you have talent, the others don't"), tramples on fragile ambitions ("you should give up... don't keep trying"), and generally carries on like the campest man on television (although he *obviously* can't be gay, because his PR company keeps telling the tabloids about his jaunts with the ladies). Sharon Osbourne's sensitive motherly routine rings equally hollow, while the complaints booth in which the gratuitously insulted can let off steam afterwards isn't a serious attempt at redressing the balance, just a cynical ruse to prevent the haemorrhaging of subsequent legal action. As for the grandiose title music, it's an appropriate metaphor for the entire series, because whether you pronounce it as Carmina Burana or Car-meena Bur-arna, the message is the same: let's call the whole thing Orff.

Despite a welter of post-production, including special effects, morphing, and snide non-contemporaneous ad-libs (clearly added after the event), the programme cannot hide its own staleness. Most of the contestants wouldn't even make the grade in the porn industry, let alone the pop world, and as for Cowell's Svengali-like forays into the doomed music and record industry, he (and the rest of us) will surely watch that business unravel before our eyes. With ITV celebrating its fiftieth anniversary this week, Nigel Pickard (its Director of Programmes) has been loudly insisting that the channel's core values haven't changed, and in a sense he's right, because its light entertainment department is as patronising as ever, its drama is still trashy and populist, and Denis Norden is still endlessly reshowing self-conscious out-takes from the cutting room floor, while ITV continues to bin many of its most important archive programmes. But there's one important difference. When the channel began, there was no fear, but now it lives in permanent dread of falling ratings, as Pickard and Chairman Charles Allen both fight for their own survival. No man can think clearly when his fists are clenched, and the results are on our screens for all to see.

It must be five years since I wrote that review, and precious little has changed. Mr Cowell is still camp, he's still regularly photographed by the tabloids "escorting a lady friend" (so he still can't be gay), and he's still critical of most of the acts who perform for him, although he's far less caustic and gratuitously nasty than he used to be. Why? Because there's a prolonged recession, here and in the US, and he's smart enough to know that people need hope and optimism in economically harsh times. When the economy was booming, public humiliation was in vogue. But now, it seems, a homeopathic dose of compassion is required. When he starts being truly nasty again, that'll be a sure sign that the economy is finally on the mend.

*Until it is, shopping channels will continue to tempt viewers with cheap tat. And so, to bring this chapter to a close, let us celebrate the life of the King of the Shopping Channel, Steve Whatley (11 July 1959 – 7 November 2005), known to both his admirers as "Gadget Man," "Mr Diamonique", "Whatters," and "Mr Zhuzh!" Here he is in action, performing his trademark act of laughing wildly at nothing much – please click on link #38 on the **TV Reviews** page on **www.badastralbooks.com**.*

I was once in the British Airways First Class Lounge (it was a media freebie – I used to review restaurants abroad) when Mr Whatley walked in with his wife, who looked like a Scout Master. Their tickets were examined, and they were both ejected. And at that moment, something deep within me danced for joy.

PICK OF THE DAY

IDEAL WORLD 2001

In all the years I spent as a restaurant critic for a glossy magazine, the most outrageous incident that befell me occurred when I was stopped at the door by a surly maitre d', and bluntly refused entry because I was wearing jeans, and wasn't wearing a tie. What snobbery and arrogance it is for a restaurant to tell its paying customers how to dress, *particularly* when they insist that we wear an item which garrotes the very tube down which the food passes. I was seething, but my watch cry has always been

TV reviews

"don't get even, get mad," so next day (affecting an accent so haughty it made Brian Sewell sound like Michael Barrymore), I phoned the very same maître d', claiming to be Prince Edward's private secretary. "The Prince will be bringing a party of six to dine," I began. "Wonderful Sir, I will prepare our best table," came the grovelling reply. "Excellent. Just one thing though, the prince cannot abide formality. I assume he will not have to wear a tie, and may wear jeans?" "No problem at all sir," came the reply. "Then why didn't you let me in last night?" I said, dropping the accent. "Don't you have *peasant* on the menu?"

Were I still working as a restaurant critic, by now I'd doubtless require a pair of the "sixty-inch waist Indigo five-pocket jeans" being flogged yesterday morning during *Pick of the Day*, on the Ideal World home shopping channel. Some would say that a sixty-inch waist is a contradiction in terms (the waist being, by definition, the narrow bit between the ribs and hips), but that didn't stop Steve ("call me Watters") Whatley declaring that "everybody is entitled to fabulous jeans," and holding up a garment so vast that even Andrea Dworkin might well have been able to squeeze inside it. Admittedly, he himself was wearing a much smaller size, dancing around and declaiming a Kurt Schwitters sound poem ("Way eh eh eh yes, way eh eh there we are, way eh eh eh jeans jeans, way ey, woe oh, good morning, ah, ah, ah, ah wooo!"), his pained phonetics doubtless due to his thirty-four-inch waist being thrust into a thirty-inch waistband. But he still has a long way to go before he'll resemble the Human Toffee Apple, as Jeremy Clarkson is known *chez* Lewis-Smith.

In case you have one of those things called a life, let me bring you up to speed on the brief but turbulent history of this laughably ramshackle ersatz QVC. Founded in April 2000 in a Peterborough industrial estate by the undynamic trio of Whatley, Paul Lavers, and Debbie Flint, it was losted a few months ago when their warehouse-cum-studio burned to the ground in a mysterious blaze (which ironically destroyed their supplies of domestic firefighting equipment), only to rise again within weeks. I say mysterious, by the way, not because I'm implying any insurance fiddle, dear me no, but because it happened not long after I'd written about the channel in this very column. And what did I say? That Lavers had "smoky good looks (as though he'd recently been in a house fire)," and that he looked like a wax dummy that had begun to melt in the studio heat. Synchronicity or what?

"So slick, so smart," enthused Watters as a sixty-inch male model waddled on, then thoughtfully showed us a label reading "wash separately" (as though there might somewhere be a washing machine so large it could possibly hold anything more, once six acres of denim had been stuffed into it). "Shopping is retail therapy," he continued, "like eating chocolate," though I've long suspected that the typical Ideal World viewer doesn't bother with such gastronomic niceties, and simply eats lard straight from the packet. Having helpfully held up a tape measure, pointed to the number thirty, and announced that "if you're in that sort of area, you'll want a thirty," he resumed his curious dancing, laughing maniacally that "it's early in the morning, no one's watching." How true, but I have bad news for Mr Whatley and his chums. It doesn't matter *what* time of day or night it is. No one's *ever* watching.

Where QVC reeks of American slickness, Ideal World's amateurishness is typically British, and that's ultimately its one saving grace. Some of those who tune in to mock presumably end up buying something, but I was able to resist the temptation, not least because a nasty dose of literally-itis ("literally check your waist... literally twenty seconds into Monday morning... literally these trousers are growing... literally punch in the numbers... literally hundreds of satisfied customers") broke out on screen. And speaking of nasty afflictions, I recalled how co-presenter Paul Lavers once had an operation, to replace his diseased oesophagus with part of his colon. So he can hardly object if I name him here as the only presenter on British TV to *literally* talk out of his arse.

Although he has been dead since 2005, Mr Whatley's ambitions in retail live on, with his perfume "Zhuzh" still available at www.zhuzh.com.

R.I.P. We shall not see his like again. Thank fucking Christ.

CHAPTER 5

SCIENCE

Nowhere on earth is the combination of ignorance and arrogance more intoxicating than when a television programme addresses itself to matters scientific. By nature, science is an area of human endeavour that requires years (if not decades) of slow and thoughtful experimentation, research, and observation, before even the barest bones of a new theory can be tentatively put forward with any confidence; whereas television is an area of human endeavour that relishes the debunking of the established consensus (often in the teeth of all empirical evidence), encourages bold speculation (frequently based on little or no evidence), and has no time for the diligent, patient, expensive, and unglamorous gathering of extensive data that is an integral part of the scientific method. In short, television is not a footnotes medium, while science consists of little else.

Consequently, the television schedules are full of science programmes whose EPG descriptions claim that they will overturn the accepted wisdom on a particular topic, yet turn out merely to be asserting highly improbable views, often through the cowardly form of the interrogative – "Has this man invented a perpetual motion machine?" "Do polystyrene wine racks cause warts?". During my one-hundred-and-forty-seven years as a television critic, I endured more than my fair share of those, as this chapter will amply demonstrate. Yet just occasionally, one comes across a presenter or producer who truly understands the art of popularising science, of simplifying the complexities without patronising the lay viewer, and of presenting the necessary evidence in a way that holds the audience's attention, rather than sending them into a coma. This chapter contains plenty of those wonderful programmes too.

The middle-class obsession with organic food has long infuriated me, so let's start with a refreshing debunking of the pseudo-science that underpins this well-intentioned but self-deluded form of agriculture.

Ch 5 SCIENCE

COUNTERBLAST

BBC2 2000

How I wish that Jack Hargreaves (a professional septuagenarian from the age of thirty-five) were still on our screens on Sunday mornings, presenting *Out of Town* in his gingham shirt to the soothing accompaniment of Francisco Tarrega's "Recuerdos de la Alhambra". From his TV studio in Southampton, he spent years offering his urban audience a quaint depiction of the countryside as an unending pastoral idyll of nestling villages, wise old framers chewing on straw, gently bleating sheep, gaily-painted Romany caravans, and cheerful peasants happily scything the corn and winnowing the grain. I must have missed the edition in which he finally confessed that the reality of traditional rural existence was somewhat bleaker, consisting of mud, poverty, disease, stench, alcoholism, suicide and domestic violence. Or the one in which he admitted that it wasn't his impeccable agrarian credentials that had landed him the presenter's job, but the fact that he was on the Board of Directors of Southern Television.

Jack has gone the way of all flesh and is now worm food, but the myth that old-fashioned rural life was a veritable Eden persists, primarily in the minds of chic, well-heeled city dwellers in Islington and Chelsea. These Woofs ("Weekends On Organic Farms") have convinced themselves that modern agriculture is the root of all evil, so they must have been choking on their pesticide-free Madeleine cakes last night when Roger Bate (director of the European Science and Environmental Forum) introduced BBC2's *Counterblast* with the words "I distrust organic food, I think there's something rotten about the whole business." However, speaking as someone who regularly orders MSG as an extra side dish in Chinese restaurants, I purred contentedly as he proceeded to expose the flawed assumptions and media hype that have frightened the gullible middle classes into paying exorbitant prices for frequently substandard, crap-covered fruit and vegetables, and demonstrated that it's not just the indiscriminate use of manure which accounts for the strong smell of bullshit surrounding the organic movement.

In support of his thesis, he had mustered an impressive array of experts, including Professor Hugh Pennington, who reminded us that "natural does not necessarily mean safe." Professor Pennington, who is an expert on e coli (a name which, like aloe vera, always sounds to me like a Northern comic's catchphrase), pointed out that it can be passed into the food chain via the cow dung that's used so liberally by organic farmers, while others revealed the presence of microtoxins in organic

TV reviews

vegetables, caused by incipient fungal infections. As for the supposedly massive quantities of chemical additives in conventionally produced food, "the total amount of pesticide residues that a person will consume in a year is equivalent in toxicity to one cup of coffee," and I recalled how my own brief flirtation with organic food had ended in ignominy after I was advised by a Woof to start putting manure on my rhubarb. Never again. From now on, it's custard or nothing.

True, the programme was visually unremarkable (television has never figured out what to do with scientists, and invariably ends up showing meaningless shots of men in white coats peering down microscopes or decanting pipettes into test tubes), but that was amply compensated for by its compelling and inexorable logic. Being Bate's personal view, he only allowed the pro-organic lobby a few minutes to respond, and their defence was emotional rather than rational, falling back on unsubstantiated claims that organic farming is better for the environment. Here again, the hollowness of those assertions was exposed, because low yields mean that, were organic farming ever to be widely adopted, vast areas of wild land would have to be turned over to agriculture, with disastrous consequences for the species that live there. By the end, I realised two things about the eco-lobby: they're even greener than I'd previously suspected, and their plans for the future of world farming put the *mental* back into environmental.

This was yet another forceful programme from the BBC Community Programme Unit, produced and directed with economy and clarity by Marcus Ryder. Myths about the moral superiority of simple rural life are nothing new (back in the mid-eighteenth century, Rousseau was already denouncing the artificiality of civilisation and promoting the idea of the noble savage), but in a world where millions are starving due to the inefficiency of old-fashioned farming methods, trying to turn the agrarian clock back to ease the consciences of rich city types is certainly irresponsible, if not plain wicked. The Third World needs our farming technology, not our self-indulgent guilt trips, although the programme surely didn't need to show footage of starving kids in Africa to make that point.

Thanks to the Channel 4 series You Are What You Eat *(2004-07), colonic irrigation has become an everyday sight on British television. Prior to that, however, the subject was generally considered unfit for family audiences, and was rarely dealt with at all (although – paradoxically – there has always been a great deal of shit floating across my television screen, as far back as I can remember). So Dr Gillian McKeith can fairly claim to be the person who first turned the giving and taking of enemas into prime-time light entertainment, rather than the innocent domestic hobby that it had previously been. Readers*

Ch 4 LIVE AND DIRECT

who have never witnessed colonic irrigation may like to experience it for themselves (albeit at one remove) by watching a textbook example at link #39 on the **TV Reviews** page on **www.badastralbooks.com**.

I said "Dr" Gillian McKeith earlier, because that is how she habitually described herself on television. In fact, her doctorate consisted of a Ph.D. that had been obtained through the mail via a distance-learning programme from the American Holistic College of Nutrition, and she had no legitimate medical qualification that entitled her to practise as a doctor in the UK.

However, four years before Dr McKeith's series began, hydrotherapist (and non-doctor) Clare Lucas had been given the opportunity by Channel 4 to do something similar, albeit in a more serious manner. What follows is a review of what may well have been the first television programme ever to tackle the delicate subject of colonic irrigation.

INTIMATE RELATIONS

C4 2000

According to an unsolicited e-mail which arrived yesterday, this is National Chip Week. The message did include the useful information that the Spanish refer to the potato as "turma de tierra" (testicle of the earth), but I'm nevertheless becoming increasingly tired of hearing that yet another day or week has just been colonised by a PR company on behalf of yet another foodstuff or medical condition. Just as I've campaigned for all juke boxes to include one blank disc (so I can pay for a few minutes' silence in the pub), so I am now planning to hire a PR company to promote 1 March as National No Day Day, thus preventing others from claiming it as National Diarrhoea Day, National Incontinence Day, or some such nonsense. I've already warned you that National Constipation Day is approaching (are we supposed to commemorate it by hopping everywhere with our legs crossed?), and it's rumoured that a National Colostomy Day may soon be declared. Well, at least I know how to celebrate that one. Instead of concluding this sentence with a full stop, I'll end it with a semi-colon;

The full colon, from caecum to rectum, was celebrated on last night's *Intimate Relations* (C4), during which hydrotherapist Clare Davies poured several quarts of warm water up what we medical men call the

TV reviews

"tradesman's entrance" of her client, Clare Lucas. This short series is exploring "what happens when the relationship between a consultant and a client is both professional and personal," and relationships seldom get more personal than one person allowing another to insert rubber tubes and large shiny metal contraptions where the sun don't shine. Sorry, but you wouldn't catch me entering the surgery of someone who has HYDRO THE RAPIST written on their front gate, and anyway I will not entertain Mr Speculum at my door. I don't even allow people to waggle a finger in my face, let alone anywhere else.

Radio 4 recently broadcast something similar to what followed, and that was pretty easy to stomach because (as they always say) on radio you make your own pictures. But last night I found myself frantically making my own pictures (mostly of raindrops on roses and whiskers on kittens) in an attempt to avoid seeing what was passing along the glass tube connected to the rubber hosing which had been inserted "up the Gary Glitter" of the recumbent client. As morbid chunks of faecal matter sluiced along the tube, the therapist told a horror story about one woman she'd treated: "A lot of sweetcorn was coming through, so I said, 'Do you like sweetcorn?'... and she said, 'It's *five years* since I ate any sweetcorn'." I suspect that's an apocryphal tale told by all hydrotherapists because, if sweetcorn *can* stay in the intestines for five years at body temperature without breaking down, how come the stray kernels which are occasionally left at the back of my fridge invariably rot within a week?

Debrett offers no advice on how to behave when such an intrusive experience is in progress, so I had to admire the sang-froid of Ms Lucas, who politely asked "are you a Virgo?" while all manner of aquatic commotions were taking place behind her. Ms Davies wasn't, but went on to explain that, as a Taurean, she took no stimulants (no tea, coffee, or wine), which may explain why she was one of the least stimulating conversationalists I've heard all year. Watching her at work, I was reminded of the proctologist who used to redecorate his hallway through his letterbox, and I found myself wondering about the wisdom of douching the bowel, thereby removing all the beneficial bacteria that naturally inhabit it. There seemed to be a close personal bond between these two women, and both were clearly looking for something extra in their lives, so why didn't they heed the advice of the old adage: with friends like these, who needs enemas?

Down at Horseferry Road, this brief space after Channel 4 News is known colloquially as "the slot." That was certainly an accurate description of last night's edition, but in reality it's more of a crucible, allowing little experiments to take place, many of which subsequently lead to bigger programmes. Last night's offering was absorbing, but it didn't convince me about the value of alternative therapies, although I have to admit that conventional medicine can be pretty dodgy too – and if you don't believe me, just read this information leaflet, which accompanied a conventional remedy purchased recently from a high street chemist: "Possible side effects include sickness, indigestion, belching, abdominal cramps, stomach ulcers, ulcerative colitis, constipation, inflammation of pancreas, skin rashes, sensitivity to sunlight, tiredness, difficulty with sleeping, irritability, depression, tremor, disorientation, ringing in ears, taste alteration, swelling due to water retention, tightness of the chest, diarrhoea, loss of appetite, vertigo, dizziness, bleeding from intestine or bloody diarrhoea, sore mouth and tongue, back pains, mouth ulcers, hair loss, drowsiness, impaired hearing, seizures, anxiety, mood changes, memory disturbances, changes in vision, bad dreams, allergic reactions, palpitations, and impotence." Apart from that though, it's perfectly safe.

For some reason, the following review about Mark Richardson, Nandrolone, and other performance-enhancing drugs has caused the name of Linford Christie to pass through my frontal lobes. Christie, you may recall, has always claimed that his late-flowering athletic career was due entirely to his own efforts, and had absolutely nothing whatsoever to do with banned anabolic steroids. Indeed, he even fought and won a libel action in 1998 against John McVicar, who did a magnificent job of representing himself in court after he had dared to insinuate in a satirical magazine that Christie's remarkable rise from 156th in the world to triumph (at an age when his track prowess should have been in decline) could only have been achieved through performance-enhancing drugs. Barely a year after Christie's victory in the courts, the IAAF gave him a two-year ban for using Nandrolone, and he was told that he would not be accredited for any future Olympic Games. Lawyers have asked me to point out that Christie has always denied the charges, that both he and Mark Richardson were cleared by UK Athletics, and that Richardson was re-instated by the IAAF following his ban.

In 1992, Christie (who had tested positive for drugs at the 1988 Seoul Olympics, but escaped sanction after the International Olympic Committee's disciplinary committee voted in his favour, by a margin of 11 to 10) succeeded Allan Wells as a British Olympic 100m champion, winning the title ahead of Frankie Fredericks, of Namibia at the Barcelona Olympic Games. In the absence of his great rival Lewis, Christie ran 9.96s in the final and, at the age of 32, became the oldest Olympic 100m champion by four years. Watch his entirely drug-free performance (so this book's lawyers assure me) at link #40 on the **TV Reviews** *page on* ***www.badastralbooks.com.***

TRUST ME, I'M A DOCTOR

BBC2 2000

So touched have I been by the patriotic media support for Mark Richardson (the latest British athlete to be suspended from competition after testing positive for Nandrolone), that I've decided to see if the press will give an honest British TV critic the same generous benefit of the doubt. Purely as an experiment, I shall arrange for the rozzers to stop me in my car, on suspicion that I've been taking an illicit substance called "alcohol" (a drug which is on the NUJ's list of banned substances, because many hacks use it to artificially enhance the speed of their column-writing). I will be asked to blow into a bag, and will be found to be a hundred times over the legal limit; but, instead of condemning me as a cheat, I fully expect the press to defend my reputation, query the accuracy of so-called "breathalyser" tests, and call for them to be banned. Then, when the case comes to court, my QC will point out that brown bread contains a substance called "yeast," which produces microscopic amounts of alcohol; and that I had accidentally eaten 875,000 brown bread sandwiches only hours before the test was taken. This scientific explanation will surely satisfy the British media and therefore, even though I've been found guilty, they will promptly declare me to be innocent.

"The use of steroids in sport is rife" declared Dr Phil Hammond during last night's *Trust Me, I'm a Doctor* (BBC2), but he too unquestioningly accepted the claims of the various athletes and bodybuilders he encountered, all of whom insisted that their extraordinary physiques had been acquired entirely through vigorous exercise, and through the drinking of high-protein milk shakes. Confrontation simply wasn't on the agenda, because television doesn't want any unpleasantness, in the form of serious investigative medicine. No, it wants light entertainment, presented by yet another whacky doctor who'll do and say anything, just so long as he doesn't have to sit all day in some draughty provincial surgery examining verrucas and haemorrhoids, but instead can bask in the warm, ego-toasting glow of the cathode rays. From Beedles and Buckman and Instant Sunshine to Harry Hill and Hank Wangford, these medics all seem to suffer from *narcissus onanis*, the unshakeable but wholly mistaken belief that the nation gave them a grant to study for six years at Barts solely so that they could then spend their time appearing on telly, performing routines in which not even a single molecule of genuine humour can be detected. Sorry, but if laughter really is the best medicine, I can only assume that the families of all these comedy doctors were wiped out long ago by tuberculosis.

Ch 5 SCIENCE

The central conceit behind last night's programme was that Dr Hammond had eight weeks to get his body into better shape, in hopes of then featuring on the cover of a men's fitness magazine. But *his* central conceit was that we would all happily spend thirty minutes watching him show off, in an orgy of self-gratification that recalled Roy Castle's worst excesses on *Record Breakers*: Phil plays the trumpet, Phil sings along with Ian Dury records, Phil flexes his muscles, skips, runs, cycles, lifts dumbbells, goes rowing, makes a video diary, even plays with his dog (incidentally, how tragically ironic it was that Mr Castle used to tell us repeatedly that "dedication is what you need," when what he really needed all along was not dedication, but medication).

Hoping that gym'll fix it, the doctor spent much of his time exercising (apparently, that's good for you), and even considered going on a cabbage soup diet to lose excess body fat (weight loss also turned out to be good for you). And the sample prepared for him by nutritionist Amanda Ursell somehow seemed a fitting metaphor for the entire programme. Thin, bland, tasteless gruel, watery and unsatisfying, very cheap and easy to make, but containing almost no nourishment whatsoever.

Was it all a dream, or were television programmes once made and presented by the reasonably intelligent? It's true that memory is a distorting lens (enlarging cultural high points like *The Body in Question*, while simultaneously diminishing the acres of dross that surrounded them), but even *The Sooty Show* was made by people with more developed critical faculties than the bunch who produced last night's farrago. The problem, of course, is that there are far more programmes being made nowadays, yet the pool of talented and competent people has remained the same size, so the result, inevitably, is dilution. Just as the overstretched medical profession increasingly relies on paramedics nowadays, so television's standards are continually dropping, with production companies willing to employ more and more half-trained staff. Let's call them paraproducers and paradirectors, along with the industry's innumerable alcoholics, also known as paralytics. Or "big brown bread-eaters," as we doctors call them.

Some programmes start out with the science, but soon transmogrify into something else. That was true of this next review, which began by looking at surgical procedures in the NHS, but quickly became an investigation into the politics of health, showing how an obsession with reducing the length of waiting lists can actually make patient care worse. John Sweeney is one of the BBC's better investigative journalists (and certainly the best to have worked on Panorama during my years as a TV critic), but he will (unfortunately for him) be forever remembered for losing his rag with a Scientologist, while making a programme about that church's more dubious practices. In normal circumstances, this

TV reviews

would not have mattered, because he could have simply edited out his tirade, but Scientologists are sufficiently canny nowadays to bring their own cameras along to record what the programme-makers are doing, which is why Mr Sweeney will never be allowed to forget this folly, which can be viewed clicking on link #41 on the **TV Reviews** *page on* ***www.badastralbooks.com.***

SWEENEY INVESTIGATES
BBC2 2006

While browsing through some old medical journals in the British Library recently, I came across a report by Dr Jorn Kristensen of Kjellerups hospital in Denmark. Entitled "An Unsuccessful Operation," it explained that a patient had arrived in surgery "to have a mole removed from his left buttock," then described how anaesthetic was administered, while the patient's genitals and buttocks were washed with surgical spirit, in preparation for the routine operation. Unfortunately, the unconscious patient suddenly broke wind, his flatus was ignited by a spark from the surgeon's electrical knife, which in turn set fire to the surgical spirit, and everything burst into flames. When the smoke died down, the surgeon saw that his patient's penis, scrotum, and buttocks had received second-degree burns, and all his pubic hair was very badly singed. A nurse's hair had also caught alight, and the fire alarm had begun ringing, so the team immediately abandoned the operation. The patient later sued the hospital for pain, loss of income, and temporary removal of his conjugal rights, and apparently still has the mole. And you thought the NHS had problems?

Well, as we know from events over the past few days, it does have problems, and last night's *Sweeney Investigates* demonstrated with disturbing clarity that there's no comical upside to the current epidemic of botched operations. The cause is the government's obsession with reducing NHS waiting lists for routine procedures like knee and hip replacements, something they've undeniably accomplished by hiring hundreds of overseas surgeons to carry out "fast track" work in private hospitals. Tony B Liar regards the dramatic reduction in waiting times as proof of success, but as one crippled patient after another told us how their lives had been ruined by incompetent surgery performed by unsupervised foreign surgeons, the phrase "more haste less speed" had never seemed so appropriate. "Good surgery is like good DIY," said Sweeney, "but bad surgery is like bad DIY." And as I looked at the lopsided cat flap (which only flaps one way) that I

Ch 5 SCIENCE

recently installed in my office door, and at the X rays on the screen where sharp-pointed metal screws were protruding through bone and poking into ligaments, tendons, and soft tissue, it was hard to know whether to laugh or cry.

The initial desire to reduce waiting times was laudable, Sweeney argued, but it takes many years for the British system to train an orthopaedic surgeon to the required standard. And recruiting foreign surgeons (who are frequently under-qualified and lacking in experience) has proved to be an extremely unwise solution, especially as many of them are not even properly vetted (an appropriate term, since one patient declared that her surgeon "shouldn't be allowed to operate on a dog"). One man recalled that, during his operation (performed under local anaesthetic), the surgeon had botched his supposedly routine knee replacement so badly that the sister began saying "we've got to call an ambulance," whereupon he was rushed from the private hospital to a nearby NHS one, with the paramedics telling him "we've got less than half an hour to save your leg." A story grimly reminiscent of the old gag about the man awakening from surgery and shouting "doctor, I can't feel my legs," only to be reassured by the medical staff "it's okay, your legs are fine... we've amputated your arms."

Some surgeons were clearly incompetent, such as Árpád Illyés from Hungary, who'd botched twelve of his first eighteen operations before the authorities stepped in to stop him. But Matthias Honl was a conscientious German doctor who knew that he needed training in the use of unfamiliar British equipment and prosthetics, and tried to get it, only to be frozen out by xenophobic British surgeons who seemed to resent his very existence. A spokeswoman for the Nuffield Group didn't inspire confidence either, glibly boasting of a "99 per cent success rate" in fast track operations, even though many of those "successes" could no longer walk unaided, and had been in great pain for up to a year. How could she be so smug when one maimed patient after another spoke of the monumental cock-up they'd experienced in hospital, just months earlier? Only in the fertility ward can a monumental cock-up *ever* be considered acceptable.

Trial by television often leaves a funny taste in my mouth, but Sweeney is an intelligent, fair and balanced judge, with a flair for presenting difficult topics in a clear and concise way. He'd even invited the Health Secretary to discuss the situation with him, but she disgracefully declined to be interviewed, and refused all twenty of the programme's applications for documents (all theoretically available under the increasingly-risible Freedom of Information Act), a sure sign that the government knows its policy is a disaster, but hasn't yet worked out how to blame someone else for the debacle. NHS surgeons are being slowed down by the need to repair the damage caused by the reckless "fast track" system, yet the lubricious

TV reviews

Tony B Liar continues to trumpet the success of his NHS reforms, refusing to acknowledge reality, just as he does over the Pandora's box he's helped to open in Iraq. When he's not proclaiming his Christian piety on chat shows, he's deceiving us into illegal wars, so isn't it about time that he was fast tracked, for amputation of that forked tongue of his? In fact, while the surgeons are at it, maybe they could amputate *all* of him?

One of the programme formats that I've pitched (so far without success) to various TV commissioning editors over the years is a show called This Week Next Week. On each edition, I'd invite economists, politicians, journalists, sports pundits, weather forecasters, and astrologers into the studio to predict what was going to happen over the next seven days; and then, a week later, I'd bring them back, confront them with their occasional successes and many failures, and ask them to explain (in front of a derisive studio audience) how their professed expertise in their subject could have led them so far astray. After all, the one sure prediction one can make about the future is that even the best-informed predictions will usually turn out wrong, due to our old friend, "unforeseen circumstances."

The following review is of a predictive scientific documentary from 2000, about the long-term future of the motor car. Not enough time has yet elapsed for the predictions it contained to be definitively declared wrong, but the mass production of hydrogen-fuelled cars still seems as far away as ever – not because the technology does not work, but because oil still retains as vice-like a grip as ever on Western civilisation. Which is a pity, because hydrogen – unlike oil – is a universally available substance, so if and when we all finally do convert to hydrogen-fuelled cars, our governments will have fewer reasons to embark on further illegal wars in the Middle East. Although (call me Mystic Vic if you will) I predict that they will still somehow manage to find a reason.

THE FUTURE OF THE CAR

DISCOVERY 2000

With Rolls Royce owned by the Germans, and Jaguar by the Americans, what car nowadays fully expresses the majestic glory of British design? For true native élan and style, look no further than Del Boy's favourite vehicle, the Reliant Robin (*aka* Plastic Pig). It stinks of oil and plastic, it has all the stability of Douglas Bader on an ice rink, its fibreglass body shatters into shards in the event of an accident, and it is therefore

Ch 5 SCIENCE

far more quintessentially British than the Aston Martin (also American-owned) frequently driven by Prince Charles. So, if the prince *really* wants to fly the flag, perhaps he too should invest in a Reliant Robin. Picture the scene. The noble sight of a fleet of Royal Blue three-wheeled Plastic Pigs (emblazoned on the side with the words "by appointment") tootling down the Mall at a funereal pace, with the Royal Ensign proudly stuck on the bonnet. They could easily dodge the paparazzi by nipping through gaps in the fence and, with a cruising speed of 15mph, there'd be no danger of anyone ending up as Royal Jelly.

However, there would inevitably be dissent from Prince Charles, the world's leading ecologist (he only got a poor second-class degree in history, but he has a direct line to God, so we can trust his judgement) and adviser on all matters spiritual (as a self-confessed adulterer and owner of several stately homes, he well understands the temptations of this world). He'd doubtless exhort his family to buy a fleet of solar-powered vehicles of the type featured on last night's *The Future of the Car* (Discovery), because they claimed to be the most environmentally friendly machines on the planet. Sadly (like the prince) none of them really worked, but I was impressed by the strides that the world's major car manufacturers are taking to produce vehicles with much higher performance and far lower amounts of noxious emissions. In fact, if they would only apply the same technological approach to princes and politicians, then society would *really* be getting somewhere.

Speaking of emissions from politicians, the programme began with footage of President Clinton, who realised some years ago that things were coming to a head and, despite repeated blows, used his oral skills to issue a challenge that was hard to swallow, yet impossible to refuse. He challenged the US car industry to produce a vehicle which ordinary Americans would want to buy and which could travel 80 miles on one gallon of petrol, and Ford, Chrysler, and General Motors are now all close to achieving that target. The key apparently lies in using aluminium bodies, which reduce the weight of a US car by three-quarters, although there is one problem. America is the centre of the world's obesity epidemic so, while cars may be getting lighter, once two corpulent gutbuckets are sitting in the front and another three in the back, the loaded weight of the typical US vehicle will remain much the same as before.

The second half of the programme looked beyond mere improvements in petrol consumption, to more radical solutions involving different means of propulsion. The Chrysler Patriot uses a flywheel (like a child's spinning top) to store energy, Toyota have experimented with a gas turbine engine, and in thirty years time it seems that we'll all be driving hydrogen-fuelled cars which will travel thousands of miles

TV reviews

without stopping (so they'd better have on-board lavatories fitted too). They're smooth, silent, and emit only water, and they'll be wondrously kind to the planet, but they didn't seem exactly thrilling to drive, and it's sad to think that the future is going to be so damn dull. It's unfair that our increasing mastery of technology isn't intensifying our sensation of real life, but alienating us from it through society's desire to be environmentally friendly, which is why I plan to stick with bumpy, loud, and smoke-belching cars for as long as I can, and also to carry on eating as much raw meat as possible. Sorry, but I didn't fight my way to the top of the food chain only to become a vegetarian.

Well-made and well-informed though it was, no programme about the future can really be judged properly until thirty years from now. For my money, it's the predictive documentaries from 1970 that are just ready for enjoying now (the ones that said we'd all be wearing bacofoil suits, flying to work on personal jet packs, and eating pills for dinner), and I'd encourage broadcasters to search their archives for such long-forgotten programmes, because they'd give us hours of pleasure if shown today. If this one turns out to be right, then the internal combustion engine is on the way out, so perhaps on second thoughts I'd better sell my car now. I know. I'll place a cunningly worded ad in *Loot* reading "For sale – Polo, mint condition." It's got a hole in it, you see, but the Trade Descriptions people wouldn't be able to touch me.

I've long maintained that many of the factual programmes that are nominally aimed at children are, in reality, intended for adults. That was certainly true of Newsround, which (during my years as a reviewer) was often the only place on British television where, for example, a viewer could have the origins of the Irish troubles or the Israel/Palestine problem fully and clearly explained.

As for science, the closest I've ever come to understanding many of the basic problems has been while watching the annual series of Royal Institution Christmas Lectures. Over the years, I've been introduced to the mysteries of astronomy, mathematics, cryptography, quantum physics, and much else. And although the 2000 series on robotics was not one of the vintage years, it still conveyed more about its subject than any number of editions of Tomorrow's World ever could.

*Professor Kevin Warwick can be seen talking about Cyborg Life atclick on link #42 on the **TV Reviews** page on **www.badastralbooks.com**.*

Ch 5 SCIENCE

ROYAL INSTITUTION CHRISTMAS LECTURES

C4 2000

Despite having found a nasty virus on my three-and-a-half-inch floppy last week (not uncommon in men of my age, I assure you), I suffer from no fear of technology. My global computer satellite TV system is equipped with an automatic language translator so advanced that by simply pushing a few buttons I can actually hear Loyd Grossman in English. I recently devised a cunning way of sending anonymous poison pen letters to my enemies on the internet, thus proving that the e-mail of the species is more deadly than the mail. But I can't log on at present, due to having been e-mailed dozens of "I-thought-I'd-send-you-this-hilarious..." Xmas card attachments of animated reindeer, each taking five hours to download, and thus blocking up my entire system. Information Superhighway? For the past week, I seem to have been stuck behind a tractor on a B road just outside Crawley.

In truth, I can't claim to be at the cutting edge of technology, which is why I've always enjoyed watching the daily *Royal Institution Christmas Lectures*, traditionally shown between Boxing Day and the New Year. For decades they were an annual fixture on the BBC2 schedules, and there was something charmingly olde worlde about the sight of some benign boffin with a white coat and a charisma by-pass attempting to combine physics with elements of pantomime as he strove to keep his juvenile audience informed and entertained. But, as with test matches, the lectures have now been poached and messed-up by Channel 4, who've shortened the coverage, zazzed up the presentation with garish lighting, zippy graphics, and video inserts, and now feed us the goodies in bite-size chunks, interspersed with advertising breaks. And the result? Well, it's still fundamentally the same, I suppose, but as I watched yesterday's lunchtime instalment, I couldn't help feeling that somehow it just wasn't quite cricket.

"Try to imagine what it would feel like to be a robot," intoned Kevin Warwick, but I had no need to imagine, because I was already watching one. Speaking in a monotone throughout, this prime example of Crimplene Man (who is also Professor of Cybernetics at Reading University) evinced no trace of emotion or humour as he methodically began to explain how his fellow humanoids learn to sense the external world. And as though the microchip had never been invented, most of his examples reassuringly seemed to involve bits of Lego or Meccano, a PP3

TV reviews

battery, a piece of string, and some infra-red sensors (passé in 1926), and the cybermen who demonstrated his prowess could only stumble about blindly, being attracted to bright white lights, and sniffing out "the highest concentration of alcohol available locally." Indeed, the lecture room soon resembled a typical nocturnal scene in Soho, except that on the streets of W1, the androids are attracted to red lights, and try to avoid blue ones.

Although Professor Warwick and his chums were clearly world leaders in robotics, the most impressive specimens were not their latest prototypes, but well-known mass-produced objects such as Aibo the cyberdog and a self-guided vacuum cleaner. The young audience seemed underwhelmed by it all (having doubtless witnessed far more impressive simulations on their Sony Playstations), and even I wasn't overly amazed by some little cars that could sense their surroundings, because my uncle once owned a pre-war Schuco clockwork car that could do exactly the same thing. A huge red-veined eyeball set me wondering where I'd previously seen such a sight (it was in the mirror yesterday morning, looking at my post-Boxing-Day eyes which resembled maps of the A roads of Great Britain), and a display of toys spinning round and round and banging into the furniture also reminded me of something I'd seen before. What was it? Ah yes. The clockwork Stevie Wonder doll, I think it was called.

My relationship with science has always been a love-hate one (love the practice, hate the theory), but I'm afraid that this series is introducing me to the subject's tedious side. I suspect that the difficulty lies with Professor Warwick, who perhaps has little experience of talking to children, and is far more at home teaching postgraduates at the University of Reading (incidentally, if there's a University of Reading, why isn't there a University of Writing and a University of Arithmetic too?). What they need is someone with a mental age of ten, so perhaps next year they'll ask *me* to lecture, and outline my latest brilliant invention. Just suppose that somebody could print all the day's news onto a piece of paper, then distribute it to shops all over the country, so we could buy it. It would be cheap, so we could carry it about with us and then throw it away when we'd finished reading it, and although it sounds implausible, it just might work. I've even thought of a name for this twenty-first century piece of new technology: I will call it "newspaper."

Given the duplicitous nature of television (where editing, lighting, soft-focus camera, and a hundred other crafty tricks can create almost any effect that a director or performer wants to conjure up), it's hardly surprising that liars have always gravitated to the medium. Sincerity is the one quality that connects the broadcaster to the viewer, and anyone who can fake sincerity at will has a promising career ahead of them inside the magic rectangle, should the world of politics not appeal to them. *However, even the most oleaginous game show host or reality show presenter would surely concede that nobody in the modern era has lied with quite the shameless aplomb of President Clinton, declaring that he did not have sex with that woman.*

*Watch again, and enjoy: go to link #43 on the **TV Reviews** page on **www.badastralbooks.com.***

That's lying on a scale that demands respect, so no wonder that it was chosen for analysis by the presenter of the following programme, which looked in depth at the science of deceit.

THE SCIENCE OF LYING

C5 2000

One of the many drawbacks of this telly reviewing lark is that one accidentally picks up the tics and mannerisms of those who live inside the magic rectangle. Over the years, I've contracted windmill arms from Magnus Pike and strabismus from Patrick Moore, but the worst problem I ever had struck recently when, after watching Anne Robinson, I was gripped by the irresistible urge to have a wink. Worse still, I spent the whole of last week winking frenziedly night and day, at first surreptitiously on the train and bus, then openly winking in public for two solid hours at the Queen Mother's Parade. I winked myself stupid and, by the time it was over, I was so exhausted I had to go home and have forty winks.

According to last night's *The Science of Lying* (C5), winks and facial tics are the surest giveaways that someone is being insincere and untruthful when they're talking to you (just fancy that, Anne). The forty-four separate muscles in our faces can form over seven thousand distinct facial expressions when we speak, and involuntary micro-expressions lasting fractions of a second will usually betray our innermost feelings, no matter how convincingly we seem to be arguing that black is really just the new white. "Politicians are the best liars, and the best detectors of liars," said the narrator, and the inevitable clip of Bill "I did not have sex with that woman" Clinton hove into view, showing him in the days before he came clean, and confessed that, yes, he had once splashed out on a frock for Monica. Which reminds me. A journalist friend who's just got back from Camp David told me yesterday about some advice which Yasser Arafat apparently gave to the President. "Next time, try goats. They don't talk."

TV reviews

"Lying is the glue that holds society together," opined one talking head, and the programme's contributors mostly seemed wholeheartedly in favour of some good honest mendacity in everyday life. A child psychologist claimed that four-year-olds can only develop their sense of individuality by telling untruths (until then, they believe that their parents can read their mind), while other hackademics commended those fibs that avoid embarrassment or make others happy. Dr Charles Ford revealed that lies emanate from the pre-frontal cortex of the brain, and told worrying tales about pseudologues who cannot distinguish between fantasy and reality, and impostors who often spend years in hospitals, masquerading as surgeons or gynaecologists. He sounded pretty convincing, but by now I was wondering: how can we be sure that *he* is a real doctor?

Certainly not by relying on the polygraph test (the famous "lie detector" machine, whose evidence was naively accepted by US courts for most of the twentieth century), because another scientist showed us just how easy it is to fool the apparatus. Just breathe a little faster and flex your sphincter as you answer the first "what is your name?" question, and after that you can tell as many porkies as you like, with little or no fear of detection. The freeze-framing of videos to capture those tell-tale micro-expressions was deemed to be a more reliable method, but a small percentage of natural born liars can outwit even that sophisticated technique, and the only potentially foolproof device seemed to be a new machine that monitors P300 brain waves. In a decade from now, it may finally be possible to tell unfailingly when someone is lying to you, although I've already developed my own method that works 100 per cent of the time with politicians. Just look at their lips and, if they're moving, they're lying.

"I saw an excellent documentary last night on C5" is the sort of phrase that might have you reaching for your polygraph machine in disbelief, but it's true. The station increasingly relies on soft porn to boost its meagre ratings, but if only they showed more quality programmes like this instead (splendidly co-produced by Lion Television and the Discovery Channel), maybe they'd find that viewers started to tune in to have their uppermost organ stimulated, rather than their lowermost. I still can't quite fathom why a 1950s typewriter was used to tap out details of the up-to-the-minute academic research into the psychology of deceit, and I felt almost sorry for the lone Professor of Ethics (or perhapth it wath Thuthex) whose pious arguments in favour of total honesty paled into insignificance alongside a university experiment which proved that students shamelessly tell an average of seven hundred lies each year. Of course, if they'd conducted the same experiment among journalists they'd have got a much higher figure, because hacks are a notoriously deceitful bunch. Honestly, they're a bunch of frauds and liars, the whole lot of them, and you can believe me when I tell you that, truly you can.

For me, Horizon represents the mixture of arrogance and ignorance of television at its most potent – regularly claiming to turn decades of rigorous academic research on its head by flying some spurious theory or other, which is seldom ever heard of again after the night of transmission. A pity, because Horizon started its long televisual life as a respectable science strand (its 1964 debut featured a memorable documentary about the theories and structures of Buckminster Fuller).

Its simple yet evocative 1977 opening titles can be seen at link #44 on the **TV Reviews** *page on www.badastralbooks.com.*

However, by the 1990s, the programme had become almost tabloidal in its lightweight approach to hefty issues, as the following review demonstrates.

HORIZON

BBC2 2002

Old people are constantly lamenting that food doesn't taste like it used to in the good old days, and they're absolutely right. Bland organic produce is everywhere nowadays, and it's becoming harder and harder to find food laced with the great taste of added chemicals, like we had when I was a lad. Yum, how I *love* those lip-smackin' E numbers, whether it's tartrazine in my soft drinks (making me so hyperactive that I have to be sent upstairs to bed), or monosodium glutamate in Chinese restaurants (which you can get free in some places). And I certainly have no fears about eating genetically modified food because, frankly, I was always told that two heads are better than one.

And when cancer eventually strikes me (I hope I get cancer of the onc, because my local hospital has dozens of oncologists, all specialising in just that area), please pump me full of conventional chemicals that make me go bald good and fast, but just might cure me at the same time. I'll certainly pass on the homeopathic remedies, thankyou very much, because as last night's *Horizon* (BBC2) demonstrated, their theoretical justification is about as convincing as that of other pseudo-sciences, like alchemy or astrology. Formulated by the German physician Samuel Hahnemann some

TV reviews

two hundred years ago, homeopathy is based on the initially plausible notion that "like cures like," but the active ingredient (anything from pollen or onion to snake venom and deadly nightshade) is always diluted trillions of times with water, until not one molecule of it is left. Which means that believing in the efficacy of homeopathic medicines is akin to thinking that somebody urinating in the Irish Sea can cure you of bedwetting if you paddle on the beach at Blackpool.

The first half of the programme was an objective overview of the subject, with hackademics on both sides of the argument professing open contempt for anyone who disagreed with them. "There's less than a chance in a billion that there's a single molecule there," scoffed research chemist Walter Stewart as he scornfully dismissed the diluted remedies, while supporters offered mostly anecdotal evidence of their value, in animals as well as in humans. Saddest of all was Dr Jacques Benveniste, a sort of Sacha Distel with a PhD whose once-brilliant scientific career was ruined in the late 1980s after he claimed to have discovered "the memory of water," only for his experiment to fall apart under close scrutiny from Sir John Maddox (editor of *Nature*) and the sceptical magician James Randi. So, according to contemporary science, a homeopathic pill is simply a placebo with nothing in it, although I suppose it *could* still have an effect on ailments like tense nervous headaches. After all, haven't you ever heard the old slogan that "Nothing acts faster than Anadin"?

"For the first time ever, we are conducting an experiment," declared the narrator, and suddenly the programme-makers moved from the role of observer to that of protagonist. Taking up Randi's long-standing $1,000,000 challenge to anyone who can prove that homeopathy actually works, they seized on the recent work of Professor Madeleine Ennis (think Mo Mowlam without the looks), and tried to replicate it under the magician's watchful eye, to determine if water really *can* retain the memory of another substance. Despite shameless attempts to invest the experiment with dramatic tension, the answer was an utterly predictable "no, of course it can't," and yet again it seemed that all scientific "proof" of homeopathic effects had disappeared as soon as Randi entered the room. And having seen how the supposed health benefits of these sugar pills can be annihilated by simple scepticism, I inevitably came away thinking that such medicines leave a decidedly funny taste in the mouth.

The people who were promoting homeopathy appeared sincere and well-meaning (Randi noted wryly that "scientists can fool themselves"), and I was more concerned by the way the once-impeccable *Horizon* has started to dilute its own integrity, and is showing signs of turning into *Horizon-Lite©*. Getting involved in a $-million challenge from a magician isn't really something that a solid science programme should be doing, while the *Top of the Pops*-style camera effects smacked of desperation, and I fear that this venerable thirty-eight-year-old strand might be taking the same populist path that *QED* went down (a move that ultimately caused *QED* to RIP). Despite the high-profile failure of this test, the programme didn't deny that homeopathic treatments are widely used in veterinary medicine (where, for reasons as yet unexplained, they do appear to work), but what do I think of alternative remedies? Well, I've tried aromatherapy, Vedic medicine, massage, Bach flower remedies, and many more, but the only one that really had an effect on me was the one where they stick needles into you. What was it called? Ah yes, *heroin*. It was pricey, but boy did it do the trick.

*Anyone still taking homeopathic remedies seriously would be well advised to check out this Mitchell and Webb sketch at click on link #44a on the **TV Reviews** page on **www.badastralbooks.com**.*

As for heroin addiction, all that talking of craving...

CONSTANT CRAVING

BBC2 2000

Elvis was the King alright. He was the Burger King, a junk food junkie who was so addicted to the stuff that I reckon he even recorded a song about it ("Love Meat Tender"). Along with his friends and acolytes he would nightly tuck into never-ending platefuls of chitlins, deep-fried squirrel, rabbit, chicken, steak, bacon, corn bread, and french fries, all washed down with a bottle or two of barbiturates, in an orgy of greed that made Henry VIII look like Karen Carpenter. We shall probably never know *exactly* what happened on the night that the King died while sitting on his throne, but it's safe to say that he probably strained too hard, and suddenly went from a full colon to a full stop. A sad end, but at least he underwent an experience of which few men can boast. For, in his death throes, Elvis presumably experienced the supremely joyful pleasures and pains of childbirth.

If Elvis were still alive today, then (apart from scratching at his coffin lid) he might be able to find a cure for his global addiction. According to last night's *Constant Craving* (BBC2), scientists have now located the pleasure centre in the brain from which our desires emanate, and they are currently developing ways to help us combat our most self-destructive urges, be they for alcohol, tobacco, or class A drugs. That's good news for society, I suppose, but bad news for me, because my favourite hobby is spotting celebrity coke-sniffers, and it looks as though the boffins are soon going to put a stop to my fun. Incidentally, I have a surefire way of identifying chronic coke-heads. I simply ask them to name the tap-dancing star of *Top Hat* and, if they answer with the name of a famous firefighter, I know that they've snorted their septums away. It's my patent "Fred-Astaire-or-Red-Adair" drugs test.

The very mention in this country of class A drugs usually causes hysteria among politicians and large parts of the media, but last night's documentary took a refreshingly dispassionate and constructive approach to the subject. "Alcohol causes far more damage than all illicit drugs put together," pointed out Dr Colin Brewer, and 90 per cent of cocaine-users are masters of their habit, so what turns the other 10 per cent into helpless slaves? Our old friend genetic predisposition was to blame, and a specific dopamine receptor gene (which enhances pleasurable sensations and cravings) has already been located in alcoholics, so there'll clearly be no more problem drinking for me. Not that I have any problem drinking, not since I bought the funnel. Nowadays, I never spill a drop.

"The music industry is a world where drugs are not totally unknown," declared the narrator with masterly understatement, and it was fascinating to watch images of the brain of a typical long-time worker in that industry, as he volunteered for a scan. When he was shown a David Attenborough-style nature programme, his pleasure centre was inert (well, I've always thought that such natural history shows are the televisual equivalent of hallucinating grey vividly), whereas the mere sight of someone handling cocaine was sufficient to cause the telltale region to glow bright red, like the tip of a lit cigarette. Speaking of which, we also heard how an Australian smoker had used an inhibiting drug called Zyban to conquer his chronic four-a-day habit, and four lighters a day was quite a habit, I'm sure you'll agree.

By the end, it was clear that vaccines rendering us immune to the pleasurable effects of all major drugs (legal or illegal) will soon be available, and the programme left us pondering the moral and philosophical implications of that scientific advance. Many addicts will be grateful for the chance to regain control over their own lives, but will it add to the sum of human happiness if we're all inoculated at birth against the mood-altering influences of a glass of Château d'Yquem, or even a humble Woodbine? By calmly raising such issues, producer/director Andrew Thompson's excellent programme demonstrated yet again the BBC's unrivalled ability to deal intelligently with serious issues, with an

Ch 5 SCIENCE

authority that ITV simply couldn't muster. Transitory front-of-camera staff may desert the Corporation in a quest for more money, but the brainiest kids on the block are overwhelmingly on the production side, and the BBC is still the undisputed home of thoughtful documentary-making. Purely by coincidence, I finally decided to give up smoking exactly ten years ago. And I can honestly say that I have missed cigarettes every single nanosecond of every single minute of every single day, ever since. So stick that in your pipe and smoke it, you killjoys at ASH.

It is a well-known fact that cigarettes are the biggest single cause of statistics. While on the subject of that dubious science, I am often asked why my reviews are invariably so negative and critical. My answer is that this is a misperception, because it's a statistical fact that 50 per cent of my reviews that appeared in the London Evening Standard were positive and full of praise. However, it's the cruel reviews that seem to lodge in the frontal lobes of readers (and TV people, and me while compiling this book), probably because it is easier for me to be funny about a programme that I hate than about something I love. Here is an example of a passably amusing review about botanical matters that is shockingly favourable, albeit at the expense of exchanging poignancy for satire.

MEETINGS WITH REMARKABLE TREES

BBC2 1998

Did I ever tell you that I hold the record for the most unanswered letters ever posted to the *Guinness Book of Records*? Perhaps it's because I always begin with the words "Dear Mr McWhirter, please forgive the formality but I can never remember whether it was Norris or Ross who was shot by the IRA." I have never received a single acknowledgement regarding any of my bids for inclusion. That's a pity, because I'm currently training a flock of sheep (equipped with oxygen masks) to breathe underwater and swim into the pudenda of menstruating whales, a feat that transforms a simple Herdwick into the world's largest organic tampon. If only Mr McWhirter would respond, I could *literally* get an entry in the *Guinness Book of Records*.

In truth, I have nothing but contempt for the ridiculous book of records, which encourages grown men to sit in baths full of custard and yodel non-stop for five days, or push peas with their nose from London to Norwich, simply because they're unable to excel at any genuinely difficult task. I'm sure that one of its oldest entrants would condemn it too (if it

TV reviews

could speak), not least because the book's worthless pages are made from the flesh and sap of its own relatives. I refer to the Bowthorpe Oak in Lincolnshire, which was featured in last night's *Meetings with Remarkable Trees* (BBC2), and is listed in the *Guinness Book* on account of its venerable age (at least a millennium) and its colossal girth. Attempting to walk around its majestic bole would be even more tiring than trying to circumnavigate Nicholas Soames, and the whole magnificent structure resembles some Brobdignagian elephant's foot, surmounted by a green Barbara Cartland fright wig.

But the most fascinating aspect of the tree was that (like so many of today's TV stars) it was completely hollow inside, and full of rot. Centuries of natural erosion by fungi, bacteria, and insects had created a vast chamber within its trunk, big enough to accommodate an alfresco dinner party for a dozen people (which is exactly what one eighteenth century owner used it for). The present owners, the Blanchard family, clearly regard it as part of the family, and use it as a play area for their children, but over the years it's also served as a cattle shed, a summer house, a pigeon loft, a shelter for geese, even a bat sanctuary. And (remembering the Orphic legends) you can bet your bippy that it's also hosted plenty of beast-with-two-backs activity in its time, although sadly I can't bet *my* bippy on anything. The Grand National cleaned me out a treat.

Spectacular photography and direction (by Rob Paton) perfectly illustrated the fascinating information gleaned from Thomas Pakenham's book, including one mesmerising eighteenth-century picture of the (then middle-aged) tree kitted out with its own front door. Of course, natural wonders always attract obsessives, which brings us to the appropriately-named Mr Green (I do hope he has a daughter named Theresa) of the Ancient Tree Forum. He was clearly aroused by his proximity to this huge gnarled *quercus* and, when he began boasting that "I haven't ever seen one this size," I suddenly remembered that Priapus was a tree god too. To be fair though, I was also becoming smitten by this oak, but I know it's bound to be a bitter-sweet affair. Why? Because there's something profoundly depressing about the day when a magnificent creature is finally laid low, and I fear that the Bowthorpe Oak is slowly but inevitably moving towards the autumn of its life. It will be a grim day when it finally falls to earth, and (as with a whale being beached, or the Eiffel Tower being dismantled) I only hope that I'm not around to see it.

Why is it always the vast, unwieldy, lumbering mega-productions that get all the PR hype, when it's short and limber programmes like this that make the TV schedules gleam? The equivalent of those fascinating feature fillers in glossy magazines, the best ten-minute documentaries simply make their point succinctly and depart, without the ponderousness and overblown portentousness of their big-budget, hour-long cousins. In this case, the scale of the Bowthorpe Oak simply dwarfed all human achievements. Giuseppe Verdi is considered remarkable because he was still writing masterpieces at the age of eighty, but what is that compared to a thousand-year-old tree that's still producing acorns? Old, yes; but geriatric, never.

*Bowthorpe Oak still stands, and can be seen at link #45 on the **TV Reviews** page on **www.badastralbooks.com**.*

Its continued existence reminds me that it's the least talented performers and presenters who seem to stay on our televisions for the longest time, whereas many of the liveliest and most animated objects, people, and organisations that I have written about over the years have long since vanished. Perhaps the least exciting performers tend to survive for so long because a large percentage of them are (like the Bowthorpe Oak) wooden and hollow?

I've just checked how many references I made to Oxford and Cambridge universities throughout my reviews, and they go into the thousands (mostly because that's where the people whose programmes I was reviewing had been educated). Television is still flooded with Oxbridge graduates, especially on the production side, and that's hardly surprising, because there are certain fundamental laws that govern human existence. In the case of the Oxbridge law, this states that if somebody attended either of our oldest universities, they'll always mention it within eight-and-a-half minutes of entering a room (or, in Jeffrey Archer's case, even if they didn't). Vorderman's law, by contrast, posits that trivia will always remain trivia, no matter how much it's tarted up to look like science or maths. And Cole's law, of course, is thinly-sliced cabbage with mayonnaise.

The sheer preponderance of Oxbridge graduates in television ought to be a cause of intense embarrassment, but it isn't, because television has never had much of a sense of shame. Indeed, during the time that I was reviewing programmes, I noticed the national sense of shame disappearing almost entirely from British life, as members of the public queued up to display their neuroses, their foibles, and even their genitalia to the rest of us. In the case of reality television, that shamelessness was disgracefully exploited by certain producers, but there was a positive side, because people with chronic illnesses and disfigurements were encouraged to seek treatment for them, rather than

TV reviews

suffer in silence for decades, as they had often previously done. Leading the field in this respect was Channel 4's admirable Embarrassing Illnesses, which allowed us to feel compassion and sympathy for the indignities suffered by our fellow men and women, while also having a good laugh at their expense. Not that there's anything funny about loose skin, of course – click on link #46 on the *TV Reviews* page on *www.badastralbooks.com*.

Or a third nipple – go to link #47 on the *TV Reviews* page on *www.badastralbooks.com*.

That'll just be God, having a little laugh at our expense by capriciously fucking up the one and only life we'll ever have (unless you believe in Reincarnation, but I don't – I've always preferred fresh milk).

EMBARRASSING ILLNESSES

C4 2001

Cancer isn't a word to be afraid of these days, we're regularly told by "experts" on daytime television, and they're right. Cancer as a *word* is nothing to be afraid of, unlike cancer as a malignant disease spreading like wildfire through the lymphatic system, which is something to be very afraid of indeed. Unless you're a newspaper columnist, of course, in which case it could be a useful career move, because developing a chronic illness means you'll never be short of something to write about. That's why I've invented the handy "Journo Insert-a-Tumour," made from attractive and durable depleted uranium. Simply slip it into a pocket near to whichever part of the body *you* want to be affected, and hey presto! – a never-ending source of newspaper copy. Unfortunately, I haven't yet perfected my design, so for now I'll just have to bore you with columns about my Liver Spots. That's not an illness, by the way, just a barbershop quartet I've formed with three other alcoholic singers.

But there are certain afflictions which, although serious, have never been the subject of first-person confessionals on the comment pages, because they're not the sort of diseases that anyone wants to admit they've contracted. To redress the balance, C4 is showing *Embarrassing Illnesses*, a six-part series devoted to sensitive and humiliating disorders, and it started last night at the very bottom by dealing head-on with piles and anal fistulas. "We spend £11 million a year on self-help treatment for piles," admitted the narrator, and if they get through that much

Preparation H in her household alone, just think how much the nation as a whole must be buying. But that wasn't strictly relevant, because what the programme was mainly trying to teach us was that the bottom needn't fall out of your world, just because the world has fallen out of your bottom.

Several couples had bravely agreed to appear (and not in silhouette either) and talk about their problems "below the equator," and it was clear from what they said that you don't really know what marriage is all about until you've stopped fancying your partner's bum, and are instead squeezing pus out of it on a daily basis. David had a massive anal fistula which needed constant draining, yet his wife insisted that "we've been drawn closer together by it," thereby proving the truth of the old adage that abscess makes the heart grow fonder. "My wife has to digitise me each morning," said another sufferer, and while I don't intend to go into details, let's just say that it involved her index finger and a service that gentlemen in Soho allegedly pay a lot of money for. But I couldn't agree with the elderly couple who declared that "when you're eighteen, you are embarrassed about your private parts." If they think that, then they've clearly never tuned into Channel 4 late on Friday nights.

One shameful disease which they didn't mention, but which is spreading rapidly through independent production companies, is called *statistis satietas*, and this show had obviously contracted a nasty dose. Flocks of uncorroborated statistics were squirted out between each batch of talking heads ("one in three people suffer from haemorrhoids... 64 per cent never seek medical treatment..."), but given the unequivocally didactic nature of the programme, the diarrhoea slick of anal-ytical data seemed forgivable. A cheerful consultant from London's St George's hospital likened his "one-stop bottom shop" to a Kwik-Fit exhaust place, and used plenty of innuendo to ease the awkwardness of talking about sphincters, colons, creams, and suppositories.

Embarrassing Illnesses is admirable, unpalatable, fascinating, and repulsive in roughly equal measure (the sight of a freshly-removed pile almost caused me to suffer an embarrassing illness myself, all over the carpet), but above all it's *necessary*, and its not-inconsiderable faults can therefore be forgiven. Why the title music sounds like the inside of a tinnitus victim's head, only the producer knows, but anything that might persuade people to get the misery of piles eradicated at source (rather than trying to ease their pain by lashing out angrily at the world around them) can only be considered *pro bono publico* (not that I've ever been a big U2 fan myself). The consultants also seemed to be much less fearsome and more humane than they were in the old days, but I suppose they have to be, given the strange and often macabre situations with which they have to deal. In fact, one consultant told me recently how he'd

TV reviews

examined a patient, and then had to tell him "I'm afraid you have cancer *and* Alzheimer's." And the patient replied, "Well, at least it's not cancer then."

The programme with the highest number of potential Science Nobel Prize-winners in it surely has to have been Ask the Family. First transmitted in 1967, everything about this BBC quiz was wrong. Ask the Family was the title, but they didn't just ask any family. The lower orders were weeded out at the selection stage, and the producer only ever chose smug, well-dressed, well-heeled middle-class families from the Home Counties. Father was usually a university lecturer, mother a primary school teacher, while the children (always two) were an endless succession of precocious Ruth Lawrence clones, wearing bottle-bottom spectacles and looking like miniature versions of their parents (though with fully-developed adult neuroses). They all dressed in matching cardigans with golf-ball buttons, and they all had one thing in common: no-nonsense ugliness. Proving once again the truth of my theory that only the profoundly unattractive have the time or the inclination to read books. The programme itself consisted of endless rounds of questions in the lateral-thinking style, and invitations to guess the identity of a close-up photograph of a domestic object, which almost invariably turned out to be a cheese grater. Was there a saving grace? Yes... the programme's presenter, Robert Robinson. He displayed the enviable skill of appearing to be deeply interested in both the questions and the answers, but look closer, and the truth would be revealed. He was interested in neither. Sadly the programme had stopped running long before I started reviewing, but here is a breathtaking example:

*Go to link #48 on the **TV Reviews** page on **www.badastralbooks.com**.*

Where you will see the sort of middle-middle-middle Englander people who, if they took drugs, would hallucinate grey vividly. "The drugs don't work" sang The Verve on their legendary album "Urban Hymns." Well, maybe not, but in their case surely it would have been worth a try anyway? Speaking of which, the unscientific and insane basis of our current drugs policy was the subject of this next review.

Ch 5 SCIENCE

UNDER THE INFLUENCE

C4 2001

Some years ago, a friend of mine spent several months in a mental hospital. Back in his teenage years, he'd walked along the slippery narcotic path that starts with a Woodbine and ends with wood polish, and although he'd conquered his addiction by the time I met him, a "flashback" episode led to his being apprehended by the police while walking along the street with a lampshade on his head, claiming (I quote verbatim) "I am a supermarket trolley making my way towards Dublin." Once incarcerated, he soon got better, but he still remembers that the communal TV set in his psychiatric ward was permanently tuned to ITV, with tape stuck over the other buttons. When he asked why, a nurse told him that BBC1, BBC2, and C4 were considered too thought-provoking (and therefore too upsetting) for patients, whereas ITV's cosy output was bland and mindless, and ideal for recuperating ex-supermarket trolleys who were temporarily off their trolleys.

    I recalled that incident last night while watching *Under the Influence* (part of C4's thought-provoking and thoroughly un-cosy *Drug Laws Don't Work* season), because the programme presented compelling evidence that tobacco is the gateway drug which tempts most addicts to take their first faltering steps along that slippery narcotic path. "It's no coincidence that most drug-addicted people smoke," declared Dr Nora Volkow (an expert on the effects of drugs on the brain), and decades of research had convinced her that "exposure to nicotine facilitates the taking of other drugs." Selecting as its starting point a study into drug use amongst clubbers (carried out at the Maudsley Hospital's National Addiction Centre), this brave and level-headed documentary examined the risks associated with various mind-altering substances, both licit and illicit, and produced seemingly irresistible proof that our society's current laws are based on a mixture of history and prejudice, rather than on any serious attempt to protect citizens from harm. Tobacco has been killing on an industrial scale for centuries, yet the government shamefully refuses even to ban cigarette advertising, preferring to concentrate on a futile battle against illegal drugs like Ecstasy, whose most harmful side-effect is that many otherwise law-abiding users end up in jail for possessing it.

    "You never see 'tobacco' written on a post mortem report, yet it causes 120,000 deaths a year," said Professor John Henry, giving us a proper perspective on Ecstasy's annual cull of ten unlucky clubbers. With a million tablets consumed each weekend, this clearly places it at the low

TV reviews

end of the danger spectrum, compared to the four thousand deaths each year from chronic alcohol poisoning (not to mention a hundred instant binge-drinking fatalities), yet the Anne Widdecombes of this world have blindly called for the incarceration of all who dare to take it. "The drug that causes most admissions to our Accident and Emergency department is alcohol," lamented one medic, and any sane observer would have been left wondering why fags and booze weren't outlawed long ago, and why Ecstasy and cannabis ("a drug without a fatal dose") haven't at least been decriminalised. But of course, the reasons are simple. The Chancellor makes billions from taxes on alcohol and tobacco, and anyway, they're the Establishment's drugs of choice.

But in pointing out the lunacy of the current situation, the programme certainly wasn't underplaying the very serious dangers of illegal drugs. Indeed, research clearly linked prolonged Ecstasy use to impaired memory and depression, and drug-influenced drivers are an obvious public risk, but those same drawbacks were even more relevant to alcohol, and the real issue here wasn't so much the drug as the user's sense of responsibility. By the end, I could only shake my head at the sheer hypocrisy of our rulers' Manichean attitude to mind-altering substances, and thank my stars that my own preferred drugs are legal. Sadly, I've only ever needed a regular supply of wine, preferably *chateau* (or "cat's water" as we say in English). Not that I have a drink problem, you understand. Well, not since I bought a funnel and a length of rubber tubing anyway. Nowadays, I don't spill a drop. Unless vomiting counts as spillage.

Most drug-related documentaries I've watched over the years should have carried a health warning in the *Radio Times* ("may cause drowsiness"), but this one fairly raced along, like *Panorama* on speed. It's sad that our government (and most of our newspapers) are unable to conduct equally objective and grown-up discussions about drugs of all types, because many of these substances could (if used sensibly) be of enormous benefit to us all, not just in the quest for pleasure, but also as relief for the terminally ill, and those in pain. Just last week, Professor Karol Sikora despairingly described palliative care as "the Cinderella in hospitals," and complained of "this belief that one should face pain bravely," and I was reminded of the chilling words I once heard Archbishop Foley utter while condemning the very idea of euthanasia. "Suffering in the last minutes of life," he declared, "helps us to share in Christ's pain and helps us to imitate Christ more closely." If such compassionate sentiments don't make even the most resilient hospice dweller lose the will to live, then I don't know what will.

Science programme presenters are a mixed bunch. Traditionally, they were plug-ugly oddballs – or apparently so – because the one-eyed monster has always had an insatiable appetite for eccentrics. It hungrily chews them up, sucks out the goodness and then spits them out, but not before corrupting them by turning their unaffected mannerisms into self-conscious parody. The downward spiral usually starts with a bow tie, but that's just the first sign. The day Magnus Pyke began twirling his arms on cue, or Patrick Moore bought a monocle for Blankety Blank, you knew that they'd sold their souls and from then on it was downhill all the way to the tabloids.

If younger readers are unfamiliar with Magnus Pyke, allow me to remind them of his cameo appearance in a Thomas Dolby video, where he is seen (and heard) shouting out the word "science!" again and again:

*Go to link #49 on the **TV Reviews** page on **www.badastralbooks.com**.*

In recent and more visually obsessed decades, scientific styles have changed, and science programmes are just as likely to be presented by glamorous women (Kate Humble today, Philippa Forrester a decade ago), or male models for underpant commercials, such as Brian Cox. Or, indeed, by the estimable Adam Hart Davies, the star of this next review. He's a man with whom I could happily go unto the jungle because, with him, what you see is what you get.

SCIENCE SHACK

BBC2 2001

There's stiff competition in the cut-throat world of undertaking, but my Dead Funny company is putting the fun back into funeral, with its latest range of products. Our Christmas catalogue include Y-shaped coffins ("ideal for burying your unfaithful spouse"), novelty condolence cards (open one up and a voice sings "sorry to hear your loved one is worm food"), and a DIY kit for recently-deceased smokers, allowing their next-of-kin to scrape the tar from the corpse's lungs (before an impromptu cremation of the mortal remains), and use it to tarmac their driveway.

  I rather feared that an impromptu cremation was about to take place on Friday night's *Science Shack* (BBC2), when Adam Hart-Davis announced his intention to grasp an electrode with half a million volts flowing through it. I don't know much about electricity, but I do know that those things aren't called "terminals" for nothing, so I was relieved when

TV reviews

all that happened was some spectacular arcing between the electrode and his fingertips, with no incineration at all. That was just one of a series of dramatic experiments which the presenter conducted while unravelling the mysteries of lightning, but although he toyed with massive forces as playfully as a kitten might toy with a ball of wool, he also stressed the potential dangers of what he was doing, for the benefit of any dimmer types who might have been watching. Or, to give them their correct scientific name, rheostats.

Hart-Davis is one of television's good guys, an amalgam of Keith Joseph and Bernard Levin, with the added spunk of John Noakes, whose ability to communicate scientific ideas in a simple way is so refined that he can make even *me* understand the principles involved (although, by next morning, I've invariably forgotten again). Some fifty people are struck by lightning in Britain each year, so as well as explaining how celestial electricity is generated (mostly by ice crystals rubbing against each other within clouds, it seems), he gave us practical advice about how to avoid being victim number fifty-one. If you're indoors when a thunderstorm erupts, don't touch light switches (a woman who did recalled how "you could smell cooking meat" as her hand fused to the patio door), and don't use the phone, or you might get a sudden nasty shock (in addition to the one you get every three months, when BT send their extortionate bill). And if you're outdoors, curl up small and balance on the balls of your feet, but don't stand under a tree, or upright in a field, and whatever else you do, don't play golf. That last point, by the way, is good advice whether there's a storm or not. *Don't play golf.*

Just as shins are devices for finding furniture in the dark, so Hart-Davis's entire body was a device for finding electric currents, as he was zapped, blasted, and jolted, with no apparent ill-effects. In what was really a Royal Institute Christmas Lecture for adults, he encouraged high-voltage sparks to leap towards him, and at one point was even mercilessly assaulted as he cowered helplessly inside an iron cage (something that will also have happened this weekend to another TV presenter, Jonathan King). The Faraday cage in question protected him from million-volt flashes which were emanating from a gigantic Tesla coil, and his electrical derring-do inspired me to conduct my own pioneering experiment after the programme had finished. And so, in a spirit of scientific enquiry, I performed my own corrective laser eye surgery by removing the back of my CD player and staring at the light beam while it was switched on. It got rid of my cataracts alright (indeed, it got rid of my eyeballs), but remember kids, don't try this at home.

Science Shack is a joy to watch, and Hart-Davis is a *mensch* who's the best advertisement for popular science since the days of Jack Hargreaves.

Unlike Rolf Harris (currently fronting BBC1's Arts Lite© strand), he's never patronising, and has valiantly resisted the temptation to develop into a fully-fledged nutty eccentric, of the type that television loves to corrupt, demean, and then jettison (Magnus Pyke, David Bellamy, and Heinz Woolf, to name but three). What's more, he also interacts well with other scientific specialists, like Dr Clive Saunders, who made a brief appearance to talk about the seemingly impossible energies generated within a thunderstorm. I wonder if he was related to Ernest Saunders, a man who also generates seemingly impossible energies? In case you can't place the name, he was one of the "Guinness Four" who received a lengthy jail sentence for fraud, was let out of prison within months, allegedly suffering from the *irreversible* condition of senile dementia, and is now running a large company in the City, making a fortune, looking better than ever, and suing the government (despite having been convicted on the basis of his own statement). Now that's what *I* call a wonder of science.

How could any book of TV science reviews omit The Sky at Night? Well, quite easily, I suppose. Indeed, if the editor of this book decides that we're running a few pages over, he'll probably cut this next review without a second thought. That's publishing for you. It's a cut-throat business.

Nevertheless, I shall try to ensure that The Sky at Night remains, because there's been no other programme quite like it in the entire history of television. What other programme, anywhere in the world, has had the same permanent presenter for more than sixty years? None. That unique accolade belongs to Sir Patrick Moore, who has been at the helm from its first airing on 24 April 1957, thereby making it the longest-running programme with the same presenter in television history.

*A short interview with Sir Patrick in his Selsey cottage can be seen at link #50 on the **TV Reviews** page on **www.badastralbooks.com.***

THE SKY AT NIGHT

BBC1 2002

The New Year Honours list has been and gone, and once again my services to the nation have been overlooked. I had let it be known that I would accept the title of KQS (Keeper of the Queen's Steradent), or RRS

TV reviews

(Roller of the Royal Spliff) to Prince Harry, but nothing was forthcoming.. No matter, because whilst browsing through a copy of *Gray's Anatomy* the other day, I discovered "the Islets of Langerhans," which sound like the birthplace of a Scottish laird or a Tolkienesque wizard, but are actually a group of insulin-secreting cells in the pancreas. And as mine are in full working order, I wish henceforth to be addressed in public as Victor Lewis-Smith MIL (Master of the Islets of Langerhans).

If the presenter of *The Sky at Night* (BBC1) ever takes a full title, I hope he'll choose the equally anatomical "Lord Moore of Uranus," in recognition of all the black holes and heavenly bodies he's probed with his impressively proportioned nine-inch refractor. For forty-five years, Sir Patrick has been the face and voice of popular astronomy, and although (as with the long-range shipping forecast) few of us understand what in heaven's name he's talking about, we're quietly reassured that at least it all seems to make sense to him. You'd think that the man and his monthly programme were as unassailable as Alistair Cooke's *Letter from America*, but the BB Cone Lite© obsession with populism has even been threatening *this* programme's integrity of late, with one recent edition even veering into astrological prediction (a pseudo-science that Sir Patrick rightly and unreservedly despises). And when our host began this month's programme by asking "Is there life on Mars?" I feared that he might be about to embark on a geriatric cover version of a Bowie classic not attempted since Peter Glaze's spirited but doomed stab at "Golden Years," weeks before he was finally pensioned off from Crackerjack.

But thankfully, it soon became clear that the show had returned to its fascinatingly incomprehensible roots, with a sober discussion about the red planet's potential for supporting life that made few concessions to the scientific illiterati. Try as I might, I know I'll never get to grips with horizontal stromatolites or the Raman spectrum of a hopanoid biomolecule, especially when filtered through the idioglossic lips of an elderly presenter who (I swear) said at one point "wazzurplay flagripmloom clitto." So, after pausing to notice that Sir Patrick is becoming increasingly Hobbit-like with every passing month (due to his head gradually retracting into his thorax), my mind began to muse on scientific matters of its own, such as how people measured the size of hailstones *before* the invention of golf balls. And whether streets in a parallel universe are suddenly plunged into gloom when a motorist accidentally leaves his car head-darks switched on.

But my attention is always re-engaged when *The Sky at Night's* special guest comes on, because (charming and knowledgeable though they invariably are) they always look like the sort of gentlemen who are helping police with their enquiries after an incident in the kiddies' swimming pool. This month's expert was straight out of the Open University *circa* 1971 (bearded, and dressed in clashing colours that produced interference lines on my screen), but he drew persuasive comparisons between the primitive extremophile life forms found in Antarctic dry valleys and the kinds of fungi and bacteria that might conceivably exist on Mars. He brought a lot of complicated equipment with him into the studio, then (in the best traditions of the British boffin) explained that it didn't work, and I found myself drifting off again, and ruminating on the myriad planets, stars, and asteroids that hurtle around in the vastness of space. Frankly, things like that don't greatly impress me and my fellow TV critics. Indeed, when we look up at those tiny twinkly points of light in the night sky, we always think "how puny and insignificant they are, and how big and important we are."

"I think Mars still has many surprises in store for us" concluded the presenter, and with that, the closing music began to play, an imposing piece by Sibelius entitled "At the Castle Gates" (and not, as I'd previously thought, "Strangling Kittens" by Dicky Bowels). Long may Sir Patrick continue to enlighten the scientific community (and fail to enlighten the rest of us), because the show is one of the few remaining links with television's simpler yet nobler origins, although I suspect that when its founder finally goes gentle into that good night, the show will vanish with him. Before that happens, I'm hoping that he'll invite *me* on as his special guest (I've already bought a clip-on beard and a seed-packet shirt with unfeasibly wide lapels), so that I can precis the recent lecture on Relativity which I gave to the British Astronomical Society. In which I argued that nothing in the universe travels faster than a bad cheque, and nothing travels slower than a suburban train.

*Peter Glaze can be viewed in the act of crucifying David Bowie's "Golden years" on a 1976 Crackerjack. Mercifully, it's only a fragment, and I hope the wardrobe mistress disposed of their costumes responsibly – you wouldn't want them going to landfill, and potentially storing up trouble for future generations: go to link #51 on the **TV Reviews** page on www.badastralbooks.com.*

Incidentally, I and my lawyers would like to make it abundantly clear that there is absolutely no connection between the previous review of Sir Patrick Moore and the following review about gay animals. Its proximity is pure serendipity. However, since you ask, I once had a conversation with Sir Patrick when I worked for BBC Radio York, and we found ourselves stuck in the back of a broken-down radio car somewhere in the middle of North Yorkshire. Lacking an opening conversational gambit, I casually asked Sir Patrick about the rumour I had heard, concerning his penchant for watching the total eclipse of the sun from an ocean liner, during the course of which he would apparently remove all his clothes. There was a frosty silence, after which Sir Patrick changed the subject.

The following review is of one of the most hilarious and memorable programmes that I saw in my entire reviewing career.

THE TRUTH ABOUT GAY ANIMALS

C4 2002

When I consider humanity's seemingly unquenchable thirst for pseudo-scientific knowledge, I'm reminded of the great Frank Zappa's succinct line: "People we is not wrapped tight." Fortune-tellers have unashamedly continued to ply their trade since 11 September, despite their complete inability to predict the worst atrocity of the past half-century (what did the clairvoyants say in advance of the attack on the WTC? They didn't say sooth). As for Uri Geller's amazing powers, I've often been astonished that a man with self-proclaimed supernatural abilities should fritter them away on party tricks like bending spoons (something that any competent conjurer can do), rather than, say, developing a cure for cancer. Though I must admit that, the last time I saw him performing on TV, I suddenly found *myself* bent double. With laughter.

Pseudo-scientific knowledge can distort our understanding of the natural world too, by reinforcing baseless prejudices, while glossing over important but inconvenient truths. The Whispering Attenbore, for example, has simply airbrushed homosexuality out of the hundreds of programmes he's made during the past thirty years, but as Scott Capurro demonstrated in last night's *The Truth About Gay Animals* (C4), it's an everyday activity for a sizeable percentage of the animal kingdom. "As far as television goes, gay creatures don't exist," he lamented at the outset, before setting off in search of documentary proof of the love that dare not bleat, moo, cluck, whinny, or bark its name. And as his journey progressed, this outspoken gay comedian skilfully demonstrated that the *truly* sick animals aren't the four-legged homosexual ones, but those narrow-minded humans who refuse to believe the evidence of their own eyes, and prefer to live in deluded and opinionated denial.

"They get this big swelling, but I don't think that's sexual," said two little old ladies (who both dress as Margaret Rutherford in *Murder*

Ahoy, and run Twyford Zoo), as they desperately tried to explain away the rampant lesbian activity of their bonobo chimps by saying they were merely "playing with each other." But the attendant who ran the monkey house later confided to Scott that "gay sex between females is very very common," and as we watched one repeatedly rubbing her gourd-size clitoris against another girl chimp's groin, it seemed impossible to disagree. In a strait-laced Dorset village, the locals similarly denied the proven existence of homosexual swans in the vicinity ("it's unnatural" being the mantra repeatedly uttered in the teeth of the evidence), while in Florida Scott uncovered the story of a man who'd beaten his dog to death simply because it enjoyed anal sex with another male pooch. "There is no such thing as homosexuality in the animal kingdom," he was told by angry homophobic residents, and he soon left town, fearful that what they *really* wanted was to eradicate that tendency in the human world too.

In Montana, he met a professor whose life's work has been the study of homosexuality in sheep, and who estimated that up to ten per cent of rams prefer anal sex with other males ("That's a rectal intromission," she declared, as she showed us a gay ovine clip, but it sounded oddly like "rectal intermission" and, until the penny dropped, I wondered if her film of two woolly jumpers playing silly buggers with each other was an ill-fated attempt at relaunching those 50s BBC between-the-programme fillers). Scott was soon inundated with clips of gay seagulls, dolphins, and buffalos, the footage (and I *mean* footage) frequently having been removed from wildlife programmes because it didn't conform to the rigidly heterosexual norms that are wrongly supposed to govern the natural world. In a superb denouement, he interviewed the fiercely homophobic Baroness Young (a woman who, ironically, dresses like a lesbian), and demolished her ill-informed arguments about normal and abnormal sex with evidence of homosexual behaviour in over *four hundred* species, besides mankind. "I don't want to see this," she countered feebly as the ignorance and spiteful hypocrisy of her views were unmasked by a succession of video clips, and when she finally dies and goes to Purgatory, I very much hope she'll be locked in a room with a few bonobo lady chimps for an aeon or two, until she learns the error of her ways.

This was starred first-class material from Diverse Productions, and producer Nick Hornby, director Helen Littleboy (what else?), and Channel 4 all deserve congratulations for an incisive, vicious, hilarious, pacey, and original documentary. If it doesn't win a Bafta or two next year, I'll eat my cat. It's nothing short of disgraceful that the likes of Attenborough have been allowed to broadcast their relentlessly straight, sanitised, blinkered view of the natural world for so long, claiming that their programmes are educational when they're actually highly

TV reviews

selective and bowdlerised. As Capurro demonstrated, such natural history documentaries ultimately do us all a disservice, because despite their thin veneer of pseudo-science, what they really show us is a very *unnatural* history indeed.

Nearly 43 years ago, the government founded the Open University, partly to allow older people to catch up on their missed education via television, but mainly so that redbrick students (and even breeze block students) could display the same snobbish contempt towards an institution of higher learning that Oxbridge students had long shown towards their Johnny-come-lately alma mater. How glorious were those early years, with bearded lecturers who looked like sex offenders appearing in seed packet shirts so garish that viewers enjoyed an extra hour of daylight in winter, and the OU excelled in every academic area, except one. Sadly (so legend has it), the Dean of Carpentry and the Dean of Woodwork weren't fully in control of their faculties, and their department had to be closed down after Jacques Derrida was appointed to the chair in Deconstruction, only for it to collapse when he tried to sit on it. "I fear you have not fully grasped the essence of my teaching," the French philosopher informed them tartly, and one only hopes that the same department hasn't now been hired to deconstruct the late, great man's coffin.

Look Around You drew on some of the DNA of OU presentation, along with some of the DNA of Tomorrow's World from the 1970s. However, its main influence was the Programmes for Schools strand, familiar to schoolchildren who grew up in the 1960s and 1970s (and even the 1980s, until video recorders made the scheduling of educational programmes during the daytime superfluous). The second series of six half-hour programmes was good in parts, but the first series of ten-minute shorts captured the mood perfectly, as it simultaneously mocked and paid tribute to the style it was satirising. It remains one of television's most brilliant but underrated (in every sense) comedic gems.

LOOK AROUND YOU

BBC2 2002

Although many social anthropologists maintain that the consumer durable which epitomised the 70s was the K Tel home haircut kit – which turned your living room into a barber's shop (Sweeney Todd-style) by ripping great clumps of hair directly out of your scalp – for me it has to be the Slimwheel. By dint of brilliant marketing, this preposterous keep-fit device was sold to millions on the basis that it could "get rid of your beer gut," and in a sense it could, because users soon found that it totally dislocated their spine, resulting in no work, no money, no beer, and therefore no beer gut. Its "simplicity" was much emphasised (although in reality it was the purchasers who were simple), and the rim left such deep ridges in the carpet that New Age travellers would frequently turn up at the door, and insist on taking pictures of the mysterious crop circles that had formed in your Axminster. And such was the strain on the human body that many users had heart attacks and died, weren't discovered until rigor mortis had set in, and had to be trundled down to the crematorium like wheelbarrows, which frankly didn't look too dressy on the obituary page.

While slimwheeling parents were on their knees, discovering the joys of a freshly strangulated hernia, their children were watching educational programmes on daytime television, very similar to *Look Around You* (BBC2). I say "very similar to" because the late scheduling of last night's seemingly innocuous maths lesson forewarned us that there would be something decidedly odd about this short didactic film, which seemed to come from a parallel universe and to be intended for pupils of *incomprehensive* schools. The familiar ITV "Television for Schools and Colleges" disappearing clock (with guitar) was followed by a lecture that captured the very quiddity of educational television in the late 70s and early 80s, right down to the opening graphics, generated in BASIC by a state-of-the-art BBC Acorn computer. And considering that most daytime television nowadays seems intended for audiences with a mental age of ten, why shouldn't some adult time slots be filled with what is ostensibly schools programming?

"This programme, *Maths*, is discussed in chapter 3.1415926 of your text book which accompanies this series" said a Jeremy Nicholas-like period voice over that oozed dispassionate authority. The man was clearly *pi*-eyed, because he proceeded to tell us that "*Maths* stands for Mathematical Anti Telharsic Harfatum Septomin," and advised us to "think of it as the language of numbers, with 1 equalling A, 2 equalling the, 3 equalling hello, and so on," then ordered us to "write that down in your copy book now." And so the wonderfully insane but plausible lecture continued, illustrated by convincingly recreated archive clips of surreal blandness, and accompanied by music generated by the sort of primitive synthesisers that ruined many an otherwise splendid album of the period (*Band on the Run* for one). You know the sound: a sawtooth buzz like a cat chewing a bee, and a "slew" effect that resembles the explosion of gastric juices from a patient on a mortuary slab on a hot summer's day, shortly after the air conditioning has failed. That sort of sound.

TV reviews

To the casual eye, it all looked like a typically dull Fourth Form maths lesson, complete with inscrutable algebraic propositions. "Imhotep is taller than Jean but shorter than Lord Scotland," droned the lecturer, but the comedy arose not just from the perfectly observed parody, but also from some exquisite flights of fancy. One minute, eight housewives were buying eight shoes for eight spiders, the next Queens Elizabeth III, IV, and V were showing off their outfits (including one royal dress that could change shape and colour at will, but also had an unfortunate propensity to burst into flames) and, best of all, two young graffitists were seen spray-painting a complex equation onto a brick wall. Well, it's better than taking E, I suppose. Although in their case, they'd probably have taken mc2, knowing that it's the same thing.

Despite the massive hype that greeted the start of *The Office*, fifty-four million people in Great Britain *didn't* watch the first episode, and over fifty-five million didn't watch the second. Having received virtually no pre-publicity whatsoever, *Look Around You* probably started out last night with fifty-six million not watching, but I'd be prepared to bet that its audience will grow steadily, while *The Office's* ratings continue to fall. Together with director Tim Kirkby, writers-producers Robert Popper and Peter Serafinowicz have created a truly original series, and as I watched the rest of the preview tape (don't miss the ghost being electrocuted and the adventures of a rectal thermometer in the weeks to come), I was reminded that I continued to tune into schools programming long after I'd left the place. Well, back in those days, there were no such things as satellite porn channels or domestic VCRs, and for a guy with no girlfriend, programmes like *The Miracle of Birth* were the only place I was ever going to see a vertical bacon sandwich (albeit accompanied by a hell of a lot of placenta). Sorry, but I was a teenage boy without a girlfriend, and pussy is pussy.

Earlier, I noted how the trend in television presenters has changed in recent decades from the traditional mad, swivel-eyed, eccentric boffin (Magnus Pyke, Patrick Moore) towards the more photogenic Brian Coxes and Kate Humbles of the present day. However, Ms Humble is by no means just an autocutie, and has demonstrated over many years that she has an impressive grasp of natural science and (as here) of chemistry, physics, and engineering, as can be seen from this clip:

*Go to link #52 on the **TV Reviews** page on **www.badastralbooks.com**.*

Ch 5 SCIENCE

ROUGH SCIENCE

BBC2 2004

Just before Christmas, I shared with you my obsessive interest in tradesmen whose professions seem predetermined by their names (citing the case of F Sharp, the erstwhile piano tuner at Harrods). Since then, I've also found out about Annabelle Giltsoff (a gold leaf picture frame restorer), Mr Todhunter (a Master of the Hounds), and a Welsh window-cleaner called Shammy Davis Junior (okay, I lied about that one), and have realised that the same phenomenon exists in television too. Throughout the 1990s, the BBC Chairman was Bland, and his reign brought us presenters like the inanely grinning Carol Smillie, the self-promoting Melvyn Bragg, and the gluttonous Loyd Gross-man, not to mention the old bag Esther Rantzen (I'm not being ungentlemanly, that's what her surname means in German). In fact, the affinity between name and behaviour often seems so precise that I suppose we should be grateful nobody ever asked Vanessa Feltz to front a sex show with Ted Rogers.

By the same token, Kate Humble didn't get the job of fronting BBC2's *Rough Science* simply because she's a pretty face. Popular science shows always need a modest and unassuming presenter to mediate between the boffins and the viewers, and she's proved highly effective in that role, being neither an egghead nor an airhead. However, the executive producer's name should, by rights, be Hugh Briss, because this current series was filmed in California's Death Valley as the Open University's Beagle 2 headed toward Mars, and the advance PR material talked boastfully about outdoing the Americans in the space race, and seeing whether a group of British scientists "could take on NASA in their own backyard." Well, given that Beagle 2 has turned out to be the dog that didn't bark in the night (nor indeed ever), the answer to that is clearly "no," and perhaps it isn't only Kate who ought to be Humble.

When I was at university, we fine arts students used to refer derisively to science undergraduates as "Fizzers," partly because it was short for physicists, partly because they did anything *but* fizz, but mainly because physiognomically they resembled a bunch of spotty teenage Magnus Pykes (and that was just the girls). However, times have clearly changed, because the boffins who'd been assembled for this series are not only smart but photogenic too, the result resembling a Hollywood audition for a cinematic version of *How!* ("starring Nicole Kidman as Bunty James, and Jude Law as Fred Dinenage"). The producer clearly wanted there to be chemistry as well as physics on the screen, so there was plenty of giggling

TV reviews

and light flirting in evidence as they set about last night's challenges, which involved calculating the size of the Archimedes crater on the moon, and the size of some meteor or other that had made a huge crater somewhere in the Arizona desert. Sorry, but I didn't catch the name of that crater, because I became distracted when the camera suddenly panned down to the front of Ms Humble's trousers, and I realised they were so tight that I could very nearly calculate the size of *her* crater.

Being deprived of their usual hi-tech equipment, the scientists were forced to improvise with what was around them, although they did have "a few basic tools" to hand (rather as chefs on those "make a three-course dinner for £5" cookery programmes always turn out to have a full spice rack, truffles, some albino caviar, and a bottle of extra-virgin olive oil). Nevertheless, there's a limit to what can be achieved with a length of string, a shaving mirror, and a bag of flour, and Kathy Sykes ended up sounding less like a distinguished academic than like my local builder, shrugging her shoulders and guestimating "Well, it's about 1200 metres... plus or minus 300 or 400 either way." To be fair, their rough calculations ultimately proved to be roughly correct, and they'd all displayed considerable ingenuity under the circumstances, especially in measuring the size of the Archimedes lunar crater with just a stopwatch and a human hair fixed to an eyepiece. Incidentally, Archimedes is recorded as having died in 212 BC, and there's one question I'd have liked the rough scientists to have answered. How the blimming heck did anyone *know* that it was 212 BC at the time?

Given the general infantilisation of much of the BBC's TV output since Greg Dyke took over, we should give thanks for the stream of intelligent and entertaining programmes that currently emanate from the once-widely-mocked Open University. But sod Dyke, because I wish to conclude today's sermon with a story about astronaut Neil Armstrong, who not only said "That's one small step for a man, one giant leap for mankind" when he stepped onto the moon in 1969, but also uttered the enigmatic remark, "Good luck Mr Gorsky." For decades, people thought he was referring to a Soviet cosmonaut rival, but a reporter recently asked him about it, and (according to my highly reputable source, *The Global Conspiracy Journal*) has finally established the truth. "When I was a kid playing in the backyard," said Neil, "my baseball landed in Mr and Mrs Gorsky's garden, in front of their bedroom window. And as I was picking up the ball, I heard Mrs Gorsky shouting at her husband: 'Oral sex? Oral sex you want? You'll get oral sex when the kid next door walks on the moon!'"

The final review in this chapter is ostensibly about science and gadgets, and pays tribute to one of Channel Five's most successful and durable shows. It is also a thinly-disguised critique of the so-called music of Michael Nyman.

THE GADGET SHOW

C5 2004

Kindly forgive the shameless plug, but I've just finished making a documentary for BBC4 (to be shown on 25th June) about the Experimental Music movement that gave us such revered composers as Cornelius Cardew, Gavin Bryars, and Michael Nyman. Coincidentally, I also recently read a newspaper article about dire British sex comedies of the 1970s, and saw a reference to a 1976 film called *Keep It Up Downstairs*, "a sex romp starring Diana Dors, Aimi MacDonald, and Francoise Pascal, with lesbian scenes featuring Mary Millington, Maria Coyne, and Olivia Munday," and (wait for it) "music composed and arranged by Michael Nyman." I was so intrigued by this coincidence that I immediately checked the maestro's official list of film scores in *The New Grove Dictionary*, which faithfully itemises *The Piano*, *The Diary of Anne Frank*, and all his Greenaway films, but has curiously overlooked his 1976 opus. Perhaps Mr Nyman has forgotten about it too, and should be reminded, because how delightful it would be if he could serenade us at a future Prom with a suite compiled from his sole contribution to the soft porn industry.

I'm not crowing at this discovery though, because I too began my career by working in the sex trade, marketing a device called the Hickey-o-matic. This was a nozzle that attached to any vacuum cleaner, thereby enabling frustrated young men to suck their own necks and impress their friends by displaying vast but plausible love bites, and the sort of horny gizmo-crazed males who used to buy it now have an entire TV programme aimed at them, *The Gadget Show* on Five. Unashamedly devoted "to boys who love their toys," it's fronted by a sultry leather-clad Suzi Perry in full Emma Peel mode, but the target audience are doubtless just as aroused by the impressive range of state-of-the-art consumer ephemerals on display. However, while Ms Perry set even my jaded pulses racing a little faster as she leapt about last night, I was less excited by the gadgetry – but only because I've reached an age when I've finally realised that it will take more than the purchase of an electronic tie rack to add new meaning to my life.

TV reviews

As if to magnify her status as a fantasy babe, the female presenter was surrounded by spindly geeks for whom the question "Do you come from the future?" might have been invented (give them a Bacofoil suit each and we're talking Planet Tharg material). Take Jason Bradbury, a bald nerd who thought he could give his jelly-mould car that F16 fighter plane feel by installing a "heads-up display" of his control panel on the windscreen, a plucky and highly dangerous attempt to impress girls that will probably result in his next report coming from an A&E ward. Or Jon Bentley, who wore the haunted expression of one of Esther Rantzen's former catamites, and spoke excellent sense in clipped Raymond Baxter tones about which televisions we should and shouldn't buy. Having researched this topic in some depth myself (day job, you know), I was delighted to hear him agree with me that most plasma screens currently available are a waste of money, and the thought of somebody spending £20K on one amuses the Schadenfreude in me, just like news stories about millionaires crashing in their helicopters. No, it's not cruel, it's just God's way of telling people that they've got too much money.

In between reports, we returned to Emma Peel and her sidekick Adrian Simpson who – in a *Which?* magazine meets Heath Robinson sort of way – were attempting to make a professional-looking film using only domestic camcorders and editors. Brandishing the type of inexpensive equipment that has allowed the amateur porn industry to flourish in recent years, they advised us to buy one with a very wide-angle lens, so perhaps they were planning to shoot Vanessa Feltz, cavorting on her nudist beach. Lastly, the editor of *Stuff* magazine ("I'm proud to be a geek") described the very latest mobile phone he was brandishing as "awesome," even though he later admitted that it didn't actually work. But sadly, nobody had yet unearthed an invention for the far more important matter of eradicating cigarette smoke from restaurants, which is a pity, because the current policy of having a "smoking section" in them makes about as much sense as having a "pissing section" in a swimming pool.

Think *Tomorrow's World* on steroids and you've got *The Gadget Show*, which combines entertaining presentation with solid and authoritative advice about what and when to buy. And if only they'd asked me to present their review about mobile phones, I could have told them all about my own Sony Ericson P900, whose clarity compares unfavourably with two cocoa tins and a piece of string, and only works (if at all) when I am *not* mobile (although to be fair, it does allow me to take photos of myself looking livid). It's got so bad that I now try to stay at home and use my land line, which is okay, except that I can no longer terminate unwelcome conversations by saying "you're breaking up, I'm going through a tunnel..." So may I interest you in my latest invention, the inflatable tunnel, specially designed for those who cannot lie convincingly. Simply step inside it, make your phone calls, and if one becomes awkward, say "Sorry, I can't hear you, I'm going through a tunnel," and put the receiver down. Who's lying?

CHAPTER 6

RAGBAG

I have called this final (and slightly shorter) chapter "Rag Bag" because it consists of reviews that didn't slot neatly into any of the themed chapters. However, I almost called it "Old Bag," because I wanted to dedicate a chapter of this book to Esther Rantzen, since she dominated the BBC schedules for most of the period that I was a television reviewer, and therefore featured more frequently in my reviews than almost any other celebrity. However, I've decided to stick with "Ragbag" for the following chapter, which consists of some of the Evening Standard reviews that embarrassed me least upon re-reading.

*The opening paragraph of this first review concerns an actor who may not be familiar to younger readers. If so, before reading it they might like to familiarise themselves with his work by clicking on the link #53 on the **TV Reviews** page on **www.badastralbooks.com**.*

COTTAGE CHEESE

C4 1997

If tragedy's what you're after, forget about Shakespeare and look instead at the rise and fall of Jason King. With bouffant hair, a tan that was not so much St Tropez as Nagasaki, and frilly shirts unbuttoned to the navel, the suave Department S star (portrayed by Peter Wyngarde) was surely the archetypal ladies' man of the early 70s. This King was no Lear, it seemed, until one afternoon in 1975, when he too was undone by cruel fate. Imagine the following scenario. Mr King. Two bottles of wine. A gentlemen's lavatory at Gloucester bus station. A brace and bit. A young crane driver called Mr Whalley. The whispered phrase "Are you handy?" A hidden ceiling, concealing members of the Gloucestershire Constabulary. A *tableau vivant* resembling a cross between a confession and a supplicant's taking of the wafer at mass. The phrase "You're nicked." A court case. The plea "I slid on some sick and went crashing through the door." Guilty. Fined ten pounds.

End of career. But that wasn't the *real* tragedy, oh no. That came next day, when the court proceedings were printed in full, and it emerged that the real name of this macho heart-throb was... *Cyril Lovis Goldbert*.

Until I read those reports, the word "cottage" had, for me, always meant Anne Hathaway rather than have-it-away, a "hole in the wall" was a place to seek fiscal rather than physical comfort, and "I need TV now" was (I presumed) a mantra uttered by those lucky few who couldn't afford the licence fee. But, as Saturday night's *Cottage Cheese* (C4) showed, the gentlemen's public lavatory is still a focal point for homosexuals, and the unconventional goings-on there are alluded to by the ample graffiti on the walls. "I was totally disgusted by it," said one man of his first encounter with this clandestine world, though he was clearly the Mary Whitehouse of the public karzee because he kept going back there to be disgusted all over again. If this were the nineteenth century, I'd be allowed to relate in Latin or Greek the various obscene messages that were scrawled on the brickwork, but suffice it to say that we saw such revolting slogans as "There was so much spunk I almost chocked." Disgraceful. How *dare* these people write on walls if they can't spell properly.

Shot in grainy monochrome with a trio of actors, the film tried to recreate the furtiveness that seems to be an integral part of the thrill of cottaging. Some gays choose to lunch outside park lavatories, waiting to pick off whoever takes their fancy, a surprisingly large percentage of whom turn out to be unhappily married men seeking consolation and not regarding such fleetingly vertical encounters as constituting infidelity (rather like weak-willed dieters who think calories don't count if you eat standing up). There's no such easy equivalent if you're heterosexual (strange, because in the eighteenth century Hampstead Heath could accommodate a panoply of sexual tastes), but I felt no envy because these tales of casual genital trysts conducted through holes in walls – amid the stench of urine and faeces and always with the potential threat of police surveillance – were hardly the stuff of everlasting love. Mark you, only Stevie Wonder and Ray Charles could *truly* achieve that, while playing tennis.

A darker psychological side soon emerged, with admissions of "I do it to get attention... I have low self esteem," and tales of random beatings and arrests that only seemed to add to the attraction for all concerned. Prosecutions are common and convictions routine, yet (would you believe it? – course you would) the professionals who most frequently enjoy the full range of facilities on offer in the cubicles are "lawyers, solicitors, policemen." Other strands of C4's *Queer Street* season have depicted extrovert and liberated West Coast gays who've come out to such an extent that you almost wish they'd go back in again, but surely that's preferable to sad hypocritical Britain where, thirty years after it was formally legalised,

TV reviews

so much homosexual life still has to be conducted in this sordid and loveless way. So it is that many gays are, literally, still in the closet.

With opening titles that made Dymo look like a Hollywood spectacular, this was altogether a cheap and peculiar offering from Domestic Films (Domestos would be more appropriate), yet it's exactly the sort of programme that C4 was set up to broadcast. So four cheers to them because, fifteen years after their foundation, they've still got the guts to do it. Public lavatories may be gloomy places but, for all that, some of the sharpest humour can be found on their walls, such as my current favourite: "The good news. They finally found Freddy Mercury's long-lost wallet. The bad news? Your picture was in it."

Before The Office hit British screens in 2001, I had only known Ricky Gervais from his excellent scatological inserts into C4's The 11 O'Clock Show (one of my favourite comedy programmes from the last 15 years). Shortly after those appearances (but before The Office was broadcast), I wrote in my diary that a fat mouthy cunt called Ricky approached me at a BBC writers' party, and informed me that "I'm working on a new sitcom... you'll really like my stuff." A year later, the first series of The Office was broadcast, and this was my reaction.

THE OFFICE

BBC2 2001

"Britain has the best television in the world," we're constantly being told, mostly by networks who specialise in stealing the very worst formats from America. From *Double Your Money* and *The Price is Right* to *Wheel of Fortune* and *Trisha*, the UK schedules have always been crammed with second-hand ideas from the States, so much so that I've recently written to the government, suggesting that it should set up an official watchdog to monitor the trade. My proposal is that this watchdog should be called Offrip, that its board should consist of a wide cross-section of society (Lady Howe, Lord Wakeham, a retired high court judge, and perhaps a bishop or two), and that just like every other public regulatory body in the country, it should have no powers whatsoever, and exist purely to be alternately mocked and ignored behind its back.

If Offrip did exist, I'd have written them a strongly-worded letter last night, drawing their attention to BBC2's latest comedy series, *The Office*.

Ch 6 RAGBAG

Formats from both sides of the Atlantic have been shamelessly plundered for this self-proclaimed "comic study of white-collar workers," most notably the first-class pseudo-documentary *People Like Us*, with a soupçon of Larry Sanders (via Bob Martin), and even allusions to an execrable ITV sitcom from 1996, also called *The Office*. It aims to capture the tedium and monotony of a nine-to-five existence, and to lampoon the pompous imbecility of the office wag, but fails miserably because parodies of dullness only succeed when they're shorter and more exaggerated than their original models. A bore in homeopathic doses can be hilarious, as demonstrated by *The Fast Show's* Colin Hunt, but a bore in real time remains simply a bore.

In case the likes of Mike Leigh and Caroline Aherne have deluded you into thinking that it's easy to capture naturalism on TV, then a few minutes in the dubious company of Ricky Gervais and his colleagues will soon set you straight. Gervais may be a patchily amusing stand-up comic, but he's clearly neither an actor (frequently garbling his lines, and barely modulating his performance) nor a dramatic writer (cramming too many words into the characters' mouths, and leaving little breathing space), and before long I found myself shouting at the screen "What did you do with the money?" (the money his mother presumably once gave him for acting lessons). With the exception of Martin Freeman, the rest of the cast were equally underwhelming, and conveyed the impression not simply of playing the roles of dull office workers, but of being actors who were bored with their characters.

Turning now to the structure, the intercutting of fly-on-the-wall sequences with monologue confessionals could not disguise the vacuity of both the dialogue and what passed for a plot. The threat of imminent redundancy hung heavy over the entire Slough office (as indeed it should over the actors), while inside David Brent (Gervais) spent his time trying to prise weakly suggestive one-liners into his every mumbled speech. His exchanges with his secretary were one prolonged trip down Mammary Lane, with lewd quips about her breasts and the age-old remark that "There's hardly a man in this office who hasn't woken up at the crack of Dawn," (the poor woman being named Dawn Tinsley, solely to expedite this one lame gag). As for schoolboy pranks like putting a stapler inside a jelly and remarking "It's a trifling matter," what can one say, and by the time Mr Brent had made Dawn cry by pretending to sack her, I was also pretty close to tears. Of utter despair.

This is the season when schedulers try to sneak their stinking disasters into the listings unnoticed, but even that doesn't fully explain what's happening to British TV comedy at the moment. How this dross ever got beyond the pilot stage is a mystery, while over on C4 they're showing five-year-old repeats of *Brass Eye*, starring a forty-year-old *enfant*

TV reviews

terrible who's still playing his schoolboy pranks in hopes of riling the ITC (and even more embarrassingly, he's planning to do more). Strangely, last night's programme didn't pick up on the aspect of office work which I hated most during my two-year stint, namely the sheer horror of trying to think of something new to say to people whom I'd pass in the corridor several times each day (the morning I found myself saying "we can't go on meeting like this," I knew it was time to quit). Looking back on that bleak period, the only real pleasure I had came from putting a dehumidifier and a humidifier on opposite sides of my desk, then sitting back and watching them fight it out to the death. Now that *was* funny.

As I predicted, the series sank without trace, and Mr Gervais was never heard of again.

Okay, I accept that it went on to become one of the most successful British comedies of all time (and has been even more successful in its US version), and the presence of Mr Gervais in any Hollywood movie, no matter how dire, is a guarantee of box office success. However, I have never changed my opinion of the manifest shortcomings of The Office, and being out of step with every other critic in the known universe has never bothered me unduly. Ten years on, I continue to believe that Mr Gervais is the Bubonic Plagiarist (a quip that I shamelessly stole from Peter Cook, who coined it to describe David Frost), lifting ideas and formats without a care; and although he cheerfully admits to this, that doesn't make it alright.

I think it's fair to say that I was correct (although by no means alone) in predicting that Britain's various wars in the Middle East in recent decades were not a good idea. The 2003 conflict was the most disastrous, murderous, dishonest, and unprincipled of them all, but we should not forget the "small war" of December 1998, in which numerous innocent Iraqis were bombed and killed, their lives sacrificed in an attempt to divert the US media from President Clinton's political difficulties over a stained dress.

Middle East TV's coverage of the bombing (in what became known as "Monica's War") can be seen at the link #54 on the **TV Reviews** *page on* **www.badastralbooks.com.**

Incidentally, as regards the 2003 war (launched after Saddam Hussein failed to hand over his non-existent WMDs), here is an interesting detail that many people have now forgotten. Shortly after it began, the journalist David Aaronovitch wrote that, if the weapons were not found, "I – as a supporter of the war – will never believe another thing that I am told by our government, or that of the US ever again. And, more to the point, neither will anyone else." As we all know, the weapons were never found, yet Mr Aaronovitch continued to be one of Mr Blair's staunchest and most loyal supporters (and an enthusiastic supporter of Western aggression in the Middle East). However, I decided long ago as a matter of principle never to believe another thing that I was told by either Mr Blair or Mr Aaronovitch, a rule of thumb that has stood me in good stead ever since.

THE GULF WAR

ALL CHANNELS 1998

There was a time when we Westerners knew how to control Johnny Wog. We'd exchange a few glass beads for vast tracts of their land, forcibly introduce them to the soporific delights of opium, or (using our astronomical knowledge to calculate precisely the next solar eclipse) threaten to make the world go dark if they didn't obey us. Sixty seconds of uncompromising Galilean science were usually sufficient to have them eating out of our hand.

But times changed, and so did foreign policy, and nowadays the West relies on B-52 bombers and Cruise missiles to quell uppity natives. War no longer breaks out, it's pencilled into our diaries and co-ordinated with TV schedulers, which is why the International Atrocity Contest flickered onto our TV sets last week to divert attention from the mother-in-law of all battles taking place in Washington, where Clinton's *Operation Rat-up-a-Drainpipe* was reaching its climax. Maybe the President couldn't destroy the Republican Old Guard in Congress, but he could certainly make mincemeat of the Republican Guard in Iraq, and I wouldn't have been surprised to hear that a rogue Tomahawk had strayed from its path and was heading directly toward the home of a Ms. M. Lewinsky.

As America Junior rushed into action alongside Uncle Sam, so too did the news journalists, scarcely able to contain their ghastly glee as they played with their latest technological toys in a bid to serve up war as entertainment. Night cameras transformed Baghdad into the Emerald City of Oz, the digital pictures so compressed and pixelated that (mercifully) the images were actually *less* clear than those from the First Gulf War. From BBC News 24 to CNN, hacks donned sombre suits and climbed onto the roof of the Iraqi Ministry of Information building, where they were allowed to look macho and unshaven (even Kate Adie) as they commentated on those nice bright lights that looked like fireworks as they flew through the air, but then fell to earth and blew or burnt unseen human beings to smithereens. Rarely was a dissenting view allowed on air (though thank God for Tony Benn, who's mad enough to become the voice of sanity at times like these), for it would be unpatriotic to protest while our boys were "in harm's way" – although, as far as I could see, the only people in harm's way were the defenceless Iraqis on the ground, trying to survive amid the combined chaos caused by vindictive trade sanctions, a power-crazed dictator, a desperate US President, and a British Prime Minister seemingly smitten by a transatlantic schoolboy crush.

A search around the satellite channels soon confirmed that the English-speaking world was hopelessly out of step with opinion elsewhere. The BBC's Jeremy Cooke lamented that "we cannot see the military sites we'd like to see," while CNN (anchored by one of those unthreatening black faces that US networks always choose, more Sidney Poitier than Winston Silcott) reminded us that Saddam Hussein is "the greatest threat to world security." I presume that Osama bin Laden, who had that distinction only three months ago, must be losing his grip. However, the Middle Eastern Broadcasting Centre (MBC) carried a permanent logo of an Iraqi anti-aircraft gunner, and reflected the anger of Arab people through vox pops and shots of a banner reading "Killing People for Monica," while many European stations expressed profound disquiet at this cowardly war being waged without UN approval. But jolly euphemisms abounded amongst English speakers, from good old "collateral damage" (killing people) to "degrade and diminish Saddam," although in the aftermath of the carnage it seems to be us, not him, who have been morally degraded and diminished.

By Saturday evening's impeachment vote, CNN's screen had split in two as its journalists slavered over a double-dose of "history in the making." And then, suddenly, it was all over. Saddam was stronger than ever, Clinton was weaker than ever, the Iraqis were left to bury their dead, TV journalists turned reluctantly back to the dull diet of workaday non-news, and tomorrow I'll go back to writing about Vanessa Feltz, because you don't want to read about my impotent rage at the stupidity and wickedness of this sick farce. Bill and Tony are both Christians, of course, and Christianity has a long tradition of slaughtering Muslims in the Middle East. Even at the end of the millennium, it seems, the Cross and the Crescent still rule our politics. As Gore Vidal remarked yesterday,

Clinton *should* be on trial, though not for trivial sexual misdemeanours or the lawyers' fetish of perjury, but for crimes against humanity. But it won't happen. After all, war has never been about who is right, but about who is left.

R.I.P

That review reminds me of what President Clinton said, when he first flashed himself to Monica and asked "What do you think of my clock, Miss Lewinsky?" "That's not a clock, Mr President." "You put two hands and a face on it, it's a clock."

I have it on very good authority that a name I coined for the former Prime Minister – "Tony B Liar" – irritated Tony Blair considerably. It was short, simple, and (unlike him) truthful, and wherever he went thereafter, banners, T shirts, and placards all screamed it out. Indeed, I like to think that, in some small way, I contributed to his supraventricular tachycardia that afflicted him in 2003 and 2004. Of course, the most shocking aspect of his cardiac disorder was the discovery that the man had a heart at all. Now, why didn't I use that line in the review..?

THE DOWNING STREET PATIENT

BBC2 2004

I was holidaying recently in the city of Twice (it used to be called New York, until a songwriter declared it to be "so good they named it Twice"), and found myself sitting in Katz's Delicatessen. As I waited for my order of sour, pickled green tomatoes to arrive (poised to connect myself via a pair of nipple clamps to a car battery and re-enact the famous scene from *When Harry Met Sally*), I recalled the first time I'd ever visited this legendary establishment, and saw Ronald Reagan's former Press Secretary, Jim Brady, being wheeled in and placed at an adjacent table. Mr Brady had been paralysed by a bullet to the head, received during the 1981 assassination attempt on the President, and knowing him to have been a staunch supporter of the pro-gun lobby, I went over and politely asked him how he felt about the issue *now*. And do you know what? He just stared blankly ahead, saying nothing and dribbling all over his lox and bagels. Really, the manners of some people.

Despite receiving several bullets himself, Reagan immediately downplayed the near-fatal incident ("Honey I forgot to duck," were his first words to his wife), just as Tony B Liar did last autumn when his heart problem first became public. Within hours, press spokesmen were assuring journalists that this was a trivial one-off incident, even though his "harmless supraventricular tachycardia" required the application of 130,000 watts of electricity to correct it, and there had even been a brief period when John Prescott was effectively (no, make that *ineffectively*) running the country. In last night's *The Downing Street Patient* (BBC2), Michael Cockerell examined the ways that post-war Prime Ministers have dealt with illness and infirmity, constantly striving to project a vigorous Alpha Male image, even on days when they're feeling (and behaving) more like an Epsilon semi-moron. And he gave us his conclusion at the outset, by observing that "when medical doctors get together with spin doctors to issue a bulletin from Number Ten, the one prescription they're rarely on is a truth drug."

Those of us who grew up laughing at the USSR's unconvincing attempts to make their moribund leaders seem dynamic in public (usually, they simply looked embalmed) were soon given pause for thought, because it transpired that, on matters of health, all Number Ten press spokesmen suffer from a curious physical deformity: a forked tongue. In 1953, for example, Churchill suffered a stroke that put him out of action for months, yet Downing Street insisted all was well, and the press dutifully colluded in what Bill Deedes referred to as "an agreement, not a conspiracy, to keep it quiet." When Eden led the nation into the disaster of Suez, his judgement was surely impaired by the mixture of barbiturates and amphetamines he was swallowing (to cope with the after-effects of a botched gall bladder operation), while Wilson began experiencing mental problems early in his final term of office, yet stayed on for several years, before wisely quitting in 1976. Unlike Mrs Thatcher, who was singularly unable to recognise that her lift was no longer stopping at all floors, and finally had to be booted out after giving the game away by declaring "we are a grandmother."

But the real target of the programme was Tony B Liar, a man who'll happily double the staff of the intelligence services to pry into everyone else's lives, yet is surprisingly reluctant to tell us the truth about his own. Hearing his sincere denials of a long-standing heart problem (intercut with compelling testimony that Bill Clinton and the Queen have known about it for years) was a sobering experience, and gave us all a yardstick by which to judge other pronouncements from this self-confessed "pretty straight kind of guy." Just as the mere mention of fleas can turn a previously itchless audience into a bunch of scratchers, so all this talk of cardiac arrests doubtless sent millions of viewers into palpitations, but at least we learned from the excellent Dr Thomas Stuttaford that the correct initial treatment for a racing heart is "to pour iced water on the patient's face," then "press on their neck." Perhaps it's just as well that I wasn't walking past Chequers in my St John's Ambulance uniform on that fateful day, otherwise I might have been tempted to press the prime ministerial neck just a little longer than was strictly necessary.

Due to the opacity of our government and the mendacity of their press spokesmen, we are the mugs who must endure only ever learning the truth about what goes on in Downing Street decades later, when the records are finally made public. But thanks to Cockerell's authoritative commentary (allied to Martin Leonard's meticulous archive research and Anthony Lee's translucent direction), we were left in no doubt as to how previous Prime Ministers have manipulated the truth, although we cannot yet definitively judge whether the current occupant of Number Ten has outdone his predecessors. Admittedly, no leader can show too much weakness in public, because (as Dr Stuttaford pointed out) "in nature, if you have a weak or injured animal, the rest of the pack is likely to turn on it," but in the case of B Liar, the strain of constant dissimulation is clearly starting to show. "He doesn't look well" observed Bill Deedes philosophically, and no wonder, considering the giant question mark that hangs over the legality of his decision to send our troops to war, a decision that has already caused the deaths of scores of British servicemen and thousands of innocent Iraqi civilians. They don't look at all well either.

Unlike most TV critics, I didn't avoid reviewing children's programmes, even those intended for pre-school kids. Why shouldn't I? I have always thought that Newsround gives a better view of the world (and more historical context) than most of the adult news, and that some of the most crafted, imaginative, and touching programmes are made for the very young. Here's a review of one of them.

UNDERGROUND ERNIE

CBEEBIES 2006

Thank God Summer's almost here at last, because with so many naked sunbathers lying face-down in the parks, I'll never be short of somewhere handy to park my bike. Cycling in June is a delight, but I shall shun the Underground, because last year I found myself trapped in a crowded carriage with no air conditioning and the heating full on during the hottest day of Summer, crammed helplessly amongst the fetid

TV reviews

oxters of dozens of sweaty strap-hanging commuters, who all looked like reluctant holders of one-way tickets on the Belsen Express. As our train stopped between stations, a baby being held just below my left ear began screaming, the lights went out, and (under cover of darkness) somebody who had obviously cooked himself a garlic Dolmio spaghetti the night before made his trousers cough, then giggled anonymously, while a woman across from me choked out "Holy Mother of Christ." Twenty minutes later, just as the baby was starting to liquefy, the lights came on again, then off, on, off, on, off, and finally on, and as we ground to a start, someone with hay fever sneezed a long glutinous stream of snot down the arm of my jacket, then blamed it on global warming.

However, I'd happily travel across the city on the perfect rail network run by *Underground Ernie*, whose animated adventures began yesterday on CBeebies. Not only is the system operated by "International Underground" almost entirely overground (passing through the sort of verdant rolling countryside beloved of Tellytubbies), but it's also immaculately clean and punctual, seldom has more than a couple of passengers to each train, and is run by staff who sing "We know we're going to get you there... your travel plans will work out fine," without a trace of sarcasm in their voices. Better still, Ernie (voiced by notorious crisp thief Gary Lineker) is "a jolly kind-hearted man," his assistant Millie "knows everything there is to know about computer technology," and the entire network is adequately maintained by one elderly engineer, a "Mr Rails, who never fails." To cap it all, there's not a single graffito spray-painted anywhere on the system, so there's no chance of encountering unsavoury messages of the type I saw recently on a wall in Oval tube station: "What do fat people do in summer? Stink."

The movement of the figures (especially their faces) was so lifelike and natural that it almost defeated the purpose of animation, but I did have some doubts about the CGI locomotives, which weren't so much rolling stock as laughing stock. Bakerloo was a gruff monocled Sherlock Holmes traditionalist, while Jubilee was a mischievous teenager obsessed with pop and technology, Victoria an elderly queen with a tiara perched on her roof, and Circle referred to herself as "a bit of a hippy chick." More bemusingly still, the series includes occasional appearances by foreign engines like Brooklyn ("all the way from the USA") and Osaka ("from Japan"), which will doubtless encourage overseas sales, but must be irritating for users of the Central line, for whom a through train that goes even as far as Ongar is but a distant memory. And although twin brothers Hammersmith & City enable you to get to the East End (which is apparently a vast nature reserve), there don't appear to be any Northern line trains at all, so in that respect, it's very much like London.

Ch 6 RAGBAG

Yesterday's adventure involved the arrival of famous pop singer Sam Seven, whom Jubilee had to transport from the airport to his hotel. To ensure Sam wasn't mobbed by thousands of desperate fans (who'd presumably be damnably difficult to animate individually), the star was travelling in disguise, but the blabbermouth engine let the secret slip, the carriage was besieged by a vast crowd of girls (whom we heard en masse, but never saw), and all seemed lost. However, the day was saved by a human oxymoron, an "Underground Entertainer" who acted as a decoy by busking Sam's latest hit, led the screaming girls away, and was personally thanked afterwards by Mr Seven. Although God alone knows why a superstar would willingly have anything to do with one of those first-position-only busker-guitarists who wish to take us by the hand and lead us through the streets of London, and whose dodgy soprano saxophones differ from lawnmowers in only one respect. Lawnmowers can be tuned.

Sid Rainey has created an engagingly electrified version of Thomas the Tank Engine, lively, well-written, and of instant appeal to those lazy little people who don't pay rent (*aka* children) who constitute its target audience. Lineker's voice-over was sometimes a little stilted, and the audio post-production occasionally needed more attention, but Millie is an excellent role model for little girls who want to become engine drivers, and I only hope that Transport for London (who'll receive a percentage of the merchandising royalties) use their windfall to make the real Underground a little more like this fantasy one. Of course, I can't claim any great expertise when it comes to producing children's programmes, because the only animated kids' character I've ever created was called "Tubby the Tumour," half Mr Man, half malignant growth. With a merry cry of "I'm a very naughty carcinogen," my lethal Mr Blobby would swim gleefully through his latest victim's lymphatic system until he reached the liver, then produce two large pieces of cloth from his pocket and chuckle "it's curtains for you." There were complaints. Bloody loads of them. And all upheld by the ITC.

The next review commemorates an attempt to resurrect one of the most witless – yet long-lived – of all television formats: Mr & Mrs. Sadly, the revamped version did not have Derek Batey as its host, and failed to find a new audience.

Many years have passed since Mr Batey last appeared on our screens, but here is a link to an early recording of him presenting the show, while on tour at Appleby Castle: go to link #55 on the **TV Reviews** *page on* **www.badastralbooks.com.**

TV reviews

THE NEW MR & MRS SHOW

CHALLENGE TV 2000

Few things in life give me more pleasure than betting on how long a celebrity marriage will last. I remember giving Mr Trump and his wife five years (and I was damn close) after watching Ivana jump out of a $3,000,000 cake (for charity, of course) and hearing Donald whisper to a friend "vagina is *very* expensive." With Zsa-Zsa Gabor, I prefer to estimate on a "per decade" basis, and I've longed admired her expert housekeeping skills: every time she gets divorced, she keeps the house. As for Vanessa Feltz, the *decree nisi* is still pending, but I've got a fiver at Ladbroke's that says it will come through by Christmas. Anyway, it's her estranged husband who's undoubtedly experienced the greatest weight loss. Apparently, he lost 600lbs of ugly fat in one weekend.

Divorce has even struck at the heart of television's greatest celebration of the matrimonial state, *Mr & Mrs*. The original quiz was an arranged marriage between those two Titans of the ITV network, HTV and Border, and together they spawned a new series every year between 1972 and 1988; but then they separated, whereupon the Welsh station shacked up with UK Living and begat some more. Entitled *The New Mr & Mrs Show*, they're currently airing on Challenge TV, and as with anything bearing that prefix (New Avengers, New Man, New Seekers, New Labour), they are but pale copies of the distinguished originals. Even the signature tune (written by Maciek Hrybowicz, not so much a composer as a Polish eye chart) isn't a patch on the old title song penned by Tony Hatch and Jackie Trent, which famously exhorted us all to "be nice to each other" and "love one another." Tony and Jackie, by the way, took their own advice to heart so much that they too subsequently got divorced, thus fully justifying the £10 each-way bet I'd placed on them.

We all know that daytime quizzes don't have the big budgets enjoyed by prime time shows, but yesterday afternoon's offering plumbed new depths in economy television. Not only had the studio audience been replaced by a poorly-dubbed laugh track, but all the contestants had been garnered from within a ten-mile radius of the Cardiff studio, thereby avoiding the expense of a few Supersaver rail tickets but lending an unmistakably parochial air to the proceedings. Suzanne and Mark (from Cardiff) didn't know what their favourite food was, while Vera and Henry (from Cardiff) couldn't remember whether they preferred male or female company, even though they'd been married for fifty-three years. "When does Henry fall asleep?" presenter Nino Firetto asked Vera, who

Ch 6 RAGBAG

solemnly replied "when he watches TV." I thankfully suffer from that condition too, but Nino's anxious glance at the elderly male figure slumped in the soundproofed box confirmed that Henry has a worse problem: he also falls asleep when he *appears* on TV.

I learned more about Andrew and Julie (from Cardiff) than I really wanted to know, including the startling news that he has "a very neat tummy button" and that she often goes bra-less in summer. But when Nino asked them "who will be deciding on your 1995 holiday?" I finally realised that I'd been conned and that, despite the claims of newness, I was actually watching stale, reheated television. Most quizzes avoid mentioning the year for that very reason, but the programme-makers had obviously reckoned that these shows would never be repeated, not least because a fair percentage of the contestants in the series must by now be either divorced, separated, or dead. Presumably, Challenge TV is aiming at the Alzheimer market, targeting those viewers who still believe they're living in the last century, and what's wrong with that?

If satellite stations need to pad out their meagre schedules with old quizzes, can't they at least give us the originals, rather than this insipid, ersatz pap? I've long been convinced that, like fine wines maturing in bottles, old videotapes ripen inside their plastic casings, and I suspect that the 76 vintage of *Mr & Mrs* is just about right for decanting now. How I'd love to savour again the shambolic charm of Derek Batey, commiserating with some octogenarian housewife who couldn't even remember how many sugars her husband took in his tea, although they'd lived together in wretched, miserable fidelity since 1923. "Never mind, it's always difficult when you're in front of the cameras," Derek would generously opine, but he was wrong. In truth, it's always difficult when you're in the full grip of senility.

I received a friendly letter from Mr Firetto after he read the review. And after carrying out mammoth research I discover that he is by no means finished in the media, dear me no. In 2000, he became the morning host on Kestral FM in Basingstoke, and he is currently presenter of the Breakfast Show on Exeter FM. Derek Batey is also in retirement, in Florida.

At the start of this chapter, I mentioned that I had almost entitled it "Old Bag" out of respect (or rather disrespect) for Esther Rantzen. In my opinion (and only in my opinion, so the lawyers tell me), few people have abused television to the extent that she did to further their own career, which is why she is widely despised within the industry. And it's also why she hasn't been able to get a regular show for many years. Those who live by the sword...

TV reviews

WOULD LIKE TO MEET... ESTHER
BBC2 2004

Hideous Esther Rantzen. How I loathed her and her daytime confessional tearfests, on which members of the public were encouraged to talk about "the hurt inside," not least because the show forced me to the reluctant conclusion that I am the only person in Britain who was never sexually abused as a child. It's true. I always had to buy my own sweets, no scout master or boys' brigade leader ever whispered those five special words, "It'll be our little secret," and although it's a bit of a bugger (if you'll excuse the phrase) to admit it, I suppose I must have been a very plain lad indeed. Having remained so shamefully unmolested during my formative years, perhaps I should now declare myself to be a victim of society, and start my own support group, where counsellors can validate my feelings by telling me to "be yourself... find your space... have some 'me' time." Or I could undergo hypnotic regression, and fabricate memories of having been abused in a past life by Genghis Khan, while taking an elephant up the Khyber Pass.

For thirty-five years, Our Lady of Rude Root Vegetables did well by doing good on television, but two years ago her show was axed, and she began fading into the media twilight. Until last night, when she popped up on *Would Like to Meet... Esther* (BBC2) to receive a physical and psychological makeover, so that after a lifetime of imperiously telling men what to do (like those wretched catamites she used to humiliate each week on *That's Life!*), she might finally learn to converse with them as equals. Her husband Desmond Wilcox kicked the breathing habit back in 2000 (not 1999, as the programme stated), and Esther confided that she now finally felt ready to start dating again, even though she's reached an age when a spot of carbon dating might seem more appropriate. Whereupon, in a fitting tribute to the disingenuousness of the entire project, she agreed to submit her television-obsessed persona to a six-week course of antidotes – but only on condition that the entire process was televised.

With the aid of a stylist, relationship counsellor, confidence coach, and body language consultant, Esther played along with the pretence that she was a mere pupil, urgently needing to be taught how to soften her image and how to flirt. But in the programme's pre-publicity, she'd already made it abundantly clear that she saw this as *her* project, having personally proposed the idea to BBC2's controller, and telling the *Radio Times* that "it might be valuable for other people to watch and identify with me." Meanwhile, the nauseatingly sycophantic narration tried to portray this latest bid for media attention as yet another example of her altruism, telling us that "Esther lives much of her life in public, leaving no time for herself," and adding the truly toe-curling observation that "she needs to indulge herself the way she indulges her audiences through her writing, charity work, and TV shows." Yet watching her dining with a male stooge whom she didn't so much converse with as interview, it was clear that she regards her entire life as one long uninterrupted TV programme, a programme in which *she* is always holding the microphone.

"Coming on screen was a gamble," she told us, before embarking on a hollow pantomime of a date by way of a denouement, "I may never work again." But in truth, she hasn't really been working in high-profile TV for some time now, and seems destined to go the way of Vanessa Feltz, Anne Diamond, and all those other media women who still crave telly, and can't accept that the only truly satisfying relationship they've ever had (the one with the camera) is finally over. "I've been trained by television critics over the years," she remarked, while justifying her alleged reluctance to accept compliments, "One of them started his column 'hideous Esther Rantzen'...," but (unless she was clairvoyant and was referring to this review) she was quoting inaccurately. What I actually referred to three years ago was "the hideous equine dentation of Esther Rantzen, half-woman, half-horse, and always the centaur of her own universe." Three years on, I'll qualify that metaphor. The old nag is now ready for the knacker's yard.

After one of my reviews of Esther appeared in print, I received a letter from Valerie Singleton, complaining about age-ism against women on TV. She was right to point out that women in television are being particularly affected by age-ism, but I ought to point out that men are also dumped and left on the shelf. I met an ex-celebrity recently (whom I will not name), who told me, "Now that I have reached a certain age, Victor, I am starting to feel my years. I don't mind admitting that I've even tried Viagra, but what's the point? I feel like a condemned building with a new flagpole. Would that gag act as a suitable link into your next review do you think?"

"Yes it would," I replied.

TV reviews

VIAGRA: THE HARD SELL

BBC2 2005

Euphemisms are curious things, because the more they conceal about the subject they're skirting around, the more they reveal about their user. When Condoleezza Rice (hmm, it's good 'n' tasty 'n' full of 'n's) talks glibly of "collateral damage," she discloses her indifference to the lives and deaths of non-Americans, and when organic farmers speak gently about sending their animals to "low-stress slaughterhouses," they display their own hypocrisy about what actually goes on in such places (perhaps they think that a slaughterhouse can be made stress-free by simply removing its first letter). Euphemisms for death are outnumbered only by those for sex, especially on television wildlife programmes, where respectable verbs such as "tupping," "siring," "servicing," and "covering" are used to disguise the bestial debauchery that's actually taking place, and recently I even heard one voice-over artiste refer to a female eel being "attended to" by males. Since then, I've been keeping my back to the wall in Selfridges, whenever an assistant at the fresh fish counter offers me a similar service.

"Erectile dysfunction" became a favourite euphemism during the late 1990s, thanks to an intensive advertising campaign by the Pfizer pharmaceutical company. As last night's *Viagra: the Hard Sell* pointed out, they'd realised that it would be less shaming for men to seek treatment for that, than for what my old granny used to call "trying to stick a marshmallow into a slot machine" (*aka* impotence), and once the name had caught on, a lucrative worldwide market quickly developed for those little blue rhomboidal pills (whose proper clinical name is *mycoxafailin*). "It's the fastest brand to spread across the world and achieve icon status," a company spokeswoman told us at the start of this Money Programme special, which looked at the phenomenal global appetite for Viagra, whose annual sales currently exceed £1.5 billion. Not bad for a company whose British laboratories are based in the humble Kent town of Sandwich, although by rights, the drug should be made in Prestatyn (alright, no more Viagra jokes).

This being a serious programme about a serious subject, viewers were allowed to see a great many penises popping up on screen. Some were thermal images, while others were graphic representations, but the biggest one of all was undoubtedly Philip Hodson (who for years used to append the letters "MA" to his name in a ludicrous attempt to pretend that he possessed some medical expertise), declaring that people nowadays expect to be sexually active until death (or even a little longer, judging from the growing interest in necrophilia on the Internet). It was older men who were initially targeted by Pfizer, with grey-haired Bob Dole fronting commercials that were soon giving thousands of retired American males the most satisfying erections they'd had in years, although they did have to be careful about using Viagra in conjunction with other medication. For example, if they were taking iron tablets as well, they could end up spinning round and round until they eventually pointed north (alright, no more Viagra jokes).

Although it had no sensational discoveries to impart, the programme did reveal a surprising level of Viagra usage (and of its arch-rival, Cialis) amongst younger men, who don't actually *need* it at all. "It's a recreational drug... taken with amphetamines, it allows you to have inhuman capabilities," said the owner of a gay hotel in Florida, but there can be serious medical consequences to over-indulgence in all-night sex sessions with multiple partners (although if somebody dies during the orgy, how do they ever get the coffin lid shut?). By the end, it was obvious that the market for anti-impotence drugs is almost limitless, so in a spirit of generosity, here are a few ideas for new products that Pfizer might care to try out. How about a Viagra chapstick, to help British men keep a stiff upper lip? Or Viagratine, a hot milky bedtime drink with the slogan "One cup and you're up all night"? Or a blend of Viagra and Prozac, so that if you *still* can't get an erection, at least you won't care?

Despite there being no anniversary, scoop, scandal, or other visible news peg to justify the making of this cut-and-paste documentary, it was nevertheless a worthwhile little programme, well narrated by Adrian Chiles (who always looks as though he's trapped in a bottle when I see him on TV, so he'd be wise to stick to voice-overs and radio). However, the script did contain several weak puns and double entendres that no serious journalist should ever sink to, and worse, it neglected to mention the recent theft of a lorryload of Viagra (by a gang of hardened criminals), which was then dumped into the Thames, causing Tower Bridge to rise up and stay up for six hours. Of course, erectile dysfunction can happen to anyone, so it should never be a cause for laughter or ridicule, and I'm not ashamed to say that I recently went to Boots to enquire about purchasing some myself. "Can I get it over the counter?" I asked. "Only if you take six," came the reply. Alright, no more Viagra jokes.

Writing about Viagra reminds me that, some years ago, I got onto a live phone-in about penis size, hosted by Richard and Judy. Posing as a consultant urologist,

TV reviews

I began by using some recondite medical terminology to describe the typical dimensions of the human phallus, then told the hosts that, in my professional opinion, there could be no doubt that Mr Madeley was by far the biggest prick in the studio.

The call was terminated shortly afterwards.

THE TRUTH ABOUT RICHARD AND JUDY

C5 2005

Back in 1989, I had lunch with the then Head of Entertainment at Yorkshire TV, a decent chap nicknamed "The Grim Reaper" on account of his penchant for sackings ("they don't pay me enough, so I need to get my kicks somehow"). When I asked him what had happened to Ted Rogers since the axing of *3-2-1*, his reply was caustic, gleeful, and terse – "finished" – although his verdict proved somewhat premature, because I subsequently saw Ted on *Good Morning with Anne and Nick*, telling filthy jokes and relaunching himself as "an alternative comedian," just as everyone else had stopped using that term (now that's what *I* call finished). The Grim Reaper also ended the TV career of Leslie Crowther (a man known as the von Aschenbach of Central Television, because he'd dyed his grey hair black in a tragically misguided bid to remain eternally youthful), so Crowther moved to Radio 2, and stayed there until his motor accident. At which point, the erstwhile presenter of *Stars In Their Eyes* began seeing stars in his own eyes (due to smashing his head against the roof of his car), and he not only became a hit on the radio, but also on the dashboard, the windscreen, and finally the pavement.

Undignified though public sackings and horizontal departures through windscreens may be, they're preferable ways of ending a media career to simply fading away. Which is what I'm certain will eventually happen to Richard Madeley, a man who suffers from delusions of adequacy and whose sole purpose in life is to end up alone in a bedsit on the South Coast, surrounded by people who can barely remember who he is (until senility sets in and even *he* can barely remember who he is). Only a tiny percentage of the population ever watch him and his wife presenting their

Ch 6 RAGBAG

daytime shows, but you'd never have guessed how marginal Madeley and Finnegan are to British life from last night's *The Truth About Richard and Judy*. "As a country, we are obsessed with them," gushed the narrator at the outset, adding that their programme is "must-watch TV," which is quite an achievement for a couple who, even on a good day, struggle to attract two million viewers.

Despite the boldness of its title, the profile that followed had more to do with PR than with honesty. Instead of in-depth research, the couple's autobiography formed the unchallenged basis of the storyline, while their detractors were noticeable chiefly by their absence, so the skeletons in their media closet were handled with a reticence that came close to absurdity. Judy's early-morning shakes and alleged fondness for alcohol were dismissed out of hand (fair enough, I suppose, because even though the Institute of Metal Fatigue use their corkscrews for research, do they look like a drinking couple?), while Richard's unscheduled appearance on Tesco's security TV cameras as he wheeled £55 of unpaid-for booze toward the car park was treated as the sort of thing that could have happened to anyone with an unusually short attention span. Personally, I always thought from the outset that the very idea of wine theft was implausible, so thank God he got off, even though the couple were, at the time, cruelly nicknamed "Pinch and Judy" (by me, I fear).

Yet even though this was more hagiography than gutsy critique, there was plenty here to remind us why they were rightly crowned as the King and Queen of Stupidvision. After bullying their way up through the regions (Richard even had a stint at Border Television, a station that once had to close down on Christmas Day because of heavy snow), the couple got lucky when they began hosting *This Morning*, a televisual zabaglione of such meaninglessness and inconsequentiality that the narrator was paradoxically correct when he enthused that "We'd never seen anything like it on our screens."

I've long suspected that Richard has to whistle when he's at stool, to remind himself which end to wipe, and numerous clips confirmed that he also suffers from premature articulation (talking before thinking), but he's long been notorious in the industry for angrily blaming researchers and directors for his own intellectual shortcomings. In fact, we heard that he was so intimidating at *This Morning* that one producer used to vomit each day before starting work on the show. Which is quite a coincidence, because that's what I used to do each morning when I had to review it.

With a script that attempted to hide cowardice behind irony, and a depressingly obvious choice of archive – Madeley as Ali G, Judy exposing her right tit (*aka* Richard Madeley) – this was cowardly stuff indeed. From the moment that the phrase "The genius of Richard

TV reviews

Madeley" was uttered, all credibility was lost, and stories about "dirty tricks" in the battle for daytime micro-ratings only served to illustrate how inconsequential and ephemeral their entire careers have been and how insignificant British daytime television is. It has now been with us for a generation, yet it remains infantile and inane in its outlook, as was forcibly brought home to me last week when I tuned into Martin Frizell's GMTV and heard a presenter state the following (I quote verbatim): "The best thing with all these floods and storms and total electrical power cuts going on is to curl up in front of the TV and watch us on GMTV." So long as your set is gas-powered, I suppose.

*If any readers wish to see Richard and Judy in action, consorting with Gary Glitter in 1992 (back in the days when people still wanted to be in his gang), then click on link #56 on the **TV Reviews** page on www.badastralbooks.com.*

Although comedy is one of the most important parts of the schedules of most television channels, I decided not to devote a chapter to the subject. Why? Because when comedy works, it's difficult to write an interesting review about it, because one simply wants to repeat the best gags from the show one has just seen. However, it's not hard to write a review about dreadful comedies, and there was never any shortage of those during my years as a reviewer. ITV provided quite a few of the worst, such as this next disaster.

MUMBAI CALLING

ITV1 2007

Stand aside ITV with your dodgy phone lines, there's a new kid on the premium-rate-call block. I've told you before about my computer that randomly dials a million numbers per hour, lets each ring just once, then hangs up (a process that costs me nothing, but tempts some people into dialling 1471 to see who the caller was, which in turn connects them to a premium rate number charging £5 per minute or part thereof), but I've recently perfected some lucrative improvements. Now when they phone back, they'll hear a recording of a stuttering man saying "th th this is er ... urgh th th th combined offices of St St Stammerers UK... (pause 5") and The National Speech Impediment line. S s s s orry you were

Ch 6 RAGBAG

d d d d d d dialled in error, but er.... (pause 10"), er... th th thank you for c c c calling anyway." Nobody could accuse a stutterer of deliberately lengthening a call, nor will they have the heart to put the phone down until his four-minute message is completed, so I'll quadruple my profits and start grossing at least a million quid a week.

However, the inescapable law of telephonic karma has already taken its revenge on me, by robbing me of thirty minutes of precious existence last night as I watched *Mumbai Calling*. Billed as "a cross-cultural romantic comedy," this pilot about English Jews trying to manage an Indian call centre with the help of their British-born Hindu accountant failed utterly as both drama and sitcom, while its observations about ethnic differences were so crass that even the notorious *Mind Your Language* would have looked enlightened in comparison. In a desperate attempt to prove that ITV can still make a successful comedy, Paul Jackson (ITV's Director of Entertainment) turned to the once sure-footed triumvirate of of Allan McKeown, Laurence Marks, and Maurice Gran (the men behind such long-running 90s shows as *Birds of a Feather* and *Goodnight Sweetheart*), but he made two serious miscalculations. He not only allowed the ever-smug Sanjeev Bhaskar to co-write the script, but also let him star in it, and the result was as bland and unpalatable as the dubious turkey served to the bemused staff in the final scene.

Bhaskar's portrayal of Kenny Gupta as a timid and lovestruck loner (complete with detachable clip-on pathos) was deeply unconvincing, but worse still was Tiffany (Sophie Hunter), the object of his affections. The boss's daughter spoke her lines in anything from a shout to a whisper (the decibel level seldom correlating to the required emotion), and the acting of both performers was so wooden that (bearing in mind how we were taught to start fires in the Wolf Cubs by rubbing two dry sticks together) I feared they might both burst into flames if they ever got into a serious writhing clinch. The script was equally abysmal, full of pitiful repartee like, "Our son has a good heart," "Well, let him donate it to medical science then!" and the even more contrived "I used to date this guy who was really big in Apple," "Apple? What was he? A maggot?" As for the moribund scene where Kenny told his staff that "There's nothing wrong with letting your hair down," while the camera panned to two turbanned Sikhs looking worried, no flowers please, just donations to your favourite charity.

As anyone who's been to India lately knows, it's a rapidly burgeoning superpower that's teeming with self confidence, and is already starting to make the West seem positively backward. Its numerous call centres are staffed by clever and personable young graduates whose spoken English is often better than our own, yet the lazy old Empire view lingered on here in condescending portrayals of the natives as funny but indolent

TV reviews

wogs like Dev (Nitin Ganatra), the friendly call centre manager who had to be sacked because he's an incorrigible fraud and scoundrel. By the time Twiggy appeared for a cameo spot as a caller from London ("My name? It's Twiggy... no Twiggy, not Piggy!"), even the cast were starting to lose the will to live, and I perversely began to enjoy the final scenes, amazed at the sitcom's unending ability to become progressively more and more dire. Indeed, by the end, I was watching with a 50–50 mixture of delight and revulsion, my predicament reminding me of the old conundrum: what's worse, a freezing cold lavatory seat, or a still warm one?

From its patronising portrayal of Mumbai to its crass Indian-Jewish theme tune (ersatz klezmer played on the sitar), this was Bollywood misrepresented as Gollywood. "If the episode is well-received," an ITV spokesman said recently, "a full series will be made," so let's hope that the entire demeaning project is now immediately shelved, because although there's definitely room on television for an intelligent comedy drama about traditional and modern lifestyles co-existing in the shiny new (yet unfathomably old) India, this isn't it. As it happens, just last month I had a long and enjoyable telephone conversation with a call centre woman in Delhi, who gave me an excellent recipe for Mangalorean crab while waiting for her screen to show her details of trains from Preston to London, and I've often been impressed by the wide gastronomic knowledge of Indians. Like Emperor Shah Jehan, who regarded a chain of Anglo-Indian restaurants so highly that, when he built that vast mausoleum in Agra, he named it after them. The Taj Mahal.

Aparently a pooja (not to be confused with a Poona) was used to bless the production offices of Mumbai Calling. It clearly didn't have any efficacy – because only one series was ever aired of this utter bilge. I have to admit that its producer, Ned Parker, used to work for my company. He was a total suckup merchant when I was his boss. Now he appears to be sucking up to his current employer, Allan McKeown. This is what he wrote about him in Broadcast Magazine:

"The television personality I most admire: Allan McKeown – Not so much a TV personality but a personality in TV, the man I now work with, Allan McKeown. He has been behind so many successful shows and his enthusiasm and passion for television is truly amazing. I spent four months with him in India last year filming Mumbai Calling for ITV and I still don't tire of his stories."

Sick-making or what?

See the health and safety nightmare epsoide and you really will not

Ch 6 RAGBAG

*keep your breakfast down go to link #57 on the **TV Reviews** page on www.badastralbooks.com.*

There are certain formats that one could predict from the outset would run for years, if not decades. And one could also predict that their success would make caricatures out of their presenters. That was certainly the case with this next programme, which continues to delight and infuriate viewers to this day.

DRAGONS' DEN

BBC2 2006

Ever since discovering that the collective noun for collective nouns is a "peculiar," I've been fascinated by terms of venery. Wildlife is a particularly rich source, with an ostentation of peacocks, a bloat of hippopotami, a murmuration of starlings, a clowder of cats, a deceit of lapwings (maybe that should be lawyers), a smack of jellyfish (or heroin addicts come to that), and a hypocrisy of animal lovers. Okay, I invented that last one, but what word could be more appropriate to describe a group of people who lapse into paroxysms of grief when told that melting Antarctic ice is preventing a herd of seals from reaching their feeding grounds, even though the first thing that those mammals would do if they got there would be to devour a hundred shoals of salmon, who surely have an equal right to life? As usual, there's a sentimental apartheid at work here: cute and fluffy equals good, slimy and scaly equals bad.

As this television critic (collective noun an "irrelevance") sat watching *Dragons' Den* last night, he not only noticed that he'd begun referring to himself in the third person (an early sign of madness), but he also started wondering what the collective noun for hypocrites might be. Well, how else could you describe Rachel Elnaugh, imperiously telling others how to run a business when her own Red Letter Days company recently went into administration, and had to be rescued by her equally haughty colleague Theo Paphitis, whose other wise investments have included pumping a fortune into Millwall FC (currently bottom of their league)? Or Peter Jones, railing obsessively at budding entrepreneurs who don't wear smart clothes, yet turning up weekly in an ill-fitting jacket

TV reviews

whose collar rises two inches above the shoulder like something in nylon polyamide from Top Man? Or the enervating Duncan Bannatyne, boasting about his chain of fitness clubs, yet looking in need of a lengthy stay at one of the nursing homes he used to run in the 90s? Or Doug Richard, who accuses over-zealous pitchers of being "prickly," yet himself behaves like a graduate from the Pol Pot School of Charm?

As a quintet, they expect inexperienced inventors to make instant decisions about exchanging 50 per cent of their brainchildren for some modest seed capital, when they themselves would hire lawyers and accountants, and take weeks to decide; so all in all, what else could I call them but... ah yes, I remember, a "decortication" of hypocrites.

As I predicted when reviewing the first series, the dragons have begun to believe in the myth of their own infallibility, as though they alone understand the vagaries of the market place. Worse, the poisoned spirit of *The X Factor* has entered their souls, and they now devote most of their time to humiliating the pitchers (attacking not just their products but their personalities too), so much so that Evan Davis's post-encounter interviews function not only as consolation, but also as safety valves against subsequent litigation.

The panellists have realised they'll thrive better in the edit suite if they sneer and snarl as often as possible, so they're constantly feigning horror, revulsion, and withering contempt, to a degree that would have them sectioned under the Mental Health Act if they weren't being filmed. Watching their narcissistic displays of competitive gurning last night, as they vied for the attention of the lens, I realised that those primitive tribes who distrust photography and refuse to have their picture taken have a valid point: cameras really *can* steal your soul.

Admittedly, most of the hopeful inventors proudly displaying their hopeless inventions should never be allowed the chance to waste other people's money, having already wasted their own. But that was no excuse for the pitifully weak puns (remember, incidentally, that a good pun is its own re-word) that the Dragons used to crush these fragile dreams, whether telling a designer of chocolate photographs that "my money would melt if I invested," or a pooper-scooper manufacturer that "it's a dog of an idea." I briefly perked up when Theo told an ad salesman that "I'd rather stick pins in my eyes than invest in your product" (perhaps he'll consider investing in my ophthalmic acupuncture kit then), but perked down again when the creator of the Yakibox (containing an imported Yakiniku grill from Japan) revealed that he didn't own the commercial rights to his product, only the commercial wrongs. As he attempted simultaneously to cook a meal and outline his business plan, he gave me time to construct the following haiku: "Chopsticks. The sole reason why the Japanese did

Ch 6 RAGBAG

not invent custard." Eat your heart out Ikkyu Sojun (though not on a Yakiniku set).

The world is full of inventors who've spotted a gap in the market without pausing to consider whether there's a market in the gap, and this programme is at its best when it allows idiot entrepreneurs to struggle and sink in the quicksand of financial reality. But the pernicious influence of Simon Cowell and Gordon Ramsay is all too evident in the panellists' desire to abuse and degrade the pitchers, rather than humanely allowing them to work out for themselves whether their cherished creations have utility or futility. However, there is still the occasional genuinely brilliant creation amongst the dross (the baby-rocking Dream Machine had a touch of deranged genius about it), which makes me tempted to pitch some ideas of my own to them, such as my state-of-the-art phoneless cord, for people who hate telephones. Or how about my new whisky diet? I tried it last week, and lost three days.

I wasn't altogether sorry when I hung up my aerial and retired from the whole TV reviewing caper. Well, celebs can be very touchy, and newspapers don't pay danger money to critics. Over the years, I had to put up with all sorts of abuse. Jack Dee's agent, Addison Cresswell, once threatened to chuck me into a car-crusher after I'd failed to write 800 words of closely argued adulation about his client. That fight (at the Groucho Club) made it to the front page of The Sun. The article, full of lies and spun to make Mr Dee and his Mr Cresswell look like victims, was written by one Andy Coulson. Mr Coulson, you remember, was the Editor of The News of The World at the time of the phone-hacking scandal, and I am delighted to say that – at the time of writing this – he appears to be having quite a bit of bother over phone-hacking allegations. What goes around comes around, Andrew.

Others who abused me (verbally at least) include Jenni Éclair. She shouted "You are a total cunt," as she drove past me in her mini car after I'd described her as spouting half an inch of meaning to every fifty feet of noise. Craig Charles offered to push me through a plate glass window (that last threat seemed particularly ironic, as he'd just been fronting an anti-bullying campaign at the time). But the oddest confrontation I've been involved in was with Bobby Davro, who also approached me at The Groucho Club (shortly after I'd reviewed his soon-to-be-axed series), and threatened to "give you a piece of my mind." As I enquired at the time, "Could a man of your intellectual dimension really afford to give away even the smallest piece of your mind?"

Thanks to the receptionists at The Groucho for holding him down while I jumped into a taxi.

TV reviews

Despite having fronted a newspaper column for fifteen years, I've actually never had any great desire to be in the limelight. Nowadays, I'm much happier producing television programmes, but there was a time when I used to make my living by performing on television and radio. So when disgruntled celebs used to write to me after a negative review, saying, "Those who can do; those who can't become critics," I was able to remind them that I not only performed, but was rather successful at it too, as the following review points out en passant.

THE COMEDY AWARDS –
16 DANGEROUS YEARS

ITV 2006

I've never been impressed by awards. Indeed, the only time I was ever hubristic enough to turn up in person to accept one (many years ago), I was humbled by falling off the stage and breaking it in half before I'd even had the chance to preen myself, and a good job too. The trophy that I broke all those years ago was a jester statuette, presented to me at the British Comedy Awards. The organisers wisely changed the design next year to a more durable jester playing card encased in a perspex block, but I suspect the ceremony itself is still as choreographed as it was when I attended, something that I only agreed to do because they'd told me beforehand that I'd won (hence my mistrust of all those "I am utterly surprised" speeches). Even though the live show is much tighter than it used to be, it can still be toe-curlingly embarrassing at times, because comedians are at their worst when they take themselves seriously, which is why I found it so enjoyable to watch last night's *The Comedy Awards – 16 Dangerous Years*. Thankfully, this compilation had dispensed with all the self-congratulatory crap, and concentrated exclusively on the funniest and most outrageous moments, thereby proving that comedians are at their best when they disrupt expectations by taking the piss out of everything, including the ceremony and (most of all) themselves.

The programme's laudable desire to shoot itself in the foot was obvious from the outset, as presenter Al Murray introduced clips of how not to host the ceremony. Those began with a time-lapse sequence of Jonathan Ross, who resembled the increasingly debauched figure in *The Picture of Dorian Grey* as he endlessly repeated the same crude gag (saying "you helped me through my difficult teenage years" to any once-attractive female celebrity who is now of a certain age), but there were some corkers too. "You can tell the difference between Ant and Dec, because Ant's on smack and Dec's on crack" deservedly brought the house down when Ross delivered it a few years ago, because McPartlin and Donnelly have always struck me as one of television's most bland and undistinguished duos, being nothing more than a double act with two straight men.

That last joke, by the way, is dedicated to Arthur Smith, a thoroughly limp man (I have my sources) who has never won a British Comedy Award, probably because he's about as funny as an outbreak of rabies in a Guide Dogs for the Blind home.

The selection of clips that followed condensed the sixteen ceremonies to their very essence, with many of the moments having stuck in my memory ever since they were first aired. There was Spike Milligan calling Prince Charles "a grovelling bastard," Dame Edna accurately describing the trophy as "this comparatively inexpensive, unimaginative, poorly-crafted object," Hugh Grant hilariously thanking "all the residents of Notting Hill, especially the West Indian community who played such an important part in the movie," and Ricky Gervais unfailingly finding the right mixture of wit, disdain, self-mockery, and general contempt (why can't his sitcoms achieve the same blend?). The presence of Archbishop Desmond Tutu and Stephen Hawking seemed odd at a ceremony for comedians, although I could understand why Simon Cowell was there, because I roar with laughter every time television's gayest heterosexual lisps onto my screen. But towering far above everyone else was the effortless genius of Paul Merton, whose funniest moment came when he walked on stage to collect an award, and began with the words "I'm only sorry I can't be with you tonight..."

This was an hour-long white-knuckle ride of a programme (expertly constructed by Michael Hurll), and if tonight's ceremony generates even half as many laughs, it will be well worth watching. Perhaps my favourite visual clip was the Malcolm-in-the-Middle acceptance speech (in which the dignified tuxedo-clad recipient was gradually revealed to be naked from the waist down), and it certainly beat the oration made on the night I won my award, not by me but by BBC executive Johnny Beerling. Mr Beerling had commissioned my thirteen-part series with the words "I want dangerous comedy," then tried to cancel it after one programme because it was "too dangerous;" but the entire series was eventually made and broadcast (thanks mainly to the late great John Walters), and it duly won a British Comedy Award. Come the big night, guess who bounded up on stage ahead of me to accept the statuette, and take the credit for having commissioned such an adventurous series? That's right. It was Johnny, the failed abortionist belatedly claiming to be the midwife.

During my time as a television reviewer, I saw the inevitable march of progress create an environment where (with a few honourable exceptions) viewers had an increasingly wide choice of increasingly dire programmes to watch. Well, that's what one comes to expect from the inevitable march of progress, which frequently seems to replace the things we enjoy in life with much better substitutes that fail to please us. That was certainly true of public transport in London, which in 2005 saw the old beloved Routemaster bus replaced by the widely loathed bendy bus, which itself has recently been replaced by a new design of Routemaster.

*The final day of one Routemaster bus can be seen at link #58 on the **TV Reviews** page on **www.badastralbooks.com**.*

And here's a tribute to one of London's lost icons (although, to avoid letters from pedants, I should point out that they can still be found on London's streets, on two heritage routes).

THE LAST DAYS OF THE ROUTEMASTER

ITV1 LONDON 2005

People put the strangest things in their mouths. Labour party bigwigs and soap actresses aside, the *Guinness Book of Records* is bulging with people who've eaten light bulbs, furniture, boulders, even entire cars, and I personally know a man who used to eat 78 records. Indeed, I'm often tempted to nibble at the CD-ROM version of the complete twelve-volume *Oxford English Dictionary* that nestles within my computer, and to video myself while I'm chewing it, though not because I wish to break any world record. No, it's just so that the next time I use a long word in conversation, and some semi-literate moron says, "Oooh, swallowed a dictionary have you?" I'll be able to reply in the affirmative, and supply him with photographic evidence.

I thought of the chap who's listed in the *Guinness Book* for having gobbled up an entire London double-decker bus (stairs and all) as I watched *The Last Days of the Routemaster*. The Hollywood-style interior mirror lights must have been a bugger to digest, but they've always struck me as quidditatively appropriate for a vehicle that contains all of life's dramas as it trundles along: love, adultery, pickpocketing, curry-vomiting, divorce, death, and fare evasion. Sadly, the final act of that long-running London drama is being played out during 2005, as the last Routemasters disappear from our city streets, and last night's programme offered a moving tribute to an icon of public transportation that's been part of our street architecture for the past fifty years. This week alone, bendy buses are taking over the number 19 route, and I fear that the aforementioned Guinness man will soon have to modify his diet, because the Routemaster itself is about to be gobbled up by history.

"Only some sort of ghastly dehumanised moron would want to get rid of Routemasters," said Ken Livingstone back in 2001, as he invested £4 million of public money to bring scores of older models back into service, and pledged to keep them operating for at least another decade. The programme had tracked down a clip of him uttering those precise words (well spotted that researcher – great programmes are created around such jewels), and used it as a refrain while turning the full force of its scorn upon him for having now reneged on that unequivocal promise. Andrew Gilligan spoke for many when he observed that "it's part of our heritage... it has style... it's designed for London," and I remembered how, as a child, I was convinced that Routemasters were simply huge red telephone kiosks, laid sideways across four wheels. Even today I can still see the similarities. Both are emblematic of London in its prime, both symbolise a solid commitment to public service reliability that has now all but vanished, and both often reek of piss.

Despite claims that Routemasters are dangerous and unfriendly to the disabled, the programme argued passionately that these criticisms (while by no means unfounded) are greatly exaggerated. A random survey indicated that the wheelchair ramps on new bendy buses frequently don't work, while responsible citizens who jump onto a moving Routemaster against all advice know that they only have themselves to blame if they fall off, although the modern temptation to limp off to one of those appalling "Have you had an accident?" no-win-no-fee telly solicitors has been one of the main reasons for the traditional red bus's demise. It also emerged that the new driver-only articulated buses are encouraging ticket evasion to the tune of £57 million a year, but my slits narrowed to mere eyes when one interviewee used that as an excuse to lament the disappearance of "those friendly conductors" from days of yore. Friendly? When I think of all the ones who, over the years, have grinned sadistically at me from the comfort of their rear platform as their bus has sped past, leaving me standing at a request stop in the pouring rain, the adjective I'd have chosen would have been *fiendly*.

TV reviews

This was a shamelessly biased programme that made little attempt to demonstrate the benefits (and there are some) of bendy buses, but it stated its case with passion and eloquence, so three cheers to that. Life shouldn't always be a carefully-balanced "on the one hand – on the other hand" *Times* leader-style c.1965, and it's right to protest about this reckless and irreversible culling, because London is losing part of its uniqueness and identity as it trades in its heritage, in exchange for the dubious benefits of soulless efficiency and global standardisation. Still, some Routemasters will be with us for another nine months yet, so *carpe diem*, leap on one today while you still have time, because they're the ideal way to see London. Why? Because most of the time you can't see out of their filthy unwashed windows, so what better way could there be to view our gloriously filthy and unwashed capital?

This next review also caused letters to flood in. Well, one letter flooded in anyway, from Vince Powell, the man who wrote the scripts for many of ITV's most dismal comedies from the 1970s and 80s.

BLESS THIS HOUSE

PARAMOUNT 2 2006

Easter is approaching, so what better way for this Christian country to commemorate our Lord's suffering on the cross than by consuming as many chocolate eggs as possible? Consisting of 1 per cent cocoa solids, 29 per cent air, and 70 per cent foil and cardboard, they'll be purchased by the millions over the next ten days (leaving the dustmen to cart away enough discarded packaging to fill yet another gigantic landfill site), but I shall eschew them in favour of a case or two of Fleurie, as I perform my annual Easter urinary miracle of turning wine into water. Incidentally, I have a friendly word of advice for those followers of Jesus who are expecting the Second Coming of the Saviour at any moment: if I were you, I'd throw away those crucifixes before He gets here. I mean, a survivor of the *Titanic* wouldn't appreciate being greeted by crowds of people wearing plastic iceberg hats, so why do Christians think that the Messiah would want to be reminded of the one truly lousy thing that happened to Him last time He was here? Worse still, if He keeps seeing images of Himself writhing on the cross, the poor old Son of God might have trouble sustaining a resurrection.

As a Lenten sacrifice, I've decided to crucify myself this week by veering away from the mainstream channels, and surveying instead the state of some of the 300-plus other channels now available on digital television. Beginning with Paramount 2, which is mainly devoted to endless reruns of fine US comedies (like *Seinfeld* and *Frasier*), but currently features 70s ITV sitcoms each weekday lunchtime, with two episodes of *George and Mildred* preceded by a double bill of *Bless This House*. Running from 1971-6, this was the last televisual vehicle for Sid James, the cheerfully sexist comedic hero to a generation of New Lads, best remembered by me for a cinema ad whose catchphrase was a filthy cackle and the words "get your teeth into something this size darling." He was advertising Walls hot dogs, by the way, those hot pink tubes of extruded kapok (with what looked like a vein running down them), drenched in the great taste of yellow flavour and red flavour, served in a box that tasted better than the contents, and convincing proof of the old saying – "Walls have ears."

Though created by Vince Powell (the genius behind such racially-misguided sitcoms as *Mind Your Language* and *Love Thy Neighbour*), many of the scripts were written by Carla Lane, and that certainly showed in the episode I watched. Sid's wife Jean (Diana Coupland) was virtually a dry run for Ria in *Butterflies*, lamenting her fading beauty and unromantic husband, and wailing "the romance has gone out of our marriage... I don't want to be a wife, I want to be a lover." Peering out through layers of mascara that gave her the appearance of a spider trapped under a pint glass, she resolved to leave Sid and find some excitement, but rapidly changed her mind when crudely propositioned in the kitchen by the grocery delivery man, played by Gareth Hunt. A man whose surname is Cockney rhyming slang for what he is, and whose career peaked with a coffee ad involving a hand gesture that could still get you hanged in Puerto Rico.

As the entire plot could be summarised in the words "Don't worry your fluffy little head about our relationship dear, just make us a nice cup of tea and get on with the washing up," I ignored most of the dialogue and listened instead to the noises the Abbott family were making. And what a strange bunch they were, a rough-voiced South African Cockney father whose grown-up children Mike and Sally (Robin Stewart and Sally Geeson) enunciated with unfathomably posh accents, and constantly used the word "cool," as each generation of youths has done since the 1940s (each thinking that they're the first to do so). "Life is like a cup of tea," declared Sally to her supposedly-separating parents, "and pathos is like the sugar in it," but all we had here was bathos, although technically, gags

TV reviews

like "you spend half your life catching fish and the other half drinking like one" could be accurately described as pathetic. As for Sally's mysterious cut-glass vowels, I suddenly thought of what Daisy Donovan's father (the Cockney photographer Terence) once said about his posh-totty daughter: "that sodding accent cost me a 'undred grand."

Sid died on stage at the Sunderland Empire in 1976, but he died every week in *Bless This House*, not through any fault of his own, but due to the witless plots and dire-logue. Still, at least those of us who grew up in the 70s can enjoy the incidental period detail – the packet of Wonderloaf, or Mike and Sally's flared trousers and hairdont's. Overall, it's a horrible, wonderful nightmare. Speaking of dreams, I'm reminded of a gag about three pals forced to share the same bed: the next morning the one on the left says, "What a dream! Sex all night!" to which the one on the right responds, "Same with me... sex all night!" "How odd," says the one in the middle, "I dreamt that I was skiing all night."

I sadly don't have permission to reproduce Vince Powell's letter, which mainly consisted of a long list of his "triumphs." This is the reply I sent him:

Victor Lewis-Smith
The London Evening Standard
2, Derry Street
London, W8 5EE

Facsimile for:

Vince Powell, Guildford

Dear Mr Powell,

Thank you for sending your CV. I notice that, sadly, you haven't worked since 1980. Even so, I feel I can offer you no work here at Associated Newspapers.

I did read the list and, yes, without exception I do remember them as being extremely dire.

Finally, may I point out that 'dire' and 'hit' are not mutually exclusive.

Yours sincerely,

Victor Lewis-Smith

Ch 6 RAGBAG

Mr Powell died in 2009.

This is his bizarre Wikipedia entry:

> Powell contributed material to the Cilla Black vehicles Blind Date and Surprise, Surprise. His first marriage ended in divorce; as did his second marriage, to Judi Smith. His third marriage, to Geraldine Moore, ended when he died.

*As for Gareth Hunt, see him in all his Alpha-male pomp with the "hand-shandy" gesture Nescafe ad here: go to link #58a on the **TV Reviews** page on **www.badastralbooks.com**.*

I have no idea what he was paid for his Nescafe ads, but I imagine that for the next 10 years he bitterly regretted doing them since since I assume that he must have been on the receiving end of constant catcalls and wanker gesticulations whenever he walked around in public. No money is worth that. He died in 2007.

I've already mentioned in this book that being accosted by angry celebrities is an occupational hazard for any television critic. However, I was also accosted from time to time by angry nonentities, such as the main actor in the following programme.

URBAN MYTH

BBC2 2002

Have you ever noticed that the promotional literature for on-train dining bears no resemblance whatsoever to reality? The leaflets invariably depict smart, scrubbed, inanely grinning staff serving fresh and delicious food to beaming, delighted, and contented passengers, but such civilised (and fictional) courtesy is a far cry from what awaits anyone who is epicurious enough to dine *chez* Railtrack (or Notwork Rail, as I insist we should henceforth call them). What really happens is that you're wedged into a cramped and filthy-stinking restaurant car (so rough that even the arms of the seats have tattoos), and are expected to pay Gordon Ramsay prices for a soggy, scalding, salmonella-ridden, inedible, microwaved bacon bun, dished up by some nose-studded maniac whose knuckles scrape along the floor, while a silicon-chip voice relentlessly

TV reviews

intones "Attention guard, disabled passenger alarm activated." That's why the motto of the railway catering industry should be: "Breakfast in Kings Cross, lunch in Peterborough... dinner in hospital."

My own disabled alarm went off yesterday, as I sat in the restaurant carriage of a train, reading the promotional literature for *Urban Myths* (BBC2), and noticed that the drama starred Mat Fraser. The bells started ringing because, several years ago, Mr Fraser cornered me in Channel 4 reception, announced that he was a highly-trained kick boxer, and threatened to "take me outside" because a column of mine had dared to include a jocular reference to Thalidomide (the drug that had caused him to be born with foreshortened arms). Being firmly opposed to all forms of physical violence (especially any form that might be inflicted upon me by a martial arts expert), I tried to reason with him by asking if he also objected to gags about gays, feminists, or Christians, and he immediately replied that those sorts of jokes were all fine by him, just not any about Thalidomide. So there we had it. He could laugh at everyone *except* himself, and saw no inconsistency in asking for equal rights *and* special treatment. How disabled can you get?

Fortunately, as BBC2's timely *What's Your Problem?* season has emphasised, most Thalidomiders have a more realistic and tolerant view of disability and society. A documentary on Wednesday night featured a Scouse stand-up comedian musing on the practical problems caused by his Thalidomide disability (such as the difficulty of "thumbing a lift to my gigs"), but last night's *Urban Myths* was desperately short on humour, partly due to Fraser's wooden acting, but also because of an arch and unconvincing script by Simon Mirren. That, in turn, was mainly because disability wasn't remotely relevant to the plot, yet kept being smuggled into it via irrelevant conversations, such as when a small boy suddenly called out, apropos of nothing, "What can you do with those hands? They're too short." "There's only one thing I *can't* do," replied Fraser pointedly, which surprised me because, ever since our brief and unpleasant encounter, I've been convinced of one thing. That the man is a complete and utter Barclay's Banker.

Being based on one of those "This happened to someone who knows a friend of mine" legends that keep a million pub conversations ticking over every evening, the main storyline did at least have a plausible and persuasive outline. Following a chance encounter with a long-lost heart throb from school (Saffron Burrows), Fraser is invited to help her clear out her recently-deceased mother's flat, located in a huge, rough, and thoroughly anonymous housing estate (though why a mother would live in an area that was pure Bermondsey, when her daughter's accent was pure Belgravia, is never explained). Their unrequited passion is rekindled, and a highly improbable sex scene gets underway, but there are no condoms in the flat, so Fraser runs to the local shop, then back, only to realise that he now had no idea behind which of a thousand identical front doors lay his panting and expectant lover. Which was ironic because, although he wasn't going to get his end away, Dame Fate had ensured that he was, nevertheless, well and truly fucked.

My criticisms of Mr Fraser's shortcomings as a performer may seem harsh, but they're not, because in his agitprop rants on the Channel 4 show *Freak Out*, he's constantly exhorting society to "see the person, not the disability," and that's what I've tried to do. Like many people on the fringes of television, his ego is substantially greater than his talent, and he could learn a lot from the example of disabled performers from earlier generations, such as Michael Flanders or Ian Dury, who achieved fame because they were skilled and imaginative entertainers, rather than through special interest pleading.

As it happens, I was fortunate enough to get to know Ian Dury a little, and he was just as gloriously cynical about his own disability as he was about everything else. Indeed, it was he who told me the joke that subsequently caused Mr Fraser to threaten me in Horseferry Road. This was it:

Q: What is the smallest pub in Britain?
A: "The Thalidomide Arms."

It wasn't really worth all the fuss, was it?

DOCTOR WHO

BBC1 2005

Watching Nazi stormtroopers on WWII in Colour some struck me that the colour footage of Adolf and his ch the menace of those grim monochrome images we all grew up I thought back to childhood episodes of Dr Who, and how t (another master race who seemed so terrifying in b&w) were forever of their paralysing power once I'd seen them in Technicolo cinema, and realised they were nothing more than giant multicolo pepperpots wearing a collection of spare parts from a Morris Mi (indicators included). Just as those Nazi uniforms were revealed high camp, so there was something hilariously effeminate about

TV reviews

red and yellow Daleks with their Sieg Heil plungers, and the realisation eventually led to me writing a mini TV series entitled "The Gay Daleks." In which two mechanised ringpiece raiders of the universe (one with a robotic poodle called KY) travelled through time and space in "The Turdis," sticking their plungers through glory holes, and meeting up in the underpants department of Selfridges with their French relatives (the Garleks... what else?).

"Experminate!" was the Gay Daleks' watchcry, and I thought of them on Saturday night, while watching BBC1's increasingly inspired revival of *Doctor Who*. For there was a butch, burnished-gold Dalek all chained up in what looked like an S&M bondage dungeon, asking itself "what am I? What am I?" and being enthusiastically tortured by a man in a rubber suit. The place turned out to be an extra-terrestrial black museum in the bowels of Utah, run by Henry Van Statten, a deranged megalomaniac played by Corey Johnson as a sort of Dr No crossed with Kevin Kline's Otto character from *A Fish Called Wanda*. "I demand orders" screamed the humiliated Dalek in a classic passive-aggressive display, and while I'm not saying he was definitely gay, I strongly suspect he knew all the words to *South Pacific*.

"But I wiped you all out!" screamed Christopher Ecclestone as ⁓oped eyes on his oldest adversary, and recalled the epic battle that ˙troyed the entire Dalek race along with the Time Lords. "Then ᵉ in the universe," replied his chained enemy, "and so are you ᵉ are the same," as the script took an unexpectedly Jungian ⁺ing that Daleks are ultimately the dark shadow of the ⁻onsciousness. The machine also became emotional with er), whining like a blocked Hoover crossed with Noel e placed a compassionate hand on its helmet, whereupon d "genetic material extrapolated" and burst into renewed ₑ life. Foolish girl. You'd think by now she'd know better ɿise with cold, heartless, self-obsessed creatures who care but themselves. What with her having been married. To

rns dramatic, imaginative, ironic, allegorical, and touching, ɘ never faltered from first to last. The classic chase and ion sequences were far more polished and fast-paced than . days, while there were some excellent jokes about a Dalek's ɪal difficulty with stairs, about how it can be disabled (apparently, ɪlles heel is its vulnerable eye), and about "searching for Daleks ɪe Internet" (apart from porn, that's just about the web's number one ₑoccupation). But this was no simplistic Manichaean battle between good d evil, as Rose discovered when she found herself in a Dr Frankenstein

Ch 6 RAGBAG

role ("you gave me life" hissed the monster she'd revived), then became an object of its obsession (like Fay Wray with King Kong), and even ended up by protecting it. And most horrifying of all, we saw what the organic insides of a Dalek actually look like, and in case you missed it, I'll try to describe what I saw. Remember that dodgy portion of Calamari ripieni con ricotta e spinaci you once ordered in a cheap trattoria, then vomited up over the taxi driver's head on the way home? That's what it looked like.

Revivals of iconic series whose time has come and gone are usually a disaster, but for once the BBC haven't put a foot wrong, and have even improved on the original. There are clever, funny, and challenging scripts here, fine ensemble acting and direction, Ron Grainer's hypnotic theme tune (although Delia Derbyshire of the BBC Radiophonic Workshop should also be credited, because she was the one who made it sound futuristic), and a backlit Billie Piper to get yet another generation of Doctor Who nerds rushing off to find the Kleenex. Ah, it all takes me back to happier simpler times when, aged ten, the Daleks were the highlight of my day, after which mummy would bake a cake, and let me lick the beaters of her food mixer afterwards. Unfortunately, she once forgot to switch off the motor beforehand, which is why, to this day, I still have to brush my teeth via my rectum.

*Talking of Fay Wray, a couple of years I found myself directing a film crew in the Hollywood Forever Cemetery which is notoriously short on lavatory facilities. Desperate, I located a large bush and relieved myself behind it, only to discover, to my horror, that I had just pissed a gallon off wee wee over Fay Wray. Subsequently, having read some of her biographies, I do not believe that I am the only man to urinate on Ms Wray. See my makeshift toilet-grave here: link #59 on the **TV Reviews** page on **www.badastralbooks.com.***

*Back in the days before I took up reviewing television, I was a producer of talk shows ("never chat shows dear boy") for the BBC. One of my most regular bookings was Kenneth Williams, not so much for his on-air performances (superb though those were), as for the delight of sitting with him afterwards, listening to his outrageous and hilarious stories. In case you've forgotten just how brilliant a raconteur he was, here's a fine and insightful appearance by him on a 1980 edition of Parkinson. Go to link #60 on the **TV Reviews** page on **www.badastralbooks.com.***

TV reviews

KENNETH WILLIAMS IN HIS OWN WORDS

BBC4 2006

It's time to update my list of classical musicians with unorthodox names, a list which will surely delight readers with an interest in scatology. I started compiling it years ago in tribute to a pianist friend of mine, who gave a recital of pieces by genuine composers with double entendres for surnames (including Fux, Blow, and Scheidt); then next year, when he was invited back to the same venue (to apologise), bravely added works by Titz, Suk, and an entire family of Bendas (check them out in Grove, if you don't believe me).

    Last time I attended one of his concerts, he also played works by Pysing, Krapp, and Kok, and I strongly suspect that his next will be the first keyboard recital in history ever to be raided by the police on grounds of taste and decency. Why? Because following a call from a colleague at the British Library, my friend's repertoire will now include pieces by Christoph Kuntze and the Franco-Russian composer Amedé Wanka.

    I told Kenneth Williams about this list years ago, as we sat together in a BBC green room, and he revealed that he too had compiled a list of scatologically-named writers and artists, including the distinguished novelist Edward Knoblock. "Vulgarity runs right through the mainstream of English literature – a genuine love of the honestly vulgar," he said to me at the time, and there he was saying it again last night, on BBC4's Kenneth Williams in His Own Words. Shown as an aperitif before the much-trailed Fantabulosa, it told his life story primarily through the medium of his many hilarious talk show appearances, and therefore lacked the darkness that was posthumously revealed to an astonished public when his diaries (authoritatively edited by Russell Davies) were published in the early 90s.

    But on the other hand, just ahead of Michael Sheen's creditable impersonation, it was wonderful to hear the real thing again, with that extraordinarily resonant voice sounding like a man who'd just undergone a full manual evacuation of the vowels.

    The talk show clips were cunningly linked by extracts from an old radio bio-mockumentary, narrated by Kenneth Horne ("he was sent to the sort of school that's very difficult to get into... it was very difficult to get out of too"). But mostly we heard Williams telling his own story about his impoverished upbringing near St Pancras, a schooling in which only literature and drama had fired his imagination, and how he'd been singled out for praise in the local paper for "his mincing step and comical demeanour" during the end-of-term play. "Honest vulgarity" was always his trademark, but I noticed that BBC interviewer Frank Bough looked decidedly uncomfortable when that phrase was mentioned, probably because jovial married Uncle Frank (whose morals proved to be as woolly as his jumpers) was thinking of his own dishonest vulgarity, which involved three-in-a-bed romps with prostitutes, cocaine snorting, bondage, and spanking. Frankly, that cad ought to have been horsewhipped on the steps of his club. Although come to think of it, at the sorts of clubs Frank frequented, you probably have to ask nicely and pay extra for a horsewhipping.

Falling prey to a common documentary misconception, clips of Kenneth in acting mode (speaking whatever lines had been composed for him by the screenwriter) were intercut with his own thoughts, as though the inner life of a thespian is inseparable from the many roles they've played. But overused clips of him saying "Infamy, infamy, they've all got it in for me" told us only that he was a genius at breathing new life into old gags, although these lapses were fortunately compensated for by some rivetting talk show clips that I hadn't seen before. Telling Michael Parkinson that "I quite look forward to death," sitting on a pouffe next to Russell Harty (that makes three then), and appearing on the doomed TV version of Just a Minute, chaired by Nicholas Parsons (recently described by a friend of mine with Exocet accuracy as "sixty-five years a cunt"). He kicked the oxygen habit far too soon for my liking, and now he's no longer to be found inside the magic rectangle, I find that I'm left with a gaping chasm that is only partially filled by Dale Winton. Which, come to think of it, is just the sort of thing that Williams himself might have said.

Clearly made on a minuscule budget, this had a whiff of one man and his Avid editing machine about it, a combination that seldom makes for avid viewing. But at least this was Williams in full flow, and director John Mullen did a workmanlike cut-and-paste job on the archive, as did Executive Producer David Okuefuna, who currently seems to be in charge of about 80 per cent of all BBC4's programmes. True, it didn't get to grips with Williams' bleak view of human existence (he called Tony Hancock "extraordinarily depressive," yet was no stranger to the black dog himself), but it was remarkable to hear that voice again, its shrill and penetrative qualities equalled by only one other celebrity. That's the human dog whistle, Maurice Gibb (of Bee Gees fame), who continued producing a monotonous high-pitched whine right up to the very end, and even beyond (because the flatlining squeal of his cardiac monitor would surely have been more musical than his falsetto backing vocals on *Night Fever*).

Printed in Great Britain
by Amazon.co.uk, Ltd.,
Marston Gate.